Stage Theories of Cognitive and Moral Development:
Criticisms and Applications

REPRINT NO. 13
HARVARD EDUCATIONAL REVIEW

Library of Congress Card Number 77-91693. ISBN 0-916690-16-4.
Printed by Capital City Press, Montpelier, Vermont 05602. Cover design by Cynthia Brady.

Harvard Educational Review
Longfellow Hall, 13 Appian Way
Cambridge, Massachusetts 02138

Stage Theories of Cognitive and Moral Development: Criticisms and Applications

ROGER LANDRUM
v   **Preface**

DEANNA KUHN
vii   **Introduction**

PATRICIA TEAGUE ASHTON
1   **Cross-Cultural Piagetian Research: An Experimental Perspective**

JOHN C. GIBBS
33   **Kohlberg's Stages of Moral Judgment: A Constructive Critique**

CAROL GILLIGAN
52   **In a Different Voice: Women's Conceptions of Self and of Morality**

DAVID ELKIND
89   **Piagetian and Psychometric Conceptions of Intelligence**

ELEANOR DUCKWORTH
108   **The Having of Wonderful Ideas**

LAWRENCE KOHLBERG
ROCHELLE MAYER
123 **Development as the Aim of Education**

D.C. PHILLIPS
MAVIS E. KELLY
171 **Hierarchical Theories of Development in Education and Psychology**

ROBERT L. SELMAN
196 **Education for Cognitive Development**

203 NOTES ON CONTRIBUTORS

Preface

Despite the best intentions of psychologists and educators to collaborate in defining the aims and means of education, the fields of psychology and education stand in uneasy relationship. William James, B. F. Skinner, Jean Piaget and other professional psychologists have attempted without notable success to articulate general conceptions of education. And, in addition to the use of psychometric tests, which some claim to be the only real contribution of psychology to education, attempts have been made in a number of other ways to apply formal psychological theories to educational practice. These include constructing curricula, formulating instructional strategies, and seeking a deeper and more accurate grasp of student behavior and the conditions under which learning occurs. The influence of psychology in American education is pervasive, a fact that is apparent in the psychological jargon used by many teachers, but it is also diffuse and often ineffectual, perhaps because the complexities of classroom settings defy the elegance of psychological theory.

There is no single, dominant psychological theory at present. Psychology is a multi-paradigmatic field and it is probably true that most educators, like most psychologists, tend to believe explicitly or implicitly in one or another psychological paradigm. "Traditional" classroom practices, in a loose sense, represent a belief in behaviorist assumptions, although this may be less a result of the intellectual influence of behaviorism than a manifestation of the fact that behaviorism is a theoretical expression of the way most Americans tend to view human nature. "Progressive" classroom practices, on the other hand, are largely based on developmental theories of psychology that are counter-intuitive for most Americans. This may account for the progressives' perpetual defensive posture in the politics of education, except in private, elite schools for young children. In any event, many contemporary "open" classrooms represent a romanticized corruption of developmental conceptions. Freudian or psychoanalytic theory is also an influence in American education, especially in preschool and primary school practices, in clinical interventions, and in such recent innovations as art therapy and encounter groups. Achievement and intelligence tests are in use almost everywhere in education, reflecting a powerful if atheoretical belief in inevitable gradations of abilities among students. In reality, all the phenomena described and explained by the various psychological theories must be operating in every classroom, if the theories have any validity. That may be why some of the most effective teachers seem eclectic and unsystematic to psychologists who are working within a single paradigm and why educational programs committed to only one psychological theory often fail to display convincing results in the classroom.

In short, the relationship between education and psychology is a labyrinth. Still, work that relates the fields is important and often fascinating, both historically and currently. These two fields and the tensions between them reflect our fundamental views of human nature and our cultural ideals. The clash of viewpoints within psychology and between educational thought and psychological theory are also basic to progress in our understanding of human behavior. Thus, the editors of the *Harvard Educational Review* take a special interest in manuscripts that explore relationships between psychology and education from empirical and theoretical perspectives and from a number of different paradigms.

The articles drawn together in this reprint explore one major branch of psychological research and theory and its implications for education: the Piagetian perspective on human development. Piagetian theory became an important influence in American education during the 1960s. Jerome Bruner's *The Process of Education,* published in 1960, drew heavily upon Piagetian conceptions of intellectual growth and stimulated an interest in Piaget's work that became central to the curriculum-reform movements of the decade. Elkind, Flavell, Ginsburg and Opper, and others published accounts—widely read in schools of education—of the research and theory-building that had been going forward under Piaget's guidance in Geneva since the 1920s. Lawrence Kohlberg, perhaps the leading exponent of this approach in the United States, picked up an early strand of Piaget's work, elaborating on and systematizing his account of the development of moral judgment in the child. Kohlberg then went on to clarify the educational implications of his own and Piaget's work for various levels of schooling. At present, so many researchers in psychology and education, pursuing diverse interests, have gathered under the Piagetian umbrella that the term "cognitive-developmental theory" has been coined to distinguish the full scope of the paradigm from the confines of Piaget's original foundation.

Cognitive-developmental theory is especially powerful not only because it details a unified view of cognitive behavior from infancy through adolescence but also because it embodies an abstract ideal of optimal cognitive development that can be taken as a guiding aim of education. Less explicitly, this theory also lays a foundation for analysis of environmental influences and human experiences that mediate the pace and determine the end-point of cognitive development. In the breadth of its view of human nature, cognitive-developmental theory parallels the earliest Western text on cognition and education, *The Republic,* in which Plato describes the classical Greek view of optimal mental development and the educational processes necessary for its attainment.

The articles in this collection do not represent a systematic introduction to cognitive-developmental theory. Rather at a more advanced and critical level of analysis they slice into the theoretical framework from various angles. Individually and as a collection, these articles will assist students of psychology and of education to grasp the view of human nature embodied in one of the most prominent psychological theories and to consider more clearly the educational propositions that have been derived from this theoretical framework.

ROGER LANDRUM
The Potomac Institute

Introduction

This collection of articles each originally appearing in the *Harvard Educational Review* can be divided into two groups, each group having, on the face of it, quite distinct intents and objectives. The articles in one group critically examine developmental theory, with respect both to underlying conceptual assumptions and to questions of empirical validation. The second group of articles explores the relevance of development theory for education.

In this introduction I would like to suggest some reasons for including in a single volume these two distinct sets of articles, one striving towards a better articulated theory and the other towards its meaningful application. The reasons emerge as we examine the problems encountered by the authors as they attempt to fulfill one or another set of objectives. In a number of important ways the meaningfulness of the educational applications of developmental theory that are proposed remain dependent on a fuller articulation and development of the theory. In turn, it is in attempts at application that the weaknesses, the insufficiencies, and the necessity of further and better articulation of the theory are most plainly exposed.

The group of articles devoted to examination of developmental theory are reprinted at a time when the theory is indeed undergoing scrutiny. In order to appreciate the complexity of this evaluation it is important to understand that a structural, or stage, theory of development rests on a number of interrelated assumptions: the concept that elements are organized into "structured wholes," the idea that these wholes are something more than the sum of their parts, the concept of qualitative reorganization or "restructuring," the claim that stage sequences are invariant and universal, and the assertion that stages are constructed through the self-directed actions of individuals.

Since the early sixties there has been a general tendency to accept Piagetian-based structural-developmental theory uncritically. Little attention has been given to the analysis of its potentially separable components, its underlying assumptions, or the appropriate methods for its empirical validation. It is of considerable interest, then, that we are now witnessing the beginnings of what may become something of an about-face. John Flavel, for example, a leading spokesman for the field, anticipates "the concept of stage will not figure importantly in future scientific work on cognitive growth" (1977, p. 249). Such comments may portend a future of unqualified renunciation of structural theory equal in fervor to its previously unqualified acceptance and equally devoid of the extensive critical analysis that the theory deserves. Exactly what, for example, would we be discarding were we to discard the stage concept? In light of such questions the appearance of articles like those reprinted here, that carefully evaluate the distinct components and claims of structural theory, can only be regarded as a step forward for the theory.

Patricia Ashton's paper deals with the issue of empirical validation. What are the appropriate methods and how do the resulting data bear on the theory? Ashton focuses on the potentially critical relevance that cross-cultural data have with respect to the questions of generality, sequentiality, and universality of stage structures, and for questions about the mechanisms governing their development. She is aware of and makes clear, however, the formidable methodological problems that must be addressed before cross-cultural evidence will be able to play a decisive role.

David Elkind deals with the conceptual, rather than empirical, issues surrounding a structural theory of development and tries to reconcile structural approaches to intelligence with traditional psychometric ones, pointing out their significant similarities as well as differences. Given the prominent role psychometric assessments and conceptualizations of intelligence have played in the evaluation of school children, Elkind's paper is an important one. He also offers his views on some practical issues that pertain to children's educational environments.

Both John Gibbs and Carol Gilligan question the assumed generality of structural-development theory. Gibbs reviews the recent research on Kohlberg's theory and finds evidence that Kohlberg's first four stages do meet the developmental criteria outlined by Piaget. Gibbs argues, however, that Kohlberg's highest stages are not true stages in the naturalistic sense. Gilligan also questions the universality of Kohlberg's sequence of stages. Based on her studies of women's confrontations with a real moral dilemma, she argues that although women's moral development shows clear structural characteristics, it differs significantly from the course followed by men.

The universality of stage sequences is a crucial question in a structural theory of development, one that cuts across all of its components. If stage sequences are not universal, for example, can their mechanisms of construction be universal? The question of universality becomes particularly important when attempts are made to apply the theory to education. As we shall see, Lawrence Kohlberg and Rochelle Mayer's claim that developmental stage advancement should become the objective of education hinges on the universality of the stage sequences they discuss. While neither the arguments nor the data offered by Gibbs and Gilligan are definitive, their questions become increasingly important as attempts are made to apply developmental theory to education.

The strongest criticism of structural theory is presented by D. C. Phillips and Mavis Kelly. They underscore the dual and commonly observed errors of hypothesizing a hierarchical stage sequence that is either logically guaranteed or inferred solely from empirical order of appearance. They also insist on an answer to the difficult question of how the structural and dynamic aspects of the theory are interrelated: does a theory of stages demand a constructivist (interactionist) account of the mechanisms of development? Is stage theory incompatible with an empiricist account of the mechanisms of development?

While the Phillips and Kelly article tackles important issues, its authors may fail to appreciate the necessarily delicate interaction between logical and empirical analysis in the articulation of a stage sequence. One can argue further that they do not take into account a sufficiently broad range of possibilities with respect to what the theory-data relationship may be. For instance, in the case of structural theory, empirical data may never perform the critical "disconfirmation function," as this function is usually conceived. One might thus be inclined to agree with critics of structural theory that it is indeed impossible to obtain data that disprove the theory. But it does not follow that empirical data are irrelevant to the theory; instead, their function may be to further articulate, refine, and elaborate on a conceptual perspective that the investigator already possesses before embarking on the collection of data (Kuhn, 1975). In this light, the structural developmental perspective is perhaps most appropriately conceived of as a paradigm in Thomas Kuhn's (1962) sense.

In any event, the remaining papers in this volume—the articles by Eleanor Duckworth and by Lawrence Kohlberg and Rochelle Mayer, and Robert Selman's discussion of Furth and Wachs's (1974), and his own, developmentally based educational programs—have a very different focus. They reflect a growing interest in the possibility of deriving educational objectives and techniques from Piagetian-based theory. Such interest has led to both specific programs, like those developed by Furth and Wachs and Selman, and to theoretical work, like the essays by Kohlberg and Mayer and Duckworth that cut across the fields of psychology and education.

Duckworth's essay has the all-too-rare virtue of being based to a considerable extent on classroom experience. Duckworth claims that it is the repeated experience of deriving ideas from one's spontaneous activities and then testing and retesting them that leads children to have more and better ideas. Underlying this view is the Piagetian notion that thinking consists of actions that the child initiates, directs, and reorganizes in the course of development. Duckworth and many other theorists of education have drawn from Piaget's notion the conclusion that educational activities must at the very least be organized around the child's own activity. As Duckworth asserts, "It is almost impossible for an adult to know exactly the right time for a given question for a given child. . . . Children can raise the right question for themselves when the setting is right." Thus her educational prescription is to place children in a cognitively rich environment where they can select and carry out the activities that will best accomplish their own intellectual development.

The same general perspective is reflected in Elkind's brief comments about education. Elkind advocates " 'interest areas' where children could go on their own for long periods of time." We cannot define and supply learning activities and materials for children, Elkind argues, "It is the child who must . . . choose the method of learning and the materials that are reinforcing to him." A more moderate version of this philosophy is represented by Furth and Wachs's experimental program, reviewed here by Selman, which is loosely organized around a set of "developmental activities" but still leaves children considerable freedom to direct the nature and pace of what they do and thus to "accomplish their own development."

Selman, however, criticizes Furth and Wachs on the grounds that their activities are not clearly derived from developmental theory or research and are therefore conceptually weak as educational prescriptions. The same criticism can actually be directed even more strongly towards the, in some sense, more radical prescriptions of Duckworth and Elkind. The idea that children prosper when permitted to direct their own intellectual activities is certainly compatible with structural developmental theory. In practice, however, we know remarkably little about how children behave in the sorts of environments that Duckworth describes, just what sorts of cognitive activities they engage in, what the functional significance of these activities is, and how these activities change over time. Without knowledge of this kind, knowledge that is both empirical and theoretical, educational prescriptions of the sort offered by Duckworth run the risk of intellectual bankruptcy. The challenge then is to better articulate the concrete nature of the constructive process. And it is in this light that the objectives of theory articulation and of theory application converge.

In contrast to Duckworth, Kohlberg and Mayer draw their educational implications exclusively from theory. Yet they confront a parallel challenge. Kohlberg and Mayer claim that developmental theory can provide "value-free" aims for education. This is so as education becomes simply a process of encouraging a natural developmental progression. Becoming "educated," in other words, amounts to attaining the highest developmental stage.

The fundamental problem facing Kohlberg and Mayer becomes apparent as soon as one begins to think about implementing their recommendations. The truth is that the stage sequences on which their argument is based are still so abstract, so vague, and so incompletely defined that it is not at all clear what they entail as structures of thought in a broad, general sense that cuts across a wide range of concrete situations. And these are exactly the terms in which educators would require the stages to be defined. For example, "attaining formal operations" cannot assume the status of a meaningful objective for educators so long as the reasoning structure of formal operations (the structure that is central to Kohlberg and Mayer's thesis) is defined solely in terms of responses to Inhelder and Piaget's (1958) dozen or so physics problems. The task therefore is to discover how Piagetian or Kohlbergian stage structures manifest themselves in the reasoning that individuals employ in a multitude of everyday situations both in and outside of school. Again, we have very little knowledge in this regard, and, again, both theory and application are in need of it in order to advance.

It is important to note that Duckworth and Kohlberg and Mayer draw their educational implications from different aspects of structural theory: Duckworth from its dynamic aspect, and Kohlberg and Mayer from its static or structural aspect. Kohlberg and Mayer's position is derived from the sequence of stages postulated by Piaget to which they award the status of educational objectives. Duckworth, in contrast, bases her educational prescriptions on Piaget's assertions about the mechanisms of stage transition. Unfortunately it is not at all clear how the educational objectives that Kohlberg and Mayer and Duckworth derive from the same theory are related. Is intellectual curiosity, initiative, and creativity—

"the having of wonderful ideas"—equivalent to attaining Piaget's stage of formal operations or Kohlberg's highest stage of moral judgment? The point is that we cannot yet even address such a question meaningfully as neither objective has been rigorously enough defined to permit a clear comparison between them.

Kohlberg and Mayer's recommendation that development (through a sequence of stages) become the aim of education must be treated as the controversial proposition that it is and debated accordingly. To invoke "natural ends" as "desirable ends" certainly gets one over the hurdle of value relativity that usually arises when trying to determine what ends are desirable. But one can commit the social scientist's naturalistic fallacy of deriving what *ought* to be from what *is* as readily in the area of education as anywhere else. Does not a society's ideology—its vision of what might be—deserve to be given a voice in the educational arena, if it is to be given one anywhere, despite the challenge of multiple values that arises in a pluralistic society? Shall we renounce traditional curriculum concerns, such as artistic expression, creative writing, or physical education, on the grounds that they do not clearly promote structural-developmental growth? Or perhaps, in a more ominous sort of intellectual circularity, shall we justify our desires that these particular areas of concern remain in the curriculum on the grounds that their structural-developmental characteristics are indeed there awaiting discovery? It is imperative that we examine very thoughtfully the questions of whether and why the developmentalist's highest stages should become an—perhaps the—aim of education.

The major point I have tried to make in the present commentary, however, has to do not so much with the merit of Kohlberg and Mayer's position but rather with the very meaningfulness of it as a proposition for education. If developmental theory does not have well-articulated objectives to offer to education as well as coherent, defensible strategies for attaining them, there is in the end nothing to debate. And it is for this reason, as I asserted at the outset, that the two groups of articles collected here, the one concerned with the development of theory and the other with its application, bear an intricate and critical relation to one another.

DEANNA KUHN
Harvard University

References

Flavell, J. *Cognitive development.* Englewood Cliffs, N.J.: Prentice-Hall, 1977.

Furth, H., & Wachs, H. *Thinking goes to school: Piaget's theory in practice.* New York: Oxford University Press, 1974.

Inhelder, B., & Piaget, J. *The growth of logical thinking from childhood to adolescence.* New York: Basic Books, 1958.

Kuhn, D. Development and learning: European and American traditions. *Contemporary Psychology,* 1975, **20,** 872–874.

Kuhn, T. *The structure of scientific revolutions.* Chicago: University of Chicago Press, 1962.

Cross-Cultural Piagetian Research: An Experimental Perspective

PATRICIA TEAGUE ASHTON
University of Florida

Over the last twenty-five years children around the world have observed and responded to researchers who pour water from beaker to beaker, roll plasticene into snake-like figures, and arrange matchsticks into a potpourri of shapes. These cross-cultural experiments have been undertaken to test Piaget's theory of genetic epistemology, which posits a hierarchical, universal, and invariant sequence of stages of cognitive development. Piagetian research in varying cultures has revealed both striking similarities and marked differences in performance on cognitive tasks, some in apparent conflict with the basic assumptions of Piagetian stage theory. In this article Professor Ashton reviews a range of cross-cultural Piagetian research, analyzes the sometimes divergent findings from this research, and suggests methodological improvements which may help to resolve past dilemmas and to further future understanding of cognitive growth in different cultures.

The classic Piagetian conservation-of-quantity experiment involves the child's ability to judge that the amount of liquid in a short, wide beaker remains the same when the liquid is poured into a tall, thin beaker. In recent years children around the globe have served as subjects for this and similar experiments designed to investigate the nature and the possible universality of cognitive structures. Piagetian research has been conducted in over one hundred cultures and subcultures from Switzerland to Senegal, from Alaska to the Amazon. This research typically has

Harvard Educational Review   Vol. 45   No. 4   November 1975, 475–506.

attempted to verify the basic structures and hierarchical stages of logical thinking, as well as to establish age trends for the acquisition of cognitive abilities and the transitions from lower to higher cognitive stages.

The Piagetian conservation-of-quantity experiments have revealed both basic similarities and striking differences among children of different cultures. Individuals in diverse cultures seem to move through Piaget's hierarchical stages in the same invariant sequence, although some cultural groups appear never to attain the stage of formal operations. Within a given stage, groups also vary in their performance on specific cognitive tasks. An eight-year-old middle-class white child growing up in the United States will respond to the "water and beaker" experiment by noting the equality of liquid in both cases, while a Wolof youngster in Senegal, West Africa, may insist that the water has changed and increased in quantity when poured into the tall, thin beaker. Piagetian experiments have also shown wide variations in performance between subgroups within the same culture. Children of pottery-making families in Jalisco, Mexico, perform better on conservation-of-substance tasks than do their peers from non-pottery-making families. These findings raise important issues concerning the validity of Piaget's theory, the nature of cultural and subcultural differences, and the general conduct of cross-cultural research.

Piaget posits a hierarchical stage theory of cognitive development characterized by qualitative changes in cognitive structures. His theory divides intellectual development into four major periods. The first stage is the sensorimotor period, generally lasting from birth to two years and characterized by learning through active manipulation of the environment. The second is the preoperational stage, lasting from ages two to seven and marked by the onset of symbolic thought. The third stage is concrete operations, lasting from ages seven to eleven, during which the child masters the concepts of identity, reversibility, and compensation. Finally, after age eleven, the child reaches the stage of formal operations, which is characterized by the attainment of a high degree of equilibrium and transcendence of the here and now. Thus, from the sensorimotor stage, when infants grope with the relationships between their own actions and their momentary influence upon the objects in their immediate environment, individuals progress to adolescence, when, with the attainment of formal operations, they are able to imagine the many concrete and abstract possibilities inherent in any one situation (Ginsburg & Opper, 1969).

This theory of cognitive development, as elucidated by Jean Piaget, has had a dramatic impact on the worlds of psychology and education. If, in fact, the cognitive structures do exist as Piaget posits, the course of cognitive development for any individual can be predicted. With this predictability, it might become possible to aid the intellectual development of the individual by presenting tasks which, during critical periods, foster upward movement both within and between stages. This potential for enhancing children's intellectual growth explains, in part, why Piaget's theory of intellectual development has become the impetus for an astounding number of research efforts in education and psychology and has stimulated significant innovations in curriculum design. The power that Piagetian theory brings to these realms rests upon the two central postulations of genetic epistemology: first, that each stage represents an underlying cognitive structure which applies not only to one or two cognitive skills but to all cognitive functions, and second, that these stages represent a universal and invariant sequence of development.

The notion of universal invariant stages holds, for example, that a child, whether in Senegal or Switzerland, will pass through concrete operations before he enters formal operations. While Piaget stresses the importance of conducting cross-cultural research to support his notion of universality, experimentation in different cultures has yielded findings which are inconclusive and often contradictory. The variation in response between the Wolof and the "WASP" illustrates a central problem: do the differences in task performance reflect the non-universality of Piagetian theory, the differences between cultures, or the failings of the cross-cultural research design?

The purpose of this paper is to survey the results of cross-cultural Piagetian research in order to assess its implications for: (1) the basic assumptions of Piagetian theory, (2) stage transition in cognitive development, (3) social factors influencing cognition, (4) the effects of schooling on intellectual development, and (5) the design and methodology of cross-cultural research. For the present, the reader is warned that in almost all previous research these factors have been highly intertwined. Conclusions attributing cross-cultural differences to any one particular factor must generally be viewed askance.

Theoretical Issues in Cross-Cultural Piagetian Research

Cross-cultural Piagetian research has typically been of two types: (1) attempts to verify whether patterns of stage transition as suggested by Piaget's research on European children hold for children in other cultures, and (2) attempts to identify cultural factors that influence patterns of cognitive development. Yet as

3

Wohlwill (1968) has noted, studies designed to investigate age trends and to identify factors affecting cognitive development have doubtful relevance to the empirical validation of the essentials of Piagetian stage theory. Verification of the fundamentals of genetic epistemology is clearly necessary before researchers will be able to draw any robust inferences regarding age trends and stage transition trends in cognitive growth or environmental factors influencing the rate of cognitive growth.

Sequence of Stage Acquisition

Although cross-cultural research on the assumptions underlying stage development theory is limited, what does exist raises intriguing questions for future investigation. Specifically, the research to date challenges the notion of invariance in the sequence of stage acquisition and the idea of a basic cognitive structure corresponding to each of Piaget's stages.

As mentioned previously, one of the basic tenets of Piaget's theory is that the sequence of stage acquisition is invariant. This assumes that a child must pass through sensorimotor operations before gaining the preoperational stage, through preoperations before reaching concrete operations, and through concrete operations before attaining formal operations. There is, unfortunately, no longitudinal cross-cultural research which examines the notion of invariance across these major Piagetian stages. Cross-cultural research does bear on the issue of invariance of developmental sequence in a narrower context, namely, development within the major stages.

Piaget (1950) has postulated an invariance in sequence in the acquisition of conservation operations within the concrete stage. He maintains that the acquisition of conservation of volume is preceded by acquisition of conservation of weight, which is, in turn, preceded by acquisition of quantity conservation. This sequential development has been termed horizontal décalage and has, for the most part, been confirmed in Western studies (Elkind, 1961a, 1961b). In support of the invariance of stages, Mohsensi (1966) also observed the same sequence of development on conservation tasks for urban and rural children in Iran as well as in Europe, and children in Papua-New Guinea exhibited the expected pattern of stage acquisition (Prince, 1968). Contradictory evidence regarding the invariance of sequence has been provided by Boonsong (1968). He found the development of conservation of quantity and weight to be simultaneous in Thai children. Hyde (1959) offered additional opposition to the Piagetian position by demonstrating that some of her Arab, Indian, and Somali subjects conserved weight but not quantity. More Australian Aborigines succeeded in tasks of conservation of weight than succeeded in conservation of quantity tasks (de Lemos, 1969). These contrary results from different cultures appear to challenge the assumption that stage development is universally invariant in sequence. But before placing overmuch faith in this challenge, we also must consider the issue of the wholeness of the cognitive structures assumed to underlie Piagetian stages.

Structural Wholeness and Intertask Consistency

A second major tenet of Piagetian stage theory is that each cognitive stage reflects a fundamental underlying structure. As Wohlwill (1968) has asserted:

> . . . essential to his [Piaget's] concept of stages is the notion of an underlying generalized mental structure through which all responses characteristic of a given stage are linked. Thus, if a particular stage is characterized by the acquisition of the logical principles of reciprocity, or inversion of transitivity, the child who has reached that stage should be able to master any and all problems involving this principle. (p. 443)

The assumption of an underlying generalized mental structure predicts that a child's performance on tasks designed to assess the same phenomenon will be highly consistent. In other words, a child who has achieved concrete operations should demonstrate this achievement consistently on related cognitive tasks.

There are, however, a considerable number of studies in both Western (Uzgiris, 1964) and non-Western (Cole, Gay, Glick, & Sharp, 1971) cultures which indicate that demonstration of conservation is dependent upon the materials used. These studies call into question the Piagetian assumption of generalized cognitive structures. The failure to demonstrate generalizability of conservation and formal operational thought across materials and situations (Feldman, 1974) leads one to question the significance of the concept of conservation as well as the notion of generalized cognitive structures. To determine the relationship among conservation tasks and other measures of intellectual development, studies investigating interrelationships among a variety of tasks measuring different processes are required. The Campbell and Fiske (1959) multitrait-multimethod approach is appropriate here and will be discussed in a later section of this paper.

The idea of a generalized cognitive structure in the Piagetian study of intelligence raises an obvious question of how, or if, this structure relates to the more traditional model of intelligence assessed in psychometric testing. Studies of children from the United States have indicated a close relationship between intelligence measured in the psychometric sense and intelligence determined in the Piagetian framework (Webb, 1974). However, a number of cross-cultural studies suggest that this relationship may differ as a result of cultural influences. Goodnow and Bethon (1966) reported that a number of their Hong Kong subjects who obtained high scores on the Raven Progressive Matrices performed poorly on conservation tasks in comparison with eleven-year-old American subjects who were superior in both the California Test of Mental Maturity and conservation performance. Heron (1971) reported similar results in his study of Zambian children: a number of his subjects failed to display conservation of weight despite successful scores on locally developed psychometric measures of reasoning ability. The validity of Heron's study is questionable, considering the small number of subjects and the lack of comparability of tests and procedures. However, the fact that similar results emerge from two independent studies in different cultural settings suggests that this is a fruitful issue for further research. In a somewhat related study deLacey (1971) found that Aborigines who had had considerable contact with Europeans performed on classification tests at about the same level as white children in a similar environment, despite their markedly lower verbal IQ scores (as measured by the Peabody Picture Vocabulary Test). While the cross-cultural validity of IQ tests is disputed, this study at least brings into question the relationship between facility with linguistic symbols and the assessment of logical thinking.

Again, we must be cautious in interpreting these results. All of the studies cited have serious weaknesses in design and testing and it is thus impossible to draw clear-cut inferences from them. Nevertheless, these suggestive findings from cross-cultural Piagetian studies strike at the heart of research in cognitive development. Specifically, they raise doubts about the Piagetian assumption of invariance in stage sequence. In addition, they challenge the existence of a generalized underlying cognitive structure and question whether any such structure corresponds to general intelligence as assessed by standardized psychometric tests.

Stage Transition

Comparative studies of the ages at which logical thinking is acquired in various cultures could provide evidence concerning the role of maturation in cognitive development. If the ages of acquisition and stage transition in other cultures correspond to age norms in Western society, it would appear that maturation is predominant in the determination of mental development. Conversely, if age trends vary across cultures, the importance of environmental influences would be supported. The task would then be to identify the environmental antecedents which account for differences in cognitive development. Unfortunately, the results are not sufficiently clear-cut to support any definitive conclusions. As was mentioned previously, while Piaget's theory postulates four major stages of cognitive development, most cross-cultural studies have been concerned with the age of acquisition of concrete and formal operations. For this reason the following review will discuss only studies related to these latter stages.

Concrete Operational Stage

The concrete operational stage of cognitive development is characterized by the child's understanding that the operations he or she performs on objects can be reversed mentally. The essential characteristic of this period has been designated *conservation*. For example, the child realizes that the quantity of a piece of clay remains the same despite changes in its shape. Conservation implies an internal system of regulations that can compensate mentally for external changes (Furth, 1969). Concrete operational thinking is typically assessed through investigations of conservation of number, length, quantity, percentage, weight, and volume.

The majority of cross-cultural studies have reported that the acquisition of most conservation skills is delayed in non-Western cultures. Heron and Simonsson (1969) compared 105 European children with 200 Zambian children on the acquisition of weight conservation. They found that whereas the proportion of European children demonstrating weight conservation increased linearly with age through the teenage years, the proportion of Zambian children attaining conservation reached a limit of 55 to 60 percent around the age of eleven. In another study in Papua-New Guinea, Heron and Dowel (1969) found a similar limit in the proportion of urban high-school students achieving conservation. They found that only half of their ten- to sixteen-year-old subjects could be classified as conservers on a nonverbal measure of conservation.

Za'rour (1971a) compared a sample of 224 elementary school children living in Beirut, with data from Almy, Chittenden, and Miller's (1966) study of elementary school children from the United States. He found that among five-, six-, and seven-year-old children in the United States, 28, 56, and 76 percent, respectively, conserved number. The corresponding percentages for Lebanese children were 0, 21, and 32. On a conservation-of-liquid task, the percentages for children from the United States were 9, 32, and 48 in comparison to 0, 4, and 22 percent for the Lebanese children. Za'rour hypothesized that the developmental lag observed in Lebanese children may be due to differences in child-rearing practices and modes of parent-child interaction. He cited the Lebanese mother's emphasis on obedience and rigid conformity as a possible explanatory factor. Za'rour also noted that the Lebanese school curriculum emphasizes verbal learning and memorization and does not seem conducive to manipulation and exploration. Poole (1968) compared 150 school children of the Hausa tribe in Nigeria with 40 children from a large junior school in the suburbs of a southern English city. The English group performed significantly better on tests of conservation than did the Hausa children.

However, not all cross-cultural studies have revealed similar contrasts in levels of cognitive development. Lloyd's (1971) results suggest that in some cases there may be minimal differences between two cultural groups. Using a modification of Almy et al.'s (1966) method for assessing conservation of liquid and number, Lloyd studied Nigerian Yoruba children ranging in age from three-and-one-half to eight years. His Yoruba subjects came from "elite" and traditional homes. He found no significant differences in performance between "elite" Yoruba subjects in Nigeria and the subjects of Almy et al.'s study in the United States. Lloyd's results also show that while traditional Yoruba subjects performed significantly lower than children from the United States on conservation-of-number tasks, they scored significantly higher on conservation-of-liquid tests.

In another study Za'rour (1971b) examined conservation among 132 Lebanese elementary school children. He hypothesized that the Lebanese children would perform better than children from the United States on tasks of weight conservation because they live in a culture with little prepackaging of materials and consequently have more experience in direct weighing. His results, when compared with Uzgiris' (1964) data on children from the United States, showed no significant differences in performance on conservation tasks. In this case, age seemed a more important influence on cognitive development than did cultural variation.

A number of cross-cultural Piagetian studies address the issue of early arrest in cognitive development in traditional non-industrialized cultures. This idea has long been prevalent. For example, Werner (1948) concluded that "development among primitive people is characterized on the one hand by precocity and, on the other, by a relatively early arrest of the process of intellectual growth" (p. 27).

An Australian study by deLemos (1969) found that only 50 percent of the adult Aboriginal subjects conserved quantity and only 75 percent conserved length. Since her part-Aboriginal children showed superior conservation performance in comparison to full-blooded Aborigines, she discussed the possibility of genetic differences. In a replication of the above study, Dasen (1972) also found that a large percentage of his adult subjects were non-conservers; however, he found no evidence of differential performance between full- and mixed-blooded Aborigines and argued for the role of environment in determining the rate of conservation acquisition. Ponzo (1966) observed that among the Kohorosciwetari and Tukano of Brazil, conservation of a discontinuous quantity (specifically, clay) seemed to be doubtful even for adults. In Greenfield's (1966) study of Wolof children in Senegal, only 50 percent of her oldest unschooled subjects (ages eleven to thirteen) were conservers, an insignificant increase over the proportion of conservers among eight- and nine-year-olds. This suggests that cognitive development as measured by conservation behavior is either arrested or significantly delayed among non-Western subjects. A study of conceptualization among unschooled Wolofs also revealed no changes in patterns of conceptualizing when eight- and nine-year-old subjects were compared with adults (Greenfield, Reich, & Olver, 1966).

There is some evidence that early arrest of cognitive development may not be irreversible. Peluffo (1962) indicated that migration of rural southern Italians to industrialized Geneva was associated with significant increases in conservation, thereby suggesting that renewed cognitive growth may result from contact with a technologically advanced society. Similarly, Jahoda (1969) attributed a significant gain in perception of causality in Ghanaian boys tested in 1968 over similar subjects tested in 1955 to improvement in the quality of teaching and related technological advancements in that nation.

In summary, it is possible to say that cross-cultural studies suggest a developmental lag for acquisition of conservation in non-Western, non-industrialized cultures. What is not clear, however, is whether this lag is due to a failure of the assessment method—that is, culturally inappropriate task materials and concomitant lack of motivation—or whether it is due to real cognitive differences between cultures. A later section in this paper will consider this important issue of cultural context.

Although most of the cross-cultural work has dealt with conservation, a number of interesting studies have investigated the cross-cultural development of classificatory skills, that is, the ability to sort objects into classes on the basis of varying characteristics. A popular task of this type requires showing a child a box of wooden beads, many brown and fewer white, and then asking the child if there are more wooden beads or more brown beads. In his study deLacey (1970) administered a battery of four classificatory tests of the type described to 86 Aboriginal children who had had little contact with Western technology and 79 high-contact Aboriginal children, as well as to a group of low- and high-socioeconomic Europeans. On all four tests, the order of performance, from highest to lowest, was: high-socioeconomic Europeans, low-socioeconomic Europeans, high-contact Aboriginals, and low-contact Aboriginals. Among the Aboriginals there was a consistent and strong direct relationship between classificatory performance and degree of contact with Europeans and their technology. It was hypothesized that the environmental difficulties accounting for the low performance of the low-contact Aboriginals might include malnutrition in fetal and early post-natal life. The author also suggested that the parallel development between different classificatory abilities might occur only where the environment is optimal and argued that his data provided preliminary support for a welfare policy requiring integration of Aboriginals with substantial European settlements. It is clear that this interpretation makes distinct value judgments in favor of Western performance patterns. In a later replication of the preceding study (deLacey, 1971), it was found that 40 urban Aboriginal children from the Northern Territory of Australia performed as well as 80 white children from a similar low-socioeconomic urban environment. This was seen as providing evidence for environmental rather than genetic effects on classificatory ability.

Price-Williams (1962) compared the performance of 80 literate and 60 illiterate children of the Tiv tribe in Nigeria, ranging in age from roughly six to eleven years, on a classification task in which the children were asked to sort models of animals known in the area and plants actually picked in the neighborhood. No difference was found between the two sets of children. Price-Williams concluded that the Tiv children, whether literate or illiterate, definitely attained concrete operational thinking, although there seemed to be a small lag in years when compared to the European standard of development.

While the studies reviewed above strongly suggest that differences in age of acquisition may indeed reflect real cognitive structural differences among cultures, it is important to note that this may be due to the impact of the environment on cognition. Dasen (1973) conducted a study that dramatically illustrates the effect of life activities on the development of concrete operational thought. As the Aboriginal language is sparse in number and measurement concepts while their living pattern requires development of spatial ability, Dasen proposed that the Aborigine would perform better on spatial tests than on measurement tests. His sample consisted of three groups of school children: a group of Aborigines who had little contact with European culture, a medium-contact group, and a group of lower-middle-class Australian and European children in Canberra. As expected, Dasen found that the Aboriginal groups performed better on the spatial tests than on the tests of conservation of quantity, weight, volume, and length. In contrast, the Canberra children performed significantly better on measurement tasks than on spatial tasks.

In a similar vein, the work of Cole, Gay, Glick, and Sharp (1971), while not essentially Piagetian, seems to have strong implications for the direction of cross-cultural research. After extensive research in classification, learning, and memory with the Kpelle of West Africa, these researchers concluded that "cultural differences in cognition reside more in the situations to which particular cognitive processes are applied than in the existence of a process in one cultural group and its absence in another" (p. 322).

The Cole et al. (1971) book and the Dasen (1973) study represent excellent examples of the insight into contextual effects that may be derived when research is carefully designed with regard to the characteristics of the specific culture using materials familiar to the culture. Cross-cultural research might profitably redirect its efforts from verification of age trends to an attempt to identify for each culture the situations in which specific cognitive processes are applied. Data from such studies could have significant practical application for designing educational experiences to match culturally preferred modes of functioning.

Formal Operational Thought

Formal operational thought is characterized by hypothetico-deductive reasoning and involves the ability to follow a hypothesis through to all possible logical conclusions, as well as the ability to deal with all possible combinations in a systematic fashion. On the basis of limited research, it appears that attainment of this stage of development is not universal. In fact, its prevalence even in Western society may not be as extensive as Piaget initially theorized. Piaget considers that a 75-percent success rate indicates the general presence of a particular thought process. But in studies of late adolescents in Western cultures, the percentage of subjects succeeding at formal operational tasks is typically between 30 and 50 percent (Kohlberg & Gilligan, 1971).

A number of cross-cultural studies have also failed to demonstrate full development of formal operations. Using Piagetian tasks requiring combinatorial thinking—the ability to systematically exhaust all possible hypotheses—Peluffo (1967) found that only 25 percent of the eleven-year-old rural children in his Sardinia sample and 20 percent of his illiterate Sardinian adult subjects attained success with similar tasks of combinatorial thinking. This result is compared to a 50-to-60-percent passing rate for his eleven-year-old subjects who were sons of workers born in Geneva or sons of clerks and professionals from Sardinia.

In a survey of 1,536 Papua-New Guinean children, Philp and Kelley (1974) found no evidence of formal operational thought. This compared with 50-percent achievement of formal operations among a New South Wales group and a 10-percent rate for a group of bilingual migrant children from Syndey, Australia. The test used was Inhelder's and Piaget's (1958) classic pendulum task, which requires the discovery of an inverse proportional relationship between the length of the string and the rate of oscillation. Philp and Kelly attributed the low rate of formal operations achievement among Papua-New Guinean children to a possible communication problem or to cultural differences.

Several studies have indicated instances where adults did not move beyond concrete modes of operation. In his study of Africans in the Belgian Congo, Maistriaux (1955) noted a consistent use of direct placement in estimating the length of a piece of wood and concluded that his African subjects operated at only the concrete stage. Greenfield (1966) reported that older, unschooled Wolof subjects depended heavily on perceptual justifications in conservation experiments. In sum, there seems to be a tendency for the application of action or perceptual modes of thinking in some "primitive" societies in contrast to the formal mode attributed to Western adults by Piaget.

Such cross-cultural inferences must be tempered, however, because the phenomena from which they are drawn are subject to different, competing interpretations. Instead of concluding that Maistriaux's and Greenfield's subjects had not achieved formal operations, we could, for example, advance the counter-hypothesis that the cultural bias in the experimental methods employed by these investigators precluded finding the formal operations which the subjects did in fact possess. Such a counter-hypothesis gains credence from the work of Feldman (1974), who found that when tasks were designed with culturally familiar materials, Eskimo children demonstrated formal operational thought. Since her subjects were successful on only one of two tasks designed to measure formal thought, Feldman suggested that this finding supports Inhelder's and Piaget's (1958) postulation of two substages of formal thought. She hypothesized that failure of the Eskimo children to demonstrate the second level of formal operations might be due to inadequacies in representational ability. In forwarding this hypothesis, she appealed to the Brunerian emphasis on the importance of linguistic competence for abstract thinking.

This notion receives support from a study by Kelly, Tenezakis, and Huntsman (1973) that suggests a close relationship between language and thought. These investigators studied 183 Greek migrant children attending English-language schools in Sydney. The children were tested for conservation of number and length in both Greek and English. Twenty-five percent who passed a language pre-test and failed to show conservation in English did conserve when tested in Greek. Although this study deals with conservation rather than formal operations, it surely has obvious implications for the formal period.

None of these studies should be considered definitive, but all of them do help alert us to the difficulties inherent in conducting cross-cultural research. Whenever a research technique developed in one culture is applied in another, investigators must be careful that inferences about cultural or social differences are not confused with cultural biases carried along with research techniques.

Social Factors and Logical Thinking

While social influences upon cognitive development have received less attention than have the effects of schooling, there are a few cross-cultural studies which suggest that this would be a fertile area for future investigation. Particularly relevant issues include (1) the effect of social goals on the development of egocentrism, (2) the differential effects of social environment upon various cognitive processes, (3) the effect of culture on moral development, (4) the effect of the cultural concept of reality on cognition, and (5) peer-group effects on cognitive development.

Several of the studies cited in the preceding section are relevant to a discussion of the influences of social factors on cognitive development. These studies speak to issues of social influences as well as age trends because the confounding of age, social experience, and other cultural variables allows for competing interpretations of cross-cultural differences. Specifically, do Papua-New Guinean subjects fail Piaget's pendulum test because they lack appropriate cognitive structures, because their experiences are different from those of Genevan youngsters, or because their notions of reality differ from those of the experimenters?

Social Goals and Egocentrism

Egocentrism, which Piaget describes as characteristic of the preoperational stage, represents the child's inability to assume the role of the other person. According to Piaget, youngsters in the preoperational stage are unable to consider points of view other than their own or to see contradictions in their own thinking. Greenfield and Bruner (1966), however, have observed that Eskimo children do not exhibit egocentrism and conclude that it is not universal but is dependent upon cultural conditions and values. These authors suggest that while Eskimo society emphasizes the importance of collective and group values, the individualistic emphasis of industrialized societies, such as the United States, results in development of egocentrism. Greenfield and Bruner (1966) demonstrated that unschooled Wolofs were unable to recognize differing points of view. This lack of relativity was attributed to a lack of self-consciousness, indicated by the absence of a distinction between an object and the corresponding thought about the object. Thus, the question "Why do you *think* this glass has more (or equal) water?" was met by silence, while the subjects readily responded to "Why *does* this glass have more (or equal) water?" Greenfield and Bruner attributed this absence of self-consciousness to the Wolofs' experiences of lack of control over their environment.

Rural vs. Urban Environment

The effect of rural versus urban environment on cognitive development is unclear. The data suggest a differential effect depending on the specific cognitive skill involved. Greenfield (1966) concluded that the urban-rural dimension was relatively unimportant in the attainment of conservation: ". . . there is a wider gap between unschooled and schooled Wolof children from the same rural village than between rural and urban school children" (p. 253). In contrast, in a study of equivalence grouping in schooled rural and urban Mexican children, Maccoby and Modiano (1966) concluded that contact with urban culture was a significant variable:

> We are struck by how much closer Mexico City is to Boston, than to a *mestizo* village. . . . The perceptual, concrete, difference-sensitive, organically oriented, village child is by age twelve in sharp contrast to the more abstract, functional, similarity-sensitive, cosmopolitan city child of the same age. (pp. 263, 267)

The contradictions suggest that the rural-urban dimension may have differential effects for different cognitive tasks. Greenfield, Reich, and Olver (1966) hypothesize that the essential difference between the rural and urban child is the difference between abstractness and concreteness, and they suggest that this variation is a result of differential exposure to problem solving and communication out of context. This issue is seriously confounded by the fact that most urban children attend school, whereas their rural peers are less apt to participate in a formal education process. Maccoby and Modiano (1966) warn that there are disadvantages accompanying the abstracting skill of the urbanized: "What industrialized, urban man gains in an increased ability to formulate, to reason, and to code the ever more numerous bits of complex information he acquires, he may lose in a decreased sensitivity to people and events" (p. 269).

A great deal of research is needed to elucidate social effects. It is insufficient to simply investigate the vague rural-urban domain. Precise specification of the critical aspects of this dimension is required.

Concepts of Social Reality

Research has indicated that cultural beliefs may have a negative effect upon the development of concrete operational thinking. Kohlberg (1968) found that among the Atayal, a Malaysian aboriginal group in Taiwan, conservation of a substance was acquired at the usual age of about seven or eight but then partially lost at ages eleven to fifteen, apparently due to conflict with adult magical beliefs.

In a modification of her initial conservation-of-liquid task, Greenfield (1966) discovered that conservation markedly increased when the Wolof children were allowed to do the pouring themselves. This procedure was effective with the unschooled children who had give explanations for non-conservation in terms of "action-magic"—the amount was different because the experimenter had poured it. Thus, instances of non-conservation were the result of cultural beliefs regarding the magical powers of an intervening human agent. This study is a powerful illustration of the crucial effect of seemingly small deviations in procedure. It argues strongly for caution in interpreting results from cross-cultural studies.

Culture and Moral Development

The question of cultural differences in moral judgment has received considerable attention in the work of Kohlberg (1971). Elaborating on Piaget's (1955) analysis of the acquisition of morality, Kohlberg describes moral development as a movement from hedonistic concerns to moral reasoning based on consideration of the abstract principles of justice and equality. Kohlberg has argued for the universality of the moral stages, which he derived from Piagetian theory. In support of this contention, he provides data in the form of responses to stories of moral dilemmas. On the basis of limited cross-cultural data representing twelve cultures, Kohlberg (1971) maintained that "all individuals in all cultures go through the same order or sequences of gross stages of development, though varying in rate and terminal point of development" (p. 175).

Simpson (1974), however, has presented vigorous criticisms of Kohlberg's methodology and his conclusions, condemning them as ethnocentric and culturally biased. She contends that Kohlberg's claim regarding the irreversibility of moral development is in conflict with actual data, and cites research indicating instances in which children have regressed in their moral thinking due to cultural influences (Havighurst & Neugarten, 1955; Kramer, 1968).

Simpson objects to analyzing a culture with techniques requiring modes of thinking not utilized within that group but rather indigenous to the culture of the investigator. She argues that principled moral reasoning may merely represent the socialization of the individual into an intellectual elite through the development of "sophisticated verbalism." Simpson also criticizes Kohlberg for inadequacies in the reporting of his cross-cultural studies: descriptions of samples, methodology, and results have not been published in sufficient detail to permit evaluation. As Simpson emphasizes, cross-cultural research in the area of moral development requires a sensitive awareness of the differential values and patterns of thinking specific to each culture. Failure to respond as expected to a moral dilemma may indicate absence of the type of thinking involved in the anticipated response, but it could also be explained by failure on the part of the experimenter to provide an appropriate situation for eliciting the desired behavior.

To provide hypotheses regarding stiuations that would elicit moral thinking, Simpson recommends a combination of ethnographic and experimental techniques in which the researcher relies on careful observation of the everyday activities of the cultural group. From this analysis, experimental manipulations could be introduced which would yield information regarding the range and frequencies of situations that evoke the reasoning processes under study. She proposes that an emphasis on discovering cross-cultural differences in moral reasoning may be of greater social significance than attempting merely to verify universal invariance.

Peer-Group Effects

West (1974) investigated the relation between early social experience and role-taking skills, that is, the ability "to put oneself in another's shoes." In comparing 108 Israeli boys from kibbutz, moshav, and city settings, West found no difference in role-taking skills resulting from variation in degree of early peer-group interaction. This result was also reported in Hollos and Cowan's (1973) study of Norwegian children. These findings suggest a conflict with Selman's (1971) report of a positive relationship between role-taking skills and moral development in his study of 60 children from the United States aged eight, nine, and ten. Further research is needed to determine the specific role of peer-group interaction in the development of cognitive skills.

Labov's theory concerning the differential treatment of various cultural groups within the experimental setting aptly applies here (Labov, 1970; Cole & Bruner, 1971). He believes that researchers do not take into account that: (a) different cultures and subcultures are predisposed to interpret experimental tasks very differently, (b) different groups place varying priorities upon the many aspects of the experimental task, and therefore (c) formal experimental equivalence does not ensure equal experimental treatment for members of different cultural groups. Although Labov specifically addresses himself to the plight of black children in "white" school systems, his criticisms apply to much of the cross-cultural Piagetian research.

Effects of Schooling on Logical Thinking

The question of the effects of schooling on development of logical thinking has been prominent in comparative research. Considerable evidence exists supporting Goodnow's (1969) assertion that there is significant variation in the extent to which different cognitive tasks are affected by varying degrees of schooling experience.

In a comparison of 60 unschooled Blacks, aged six and nine, from Prince Edward County, Virginia, with 60 schooled Blacks from a middle-size, northern industrial city, Mermelstein and Shulman (1967) found there were no significant differences between the groups on verbal and nonverbal conservation-of-quantity behavior. However, the unschooled group's performance was inferior on a verbal classification task, supporting the conclusion that schooling has a differential effect on development of various aspects of logical thinking (Sigel & Mermelstein, 1965). This conclusion derives further support from the research of Goodnow and Bethon (1966), who compared a group of 81 unschooled Chinese children in Hong Kong with 32 children from the United States. They concluded that lack of schooling did not affect their subjects' performances on conservation tasks but did significantly depress performance on the formal operational task. Similarly, Peluffo (1967), in a comparison of southern Italian immigrant children and native-born Genevans, found that an agricultural milieu was sufficient for acquisition of substance but lack of schooling and underdeveloped milieu resulted in failure to acquire formal operational thinking.

From these results, Goodnow concluded that conservation of mass and weight was a rather sturdy cognitive ability, less affected by lack of schooling than tasks requiring words, drawings, or visual imagery. This conclusion has been supported by recent research with Korean and Costa Rican children by Youniss and Dean (1974) who found milieu differences on imaging problems but not for typical conservation judgments. Goodnow (1969) hypothesized that the less vulnerable tasks may be those for which the child has an action model, and that the critical skill for demonstrating a more generalized ability may be versatility in the use of different sources of information and different models, an interesting issue for future research.

The effect of schooling on conservation appears to be related to the quality of schooling. Philp and Kelly (1974) reported that schooling had a positive effect on conservation of quantity and length and on formal thinking, particularly when the schooling was in the child's vernacular. Prince (1968) conducted a survey of 2,700 school children from primary grade three to Form III of high school in three distinct regions of the territory of Papua and New Guinea. He found that school grade was more significant than calendar age in determining cognitive development, suggesting that education may be a major factor in this area. In contrast to the Philp and Kelly results, Prince reported that English-language education was more effective in developing physical concepts than was vernacular education. Greenfield (1966) demonstrated that virtually all Wolof school children in Senegal achieve conservation by grade six while only 50 percent of unschooled Wolofs ever achieve conservation.

In some cases schooling has been found to have a detrimental effect upon cognitive development. Goodnow and Bethon (1966) noted a decline in conservation from 62 percent at age ten to 40 percent at ages twelve and thirteen in some Chinese schools; this decline was attributed to poor textbooks, poor teachers, and poor methods. Goodnow (1969) further analyzed the situation in discussing the tendency in some Hong Kong schools to encourage students to depend on books and adults "as the sole arbiters of what many aspects of the world were like," thus leaving the children "unable to bring their own experiences to bear on a task defined as a 'book' task" (p. 457). Heron (1971) obtained similar results in a study of weight conservation in Zambian children. When they left school at the age of fifteen, 40 to 50 percent of the urban Zambian children could conserve weight, but a higher proportion of *younger* Zambians were conservers. In short, the evidence seems to indicate that attempts to account for the development of conservation are relatively futile without specification of the nature of the schooling. Some types of schooling seem to promote acquisition of conservation (Greenfield, 1966; Philp & Kelly, 1974); other types seem to suppress it (Heron, 1971; Goodnow, 1962).

A number of hypotheses have been offered to account for the effects of schooling on cognitive development. Greenfield and Bruner (1966) have attributed cognitive growth primarily to the school's emphasis on the use of written language requiring "out of context" teaching and learning. Hollos and Cowan (1973) provide preliminary data on this question. In a comparison of three social settings in rural Norway—a farm community, a village, and a town—48 male and female children seven, eight, and nine years of age were tested for conservation. The investigators conclude that their results do not support Bruner's hypothesis; language stimulation and schooling do not seem to play a major role in the development of logical operations. Goodnow's (1962) Hong Kong study suggests that the school's reliance on written language, book information, and learning out of context, without a firm foundation upon concrete experience, results in suppression of conservation.

Scribner and Cole (1973) hypothesize that among non-Western cultures and certain Western subcultures the school's emphasis on language and out-of-context learning is contradictory to learning in everyday life. These authors related the linguistic out-of-context aspect of the school to the tendency of schooled children to generalize rules and operations across tasks and to use language to describe the tasks and their responses, characteristics which account for the superior performance of schooled children on many cognitive tasks. However, serious learning problems can result if the school is perceived as a hostile institution:

> The school's knowledge base, value system, and dominant learning situations and the functional learning systems to which they give rise are all in conflict with those of the student's traditional culture. . . . The antagonism the schools generate by their disrespect for the indigenous culture and by ignorance of its customs almost guarantees the production of nonlearners. (p. 558)

Scribner and Cole (1973) suggest that the observational, nonverbal aspects of informal education be investigated for possible advantages which could be incorporated into the formal system. In addition, they recommend research into the effects of the interaction of the formal and informal systems that necessarily operate in the school. They argue that such research is essential for determining the cognitive consequences of education.

Another hypothesis that has been put forth regarding the nature of the effects of school on logical thinking is more compatible with Piagetian thinking than is Bruner's linguistic explanation. In her discussion of the positive effects of Western schooling, deLemos (1969) cited the use of Cuisenaire rods and other concrete, manipulative materials in the school. From this, it might be inferred that the opportunity for active manipulation is crucial for the development of concrete operations. Further support for the importance of active manipulation in the development of logical thought is provided by Price-Williams' (1962) study of African Tiv children. He observed that, with the opportunity to manipulate familiar material, illiterate children achieved conservation at about the same time as schooled children. The role of manipulation in acquiring conservation is further substantiated in a study by Price-Williams, Gordon, and Ramirez (1969) which demonstrated that unschooled pottery-making children acquired conservation at the same time as schooled children.

In hypothesizing the importance of manipulation in the development of logical thinking, one should note that the nature of the concrete manipulative activity must be based upon the stage of cognitive development at which the child is presently operating. This necessity is illustrated in a study by Prince (1968), who examined acquisition of conservation in children from Papua and New Guinea. Prince expressed surprise that work with the Dienes material, which seemed directly related to the concept of conservation and logico-mathematical thinking, failed to induce conservation, while experiences in measurement estimation succeeded in facilitating it. A possible explanation might be derived from Lovell's (1961) warning that the Dienes material requires the ability to manipulate one variable at a time while holding other variables constant—a formal operation. Thus, Piagetian theory, based as it is upon hierarchical development, would predict failure with the Dienes material at the concrete stage.

Emphasis upon concrete experience in the development of logical thinking does not imply that the importance of experiences in symbolic representation is being de-emphasized. However, the dependence of representational thought upon concrete activity must be recognized. The relationship as postulated by Piaget is hierarchical; therefore, formal operations are dependent upon the development of concrete operations; representational thought is dependent upon schemas developed from participation in sensorimotor activities. This interrelationship of manipulation and symbolic representation in the development of con-servation has been demonstrated by Sonstroem (1966). In this study the develop-ment of conservation was dependent upon a training procedure requiring both active manipulation and labeling; neither alone was effective. Thus, the most reasonable explanation of schooling effects may require a synthesis of the Piagetian and the Brunerian positions.

In summary, the evidence suggests that schooling does exert an influence upon cognitive development. Education that offers an opportunity for concrete, man-ipulative activity promotes development of logical thinking. In addition, research supports the notion that as school children are forced to talk about objects in the absence of specific referents, they learn to appreciate the process, rather than the specific product, of discriminating the relationships among objects. As they are encouraged to speak of ideas *about* other ideas (far removed from the sensory foundations of the abstract relationships present), they learn to use previously induced rules to develop new logical arguments. Their goals, therefore, become more far-reaching than those related to the completion of specific and clearly delineated concrete tasks. Furthermore, children within the school experience seem to attain a heightened awareness of what it is they actually "know." Because they are forced to code and re-code their information along increasingly abstract dimensions, schooled children are more conscious of the mechanisms by which they solve logical problems. In short, because children must generalize in order to survive in the milieu of the classroom, they become skilled at transferring learning from one task to another (Vygotsky, 1934/1962). Schooling, however, does not seem to be critical for the development of conservation, since there is evidence of conservation among the unschooled. In contrast, schooling, because of its emphasis upon symbolic thinking, may be crucial to the development of formal thought processes, at least as measured by performance on tests of com-binatorial thinking. It seems most important that school activities be related to the child's developmental level if formal education is to have a positive influence on cognitive development.

Information derived through cross-cultural analysis of formal and informal schooling effects may have significant implications for educational planning. Scrib-ner and Cole (1973), for example, have questioned the school's almost exclusive dependence on linguistic communication. They suggest that aspects of the in-formal learning system may be profitably utilized in the school setting.

The Cross-Cultural Research Design

A great weakness of cross-cultural research, and one which has limited its complexity, is the quality and nature of their methodology. Developmental cross-cultural studies have, for the most part, been simply designed—usually involving a relatively small sample and comparing two groups within a single age category. The two groups are generally compared by means of simple t-tests, or univariate analyses. Needless to say, it is appropriate to question the applicability of such simple designs to the study of so complicated a process as cognitive development. Cross-cultural studies notwithstanding, many basic questions remain unanswered. The nature of conservation (Flavell, 1971), the significance of the stage concept, and the specific factors influencing cognitive development (Brainerd, 1973; Furby, 1971) are some of the issues in need of further study. Since the technology exists for the implementation of sophisticated analyses, it is certainly reasonable to begin to apply them in the study of intellectual development.

The pages that follow consider procedures for devising more sophisticated cross-cultural research aimed at advancing cognitive developmental theory. Specifically, they take up the procedures of experimental anthropology, longitudinal studies, multitrait-multimethod approaches, quasi-experimental designs, and multivariate analysis.

Experimental Anthropology

The research of Cole and his associates has dramatically demonstrated the situation-specific nature of many experimental findings in cross-cultural settings (Cole & Bruner, 1971). Their studies have served to invalidate many of the sweeping generalizations regarding the cognitive deficiencies of non-Western cultures. Performance differences on a single task may be due to any number of causes not specifically related to cultural differences. Labov (1970), in his attack on the "cultural deficit" hypothesis regarding the linguistic inferiority of the black American child, has emphasized the inadequacy of the experimental method as it traditionally has been employed:

> With human subjects it is absurd to believe that identical stimuli are obtained by asking everyone the same question. Since the crucial intervening variables of interpretation and motivation are uncontrolled, most of the literature on verbal deprivation tells us nothing of the capacities of children. (p. 171)

The same might be said of the literature of cross-cultural research in general.

Cole et al. (1971) have provided a model for devising meaningful milieu research which they term "experimental anthropology." This approach requires a rapprochement between the anthropologist, linguist, and psychologist. Prior to design of the research, an ethnographic analysis is conducted in concert with an anthropologist and linguist. This analysis yields guidelines regarding the form for conducting the experiment and assists in identifying relevant variables. After the ethnographic analysis, the researcher begins by designing stimulus materials for the specific culture under study (Cole & Scribner, 1974). When an experimental treatment yields differential results, modifications of the experimental treatment are developed based on anthropological observations of the culture. This procedure is repeated until the particular cultural variables responsible for the difference are isolated.

Cross-cultural studies are notorious for reasoning backwards from results to causes. Through the use of experimental anthropology, hypotheses based on cognitive theory could be generated from an examination of specific characteristics of the culture. If such hypotheses so-generated can then be experimentally confirmed, one would have a more powerful defense of the theory than the conjectural statements of cause or the rationalizations of results that typically appear in descriptive cross-cultural studies can hope to offer. Experimental anthropology can provide data depicting the cultural situations in which specific factors of cognition may be expected to operate, and thus can yield the basic data for deriving hypotheses for testing theoretical issues.

Triandis (1974), reviewing Cole and Scribner's (1974) work, emphasizes the significance this approach may have for the social sciences:

> . . . the purpose of this discipline [experimental anthropology] will be to discover relationships between ecology and social structure, patterns of interpersonal relationships, and behavior. Psychological theory will aim at cross-cultural generality so that cultural variables will become embedded in theories of perception, skills, personality, and behavior. Such a movement may well become so important as to seriously modify the mainstream of both psychology and anthropology. If that happens the new discipline may absorb the parent disciplines and become the mainstream. These developments also have profound implications for education (how to structure educational experiences so that children can take full advantage of special skills developed in their particular ecologies), sociology (how the ecology of social class affects cognitive functioning and how such functioning generates different types of institutions), economics (how different ecologies result in particular viewpoints that make specific economic policies more or less appropriate in different parts of the world), and political science (how ecologies may result in

differences in the optimal political systems). In short, the books reviewed here (Cole & Scribner, 1974; Berry & Dasen, 1974) may be the first ripple of a major storm in the social sciences. (p. 492)

Longitudinal Studies

Wohlwill (1970) has emphasized the need for longitudinal, correlational studies to elucidate the functional interrelationships between conservation and other aspects of cognition. Such research is needed in order to validate the sort of developmental inferences which are now being drawn from cross-sectional studies. The danger is cross-sectional studies like that of Goodnow and Bethon (1966) and many of the other studies cited previously is that differences in performance on cognitive tasks between two age groups may be interpreted as a developmental phenomenon whereas the differences may in fact derive from some other difference between the groups besides age. Until particular individuals are traced throughout the course of the presumed developmental sequence, it will be impossible to be sure that developmental sequences inferred from cross-sectional studies do actually exist.

Research in a cross-cultural context provides a uniquely potent setting for devising natural experiments. Laboratory experiments which artificially manipulate learning variables may grossly misrepresent true developmental trends. In contrast, field experiments designed to evaluate the effect of "real" experimental differences are more likely to yield an accurate representation of developmental changes as they actually occur in the child. Thus, cross-cultural research may well hold the answer to whether the process of acquisition is the same in all cultures, that is, whether the concepts or rules that result in conservation differ according to culture or subculture. Research regarding the effects of training on conservation suggests that practice on conservation is less effective in inducing conservation than experience with other concepts and rules (Wohlwill, 1970). Cross-cultural longitudinal research may be able to specifically identify the critical concepts and rules.

Specific Dimensions

Following Piaget's directive, cross-cultural research has attempted to ferret out the effects of biological, social, educational, and cultural factors on cognitive development. However, this research has consistently concerned itself with gross categorizations of these factors: for example, urban versus rural, schooled versus unschooled. As Goodnow suggested (1969), it is critical that research begin to delineate these factors into more specific and consequently more meaningful dimensions if this research is to advance theory. Examples of such dimensions have been gleaned from a variety of sources: mode of parent-child interaction and child-rearing practices, type of play, sex-role typing, quality of nutrition, and linguistic structure (Goodnow, 1969; Dasen, 1972). The diversity of social relationships evident across cultures may have a powerful effect upon the cognitive development of the child. This area of research has been neglected.

Multivariate Analysis

Related to the identification of specific dimensions is the multivariate analysis method. Obviously, variables do not operate singly in the cultural context. To adequately represent milieu influences, it is essential that our research designs permit analysis of the interaction effects of various factors in order to reflect the complexity of the cultural environment. Factorial designs that permit the investigation of interaction effects could help unravel the web of cultural influences. Multivariate analysis, which permits the analysis of the effect of more than one variable on more than one outcome, may provide evidence regarding the effect of specific cultural factors on a variety of cognitive dimensions.

Various researchers (Goodnow, 1969; Heron, 1971; deLacey, 1971) have suggested that the pattern of cognitive abilities may vary across cultures as the result of different experiences. Buss and Royce (1975) described a procedure for utilizing the methodology of multivariate factor analysis in an effort to more effectively operationalize various organismic development concepts. A good example might be operationalizing the dual processes described by Piaget as underlying intellectual functioning, that is, assimilation—taking in experience—and accommodation—adjusting to the environment.

The Buss and Royce (1975) procedure might be employed to demonstrate operationally (1) the ways in which structure becomes increasingly differentiated with age, (2) cultural differences in cognitive structures, and (3) shifts in patterns as a result of changes during the transitional period, which Flavell (1971) suggests may be significantly more complex than heretofore anticipated.

Furby (1971) has been particularly helpful in developing a theoretical framework for interpreting cross-cultural studies of conservation. This author postulates an analysis of conservation as a function of type of culture (empirical versus magical), degree of technical development (manual versus automated), and schooling. Other more limited cultural dimensions should be considered as potentially relevant to cognitive growth. Furby's model could be broadened to encompass other Piagetian constructs and might profitably be extended to a multivariate design in which various Piagetian factors, such as transitivity and classification skills, as well as conservation, are included.

Multitrait-Multimethod Matrix

As discussed in the sections concerned with theoretical issues, there is also a need for further evidence regarding the sequential development of operational thinking, the interrelationships between the various types of conservation, and the nature of conservation itself. Unfortunately, Piagetian research in this area is beset with methodological problems, as illustrated by Brainerd (1973). In two studies, the first with 60 white Canadian second graders and 60 white American second graders, and the second with equal numbers of white Canadian kindergarteners, first graders, and second graders, Brainerd examined the order of emergence of transitivity, conservation, and classification skills for the concepts of length and weight. Brainerd's principal findings were inconsistent with Piagetian theory: transitivity appeared prior to both conservation and classification, and conservation emerged before classification. These results regarding the order of emergence of these skills have practical significance, because elementary school mathematics programs have been developed with the assumption that there is no optimal order. Other Piagetian research has also yielded contradictory data concerning the order of emergence. Brainerd speculated that such contradictions in results may be due to failure to equate methodologies, with the result that invariant sequences are produced where they do not exist or actual sequences become masked.

Campbell and Fiske (1959) proposed a paradigm for dealing with this methodological problem, which has yet to appear in cross-cultural Piagetian research. Their multitrait-multimethod matrix is a validation procedure applied among tests of at least two traits, each measured by at least two methods: "Measures of the same trait should correlate higher with each other than they do with measures of different traits involving separate methods. Ideally, these validity values should also be higher than the correlations among different traits measured by the same method" (p. 104). As Cole et al. (1971) have cautioned: ". . . whenever we want to use an explanation that requires us to assume that one group 'has a process' while another does not, our interpretation is open to question. It is always possible that further experimentation would turn up evidence of the hypothetical process under proper circumstances" (p. 228). Considerable evidence should be required before conclusions are formulated. There will always be doubt that the same results would obtain given different circumstances. The use of multiple experiments systematically varying methodology and traits can, it is hoped, help reduce this doubt.

Quasi-Experimental Designs

The requirements of full control of experimental treatments and random assignments of subjects to treatment conditions—essential conditions of the psychological experiment—are rarely met in cross-cultural research, because there is little opportunity for controlling cultural variations. The cross-cultural setting, however, is most appropriate for the utilization of the quasi-experimental designs described by Campbell and Stanley (Campbell & Stanley, 1963; Dasen, 1972). The purpose of these quasi-experimental designs is to insure equivalence of groups and reduce the threats to external and internal validity that plague cross-cultural studies.

The time-series design also seems appropriate for cross-cultural research. This approach requires periodic measurement of a group and the introduction of an experimental treatment at some point in the series of measurements. For example, conservation tasks might be presented to children from varying cultures before and after the introduction of a special cultural variable, say some new technological advance. The counterbalanced design suggests the possibility of providing a number of training experiences to differing cultural groups to determine if there is an interaction effect on culture with technique. With this design, one group might use method A and another method B for the first half of the experiment and then exchange methods for the last half of the experiment. In this manner, both groups receive both treatments at some point, and the investigator is able to compare their differential reactions to the same treatment.

In the design of cross-cultural experiments of these types, the methods of experimental anthropology, as discussed earlier, must be brought into play. Thus, in the great deal of cross-cultural research that has concentrated on the acquisition of conservation, some findings have been interpreted as evidence of retardation of conservation in some cultures. However, these findings may be the result not of genuine cultural differences in cognitive ability, but of unfamiliarity with materials or lack of motivation among subjects.

Effective research into these areas demands more adequately designed research studies. Cross-cultural experimentation should begin with a thorough collaborative study, by anthropologists and linguists, of the cultures to be considered. Such a study would help to determine appropriate techniques and to identify cultural variables that might be expected to have an impact on cognitive development. These data should be used in generating predictive hypotheses derived from existing cognitive theory. Samples should be large and as representative as possible; highly specific descriptions of the nature of the sample should be provided; comparison groups should be determined on the basis of rather specific and limited differences, and these differences should be thoroughly delineated. Designs should be employed which permit examination of complex interactions. Problems should deal with significant theoretical issues rather than with mere efforts to validate age trends. Studies should involve multiple experimentations to provide significant insights into the issues examined, such that each additional culture added to the study provides one more replication in which to test out the generalization (Holtzman, 1968).

The application of complex research design to Piagetian questions in a cross-cultural context opens up exciting possibilities for significant contributions to developmental theory. By designing studies to investigate cognitive development in varying cultural settings, researchers may produce the natural experiment that has the potential advantage of being representative of cognitive developmental processes as they actually operate in the environment.

References

Almy, M., Chittenden, E., & Miller, P. *Young children's thinking*. New York: Teachers College Press, 1966.

Boonsong, S. The development of conservation of mass, weight, and volume in Thai children. Unpublished master's thesis, College of Education, Bangkok, Thailand, 1968.

Brainerd, C. J. Order of acquisition of transitivity, conservation and class inclusion of length and weight. *Developmental Psychology*, 1973, **8**, 105–116.

Buss, A., & Royce, J. Ontogenetic changes in cognitive structure from a multivariate perspective. *Developmental Psychology*, 1975, **11**, 87–101.

Campbell, D., & Fiske, D. Convergent and discriminant validation by the multitrait-multimethod matrix. *Psychological Bulletin*, 1959, **56**, 81–105.

Campbell, D., & Stanley, J. Experimental and quasi-experimental designs for research on teaching. In N. L. Gage (Ed.), *Handbook on research on teaching*. Chicago: Rand McNally, 1963.

Cole, M., & Bruner, J. Cultural differences and inferences about psychological processes. *American Psychologist*, 1971, **26**, 867–876.

Cole, M., Gay, J., Glick, J., & Sharp, D. *The cultural context of learning and thinking*. New York: Basic Books, 1971.

Cole, M., & Scribner, S. *Culture and thought: A psychological introduction*. New York: Wiley, 1974.

Dasen, P. R. Cross-cultural Piagetian research: A summary. *Journal of Cross-Cultural Psychology*, 1972, **3**, 23–39.

Dasen, P. R. The influence of ecology, culture and European contact on cognitive development in Australian Aborigines. In J. W. Berry & P. R. Dasen (Eds.), *Culture and cognition: Readings in cross-cultural psychology.* London: Methuen, 1973.

deLacey, P. R. A cross-cultural study of classificatory ability in Australia. *Journal of Cross-Cultural Psychology,* 1970, **1**, 293–304.

deLacey, P. R. Classificatory ability and verbal intelligence among high-contact Aboriginal and low socioeconomic white Australian children. *Journal of Cross-Cultural Psychology,* 1971, **2**, 393–396.

deLemos, M. M. The development of conservation in Aboriginal children. *International Journal of Psychology,* 1969, 4, 255–269.

Elkind, D. Children's discovery of the conservation of mass, weight, and volume: Piaget replication study II. *The Journal of Genetic Psychology,* 1961, **98**, 219–227. (a)

Elkind, D. Quantity conceptions in junior and senior high school students. *Child Development,* 1961, **32**, 551–560. (b)

Feldman, C., Lee, B., McLean, J., Pillemer, D., & Murray, J. *The development of adaptive intelligence.* San Francisco: Jossey-Bass, 1974.

Flavell, J. Stage-related properties of cognitive development. *Cognitive Psychology,* 1971, 2, 421–453.

Furby, L. A theoretical analysis of cross-cultural research in cognitive development: Piaget's conservation task. *Journal of Cross-Cultural Psychology,* 1971, 2, 241–255.

Furth, H. *Piaget and knowledge: Theoretical foundations.* Englewood Cliffs, N.J.: Prentice-Hall, 1969.

Ginsburg, H., & Opper, S. *Piaget's theory of intellectual development: An introduction.* Englewood Cliffs, N.J.: Prentice-Hall, 1969.

Goodnow, J. A test of milieu effects with some of Piaget's tasks. *Psychological Monographs,* 1962, **76** (36, Whole No. 55).

Goodnow, J. Problems in research on culture and thought. In D. Elkind & J. Flavell (Eds.), *Studies in cognitive development.* New York: Oxford University Press, 1969.

Goodnow, J., & Bethon, G. Piaget's tasks: The effects of schooling and intelligence. *Child Development,* 1966, **37**, 573–582.

Greenfield, P. On culture and conservation. In J. Bruner, R. R. Olver, & P. Greenfield (Eds.), *Studies in cognitive growth.* New York: Wiley, 1966.

Greenfield, P., & Bruner, J. Culture and cognitive growth. *International Journal of Psychology,* 1966, **1**, 89–107.

Greenfield, P., Reich, L., & Olver, R. R. On culture and equivalence II. In J. Bruner, R. R. Olver, & P. Greenfield (Eds.), *Studies in cognitive growth.* New York: Wiley, 1966.

Havighurst, R., & Neugarten, B. *American Indian and white children.* Chicago: University of Chicago Press, 1955.

Heron, A. Concrete operations, "g" and achievement in Zambian children. *Journal of Cross-Cultural Psychology,* 1971, **2**, 325–336.

Heron, A., & Dowel, W. Weight conservation and matrix-solving ability in Papuan children. *Journal of Cross-Cultural Psychology,* 1973, 4, 207–219.

Heron, A., & Simonsson, M. Weight conservation in Zambian children: A non-verbal approach. *International Journal of Psychology,* 1969, 4, 281–292.

Hollos, M., & Cowan, P. Social isolation and cognitive development: Logical operations and role-taking abilities in three Norwegian social settings. *Child Development*, 1973, **44**, 630–641.

Holtzman, W. H. Cross-cultural studies in psychology. *International Journal of Psychology*, 1968, **3**, 83–91.

Hyde, D. M. *An investigation of Piaget's theories of the development of number.* Unpublished doctoral dissertation, University of London, 1959.

Inhelder, B., & Piaget, J. *The growth of logical thinking from childhood to adolescence.* London: Routledge & Kegan Paul, 1958.

Jahoda, G. Understanding the mechanism of bicycles: A cross-cultural study of developmental change after thirteen years. *International Journal of Psychology*, 1969, **4**, 103–108.

Kelly, M., Tenezakis, M., & Huntsman, R. Some unusual conservation behavior in children exposed to two cultures. *British Journal of Educational Psychology*, 1973, **43**, 181–182.

Kohlberg, L. Early education: A cognitive-developmental view. *Child Development*, 1968, **39**, 1013–1062.

Kohlberg, L. From is to ought. How to commit the naturalistic fallacy and get away with it in the study of moral development. In T. Mischel (Ed.), *Cognitive development and epistemology*. New York: Academic Press, 1971.

Kohlberg, L., & Gilligan, C. The adolescent as a philosopher: The discovery of the self in a postconventional world. *Daedalus*, 1971, **100**, 1051–1086.

Kramer, R. *Moral development in young adulthood.* Doctoral dissertation, University of Chicago, 1968.

Labov, W. The logic of nonstandard English. In F. Williams (Ed.), *Language and poverty*. Chicago: Markham, 1970.

Lloyd, B. The intellectual development of Yoruba children: A reexamination. *Journal of Cross-Cultural Psychology*, 1971, **2**, 29–38.

Lovell, K. *The growth of basic mathematical and scientific concepts in children.* London: University of London Press, 1961.

Maccoby, M., & Modiano, N. On culture and equivalence I. In J. Bruner, R. R. Olver, & P. Greenfield (Eds.), *Studies in cognitive growth*. New York: Wiley, 1966.

Maistriaux, R. La sous-évolution des noirs d'Afrique: Sa nature, ses causes, ses remèdes. *Revue de la Psychologie des Peuples*, 1955, **10**, 397–456.

Mermelstein, E., & Shulman, L. S. Lack of formal schooling and the acquisition of conservation. *Child Development*, 1967, **38**, 39–52.

Mohsensi, N. *La comparaison des réactions aux épreuves d'intelligence en Iran et en Europe.* Thèse de l'université, University of Paris, 1966.

Peluffo, N. Les notions de conservation et de causalité chez les enfants provenant de différents milieux physiques et socioculturels. *Archives de Psychologie*, 1962, **38**, 275–291.

Peluffo, N. Culture and cognitive problems. *International Journal of Psychology*, 1967, **2**, 187–198.

Philp, H., & Kelly, M. Product and process in cognitive development: Some comparative data on the performance of school age children in different cultures. *British Journal of Educational Psychology*, 1974, 44, 248–265.

Piaget, J. *The psychology of intelligence.* London: Routledge & Kegan Paul, 1950.

Piaget, J. *The moral judgment of the child.* New York: Macmillan, 1955.

Ponzo, E. Acculturazione e detribalizzazione. *Rivista de Psicologia Sociale*, 1966, 13, 41–107.

Poole, H. E. The effect of urbanization upon scientific concept attainment among Hausa children of northern Nigeria. *British Journal of Educational Psychology*, 1968, 38, 57–63.

Price-Williams, D. R. Abstract and concrete modes of classification in a primitive society. *British Journal of Educational Psychology*, 1962, 32, 50–61.

Price-Williams, D. R., Gordon, W., & Ramirez, M., III. Skill and conservation: A study of pottery-making children. *Developmental Psychology*, 1969, 1, 769.

Prince, J. R. The effect of Western education on science conceptualization in New Guinea. *British Journal of Educational Psychology*, 1968, 38, 64–74.

Scribner, S., & Cole, M. Cognitive consequences of formal and informal education. *Science*, 1973, 182, 553–559.

Selman, R. The relation of role-taking to the development of moral judgment in children. *Child Development*, 1971, 42, 79–81.

Sigel, I. E., & Mermelstein, E. *Effects of nonschooling on Piagetian tasks of conservation.* Paper presented at the meeting of the American Psychological Association, Chicago, September 1965.

Simpson, E. L. Moral development research: A case study of scientific cultural bias. *Human Development*, 1974, 17, 81–106.

Sonstroem, A. M. On the conservation of solids. In J. Bruner, R. R. Olver, & P. Greenfield (Eds.), in *Studies of cognitive growth.* New York: Wiley, 1966.

Triandis, H. C. Psychologists on culture and thought. *Reviews in Anthropology*, 1974, 1, 484–492.

Uzgiris, I. C. Situational generality of conservation. *Child Development*, 1964, 35, 831–841.

Vygotsky, L. [*Thought and language*] (E. Hanfmann & G. Vakar, Eds. and trans.). Cambridge: The M.I.T. Press, 1962. (Originally published, 1934.)

Webb, R. Concrete and formal operations in very bright 6- to 11-year-olds. *Human Development*, 1974, 17, 292–300.

Werner, H. *Comparative psychology of mental development.* New York: Follett, 1948.

West, H. Early peer-group interaction and role-taking skills: An investigation of Israeli children. *Child Development*, 1974, 45, 1118–1121.

Wohlwill, J. F. Piaget's system as a resource of empirical research. In I. E. Sigel & F. E. Hooper (Eds.), *Logical thinking in children.* New York: Holt, Rinehart & Winston, 1968.

Wohlwill, J. F. The place of structured experience in early cognitive development. *Interchange*, 1970, 1, 13–27.

Youniss, J., & Dean, A. Judgment and imaging aspects of operations: A Piagetian study with Korean and Costa Rican children. *Child Development*, 1974, **45**, 1020–1034.

Za'rour, G. The conservation of number and liquid by Lebanese school children in Beirut. *Journal of Cross-Cultural Psychology*, 1971, **2**, 165–172. (a)

Za'rour, G. Conservation of weight across different materials by Lebanese school children in Beirut. *Science Education*, 1971, **55**, 387–394. (b)

Kohlberg's Stages of Moral Judgment: A Constructive Critique

JOHN C. GIBBS
Harvard University

Lawrence Kohlberg's work on moral judgment posits a typology of six hierarchical stages which form a Piagetian developmental sequence. The last two stages have occasioned widespread controversy in developmental psychology because of their rarity and the claim that they represent morally and structurally higher forms of reasoning. In this article, John Gibbs distinguishes between naturalistic and existential themes in modern psychology and outlines the empirical criteria that identify a naturalistic or Piagetian sequence. He then argues that the first four stages of Kohlberg's typology meet the criteria for a naturalistic developmental sequence but the higher stages instead appear to be existential or reflective extensions of earlier stages. The conclusions Gibbs reaches have considerable significance for clarifying the relationships between the highest forms of moral and social thought and development, experience, and education.

Two of the most fundamental themes in modern psychology are evident in Lawrence Kohlberg's widely known work on moral judgment. The first theme is the "naturalistic" argument that the development and expression of human behavior reflect spontaneous constructive processes characteristic of life in general. The naturalistic theme owes its modern impetus mainly to Jean Piaget but was also expounded by J. M. Baldwin, Heinz Werner, and John Dewey. The second theme is the "existential" argument that awareness of self and efforts to come to terms with this awareness are keys to understanding the human phenomenon. Found in the writings of William James and symbolic interactionists such as George Herbert Mead, this theme has been propounded most extensively in the works of Erich Fromm.

* This article is an elaboration of a paper presented by the author at the meeting of the Jean Piaget Society, Philadelphia, June 1976. I wish to thank John Broughton, Valerie Gibbs, Bob Kegan, Clark Power, and Bob Selman for their many helpful comments on the article's preliminary versions. I also wish to thank Larry Kohlberg for encouraging me to develop several of these ideas.

Harvard Educational Review Vol. 47 No. 1 February 1977, 43–61.

In Kohlberg's work, where the naturalistic theme is primary, the human subject is portrayed as gradually constructing a sequence of moral-judgment "stages" by interacting with universal features of the social environment. Significantly, Kohlberg makes no explicit use of two suppositions which underlie Piaget's version of naturalistic stage theory. The first supposition, *universality of form,* states that stages should be commonly found among members of the species from birth to maturity; the second, *unconsciousness of process,* is that stage behavior derives from implicit or unconscious processes and systems. While Kohlberg's stages 1 through 4 are characterized by the naturalistic assumptions and can be understood as developmental stages in the Piagetian sense, the existential theme dominates stages 5 and 6, which are not universal and are achieved only through meta-ethical reflection. The "construction" of stages 5 and 6, writes Kohlberg (1973a), "seems to require experiences of personal moral choice and responsibility usually supervening upon a questioning period of 'moratorium' " (p. 180), and the more specific questioning of ethics or morality proceeds "from a standpoint outside that of a member of a constituted society" (p. 192). Individuals who achieve the highest stages turn upon and question the ethics used during childhood. My argument will be that the naturalistic and existential themes in Kohlberg's work should be more clearly distinguished.

Kohlberg's First Four "Stages": A Review

Since Piaget's studies in the early 1930s of the development of children's social play and moral judgment, researchers have tested and extended his early findings. Much of their work has dealt with specifically "moral" judgment: prescribing, evaluating, and justifying with reference to socially good and right action (cf. Frankena, 1973, pp. 43–53). In the 1950s, Kohlberg reviewed and identified consistently replicated findings. On the basis of this review and his own research on adolescents and younger children, Kohlberg (1958) established a typology of six stages in the development of moral judgment.[1] A second strand of research stemming from Piaget's early work has focused on social development. For example, Melvin Feffer (1959) and John Flavell (Flavell, Botkin, Fry, Wright, & Jarvis, 1968) have used innovative methods to investigate the child's developing ability to coordinate social perspectives in interpersonal relations or communication. More recent research by Selman (1971) and Chandler (1973) refines the stage typologies which emerged from Feffer's and Flavell's earlier studies. Selman's "social perspective-taking" stages were identified and defined in collaboration with Kohlberg and are explicitly hypothesized as corresponding to respective stages in Kohlberg's scheme.

The first four of Kohlberg's stages are the most common and best researched, and as such they are the most likely candidates for defining a "stage" sequence which is natural in a Piagetian sense. At this point they are posited as candidates for a verified stage sequence in the Piagetian sense and will be referred to as *orientations.*

---

[1] Questions of methodological theory and practice associated with research on Kohlberg's theory have been discussed in recent psychological literature (Broughton, 1976; Gibbs, Kohlberg, Colby, & Speicher-Dubin, 1976; Kurtines & Greif, 1974; Simpson, 1974).

Kohlberg's early orientations relate so closely to social perspective-taking that my description will consider both.

The First Four Stage Candidates in Moral Judgment

The features which perhaps best define and distinguish the moral-judgment orientations are the respective ways in which moral prescriptions or evaluations are justified. The now famous Heinz dilemma, originating from Kohlberg's work, has proven an especially good research vehicle, permitting the elicitation of different ways of justifying moral judgments concerning relations between life, law, punishment, and conscience. Heinz's wife is dying of a cancer that only a newly discovered drug, which Heinz cannot afford, may cure. Heinz's dilemma is whether to try to save his wife's life by stealing the drug, or obey the law and let his wife die. This dilemma provides the context for my review and evaluation of research on moral judgment.

Orientation 1: Justifying moral prescriptions or evaluations by appeal to the physical consequences and literal features of an action. The outstanding feature of many young children's moral judgments is their attention to the concrete or literal aspects of an act rather than to the intentions of the actor. Telling a lie is judged as naughty if it is a "big" untruth; that is, if it is an obvious departure from reality. This literal criterion is used even when the intention to deceive by means of the untruth is suggested to the child as an alternative standard for judgment (Piaget, 1932/1965; cf. Graham, 1972, pp. 207–217). Young children with this orientation explain their conceptions of parental authority in terms of grown-ups' superior size, strength, and mobility (Kohlberg, 1966). In studies using the Heinz dilemma (see Kohlberg, Colby, Gibbs, Speicher-Dubin, & Power, 1976), those who judge that Heinz should be punished if he is caught stealing the drug justify their response by appealing to the literal fact of the transgression: "What should the judge do? *Put him in jail.* Why? *Because he was caught stealing. He has to go to jail.*"

The tendency of young children to focus on immediate or literal actions in justifying their moral judgments is primarily observed in their judgments of others' conduct. Young children often use intentionality when defending their own behavior as not naughty (Piaget, 1932/1965, pp. 125–126) or when a socio-moral situation has been simplified by excluding more literal considerations (Bergcross, 1975; Caruso, 1943). Understanding intentionality in personal or simplified, but not interpersonal, contexts suggests among several possibilities that the literal focus stems from a difficulty in coordinating social perspectives. Reflecting such a difficulty is the following response of a child who is a literal moral judge:

Q. What would you do if your wife was dying and you needed the drug but couldn't pay for it?

A. I'd rob the store.

Q. Why would you do that if it's against the law?

A. Because my wife was dying.

Q. What would you do if you were the judge?

A. I'd send Heinz to jail because he robbed the store.

Q. Wouldn't the judge think he would steal in that situation?

A. Yes, he might let him go free then.

(Selman & Byrne, 1972, p. 44)

As Selman and Byrne point out, "The subject does not seem to consider that the judge would consider the husband's reasons until the interviewer has put the judge in the husband's situation. . . . The subject does not relate conflicting perspectives" (p. 44).

Orientation 2: Justifying moral prescriptions or evaluations by appeal to the actor's pragmatic needs and instrumental intentions. By age seven or eight, children usually begin to evidence in their justifications a less literal understanding of interpersonal moral conduct. Medinnus (1962) found with increasing age a dramatic decline in literal themes such as "you get punished" or "it's naughty" and a sharp increase in more judgmental themes such as "you don't get any place, it just leads to more lies," and "you always get found out anyway." Zarncke (1955) obtained similar results and pointed out that many of the judgmental reasons sounded rather pragmatic—for example, "once you've told a lie, nobody believes you again." The pragmatic or instrumental orientation in moral justification is especially clear in Heinz-dilemma justifications—you should steal because you need your wife, because she may return the favor someday, because that druggist has it coming, and so on. Piaget (1932/1965) found enough indications of a pragmatic or instrumental character to moral justification in mid-childhood to refer to an intermediate "phase" of "crude equality" or "reciprocity as a fact" (p. 323). The character of the role taking that underlies such moral justifying is most readily represented in relation to the role taking impilicit in the third moral judgment orientation.

Orientation 3: Justifying moral prescriptions or evaluations by appeal to shared interpersonal and characterological values. The third orientation, which usually emerges as the child approaches adolescence, entails a shift from a pragmatic view of moral intentions to an appreciation based on shared interpersonal values. The judgment that one should tell the truth or keep one's promises is justified not on pragmatic grounds (for instance, that you can do more things if people believe in you), but instead by appealing to the need to share in mutual trust and to show good character. Coie and Pennington (1976) found that it is not until adolescence that subjects make judgments of social deviance by reference to "a shared perception of that which is proper" (p. 412). Responding to the Heinz dilemma, subjects with this orientation recommend that the judge be lenient not because the judge understands Heinz's pragmatic motives but because the judge appreciates Heinz's good intentions (for example, "the judge should see why he did it—he should let him go free and give him a warning because he did it from the goodness of his heart"). Similarly, Piaget (1932/1965) found the twelve-year olds in his sample willing to do a favor for a friend in need, even if the request were unfair "from the point of view of equality," if the act could be understood "as a free manifestation of friendliness" (p. 283; cf. Rushton, 1976, pp. 902–903). Selman and Byrne describe the role-taking transition from the second to the third orientation as one from "sequential" perspective-taking to stepping "outside the two-person situation" and achieving a "third-person perspective on the dyadic situation" (1973, p. 5; 1974). Piaget (1932/ 1965) epitomized the role-taking transition as one from "reciprocity as a fact" to "reciprocity as an ideal" (p. 323).

Orientation 4: Justifying moral prescriptions or evaluations by appeal to societal requirements and values. Not until adolescence or late adolescence are social institutions such as law understood as instruments serving social order and the common good (e.g., Adelson, Green, & O'Neil, 1969). Justifying leniency for Heinz on the basis of Heinz's good intentions is no longer sufficient; there is a new focus upon the implications of good or bad character for *society*: for example, "Heinz's motives for stealing the drug were humanistic . . . jail might turn this solicitous individual into a callous criminal *which would, obviously, make him a dangerous addition to society upon his release*" (italics added). Persons in institutional relationships are now appreciated in relation to an overall perspective on society, just as interpersonal relationships are already appreciated from an overall perspective. Society is no longer perceived in terms of a dyadic relationship, but as a systematic structure comprised of a set of relationships (Edwards, 1975; Selman & Byrne, 1973).

These four orientations are the strongest candidates for defining a developmental stage sequence in the Piagetian sense.

Are the Four Orientations Piagetian Stages?

A consistent feature of Kohlberg's writings on moral development is the claim that his moral-judgment orientations satisfy Piagetian stage criteria (Piaget, 1971a, pp. 16–25). The four main empirical criteria are:

1. Each stage should evidence an underlying generality or consistency and a correspondence to analogous structural stages in other domains of development.

2. There should be a resistance to extinction or regression; that is, a naturally upward tendency should mark stage development.

3. Facilitated rates of stage development should be found for subjects in an experientially rich environment.

4. Upward movement through the stage sequence should be gradual and consecutive.

A fifth criterion for defining stages is explicit in Piaget's stage theory but only implicit in Kohlberg's writings:

5. The stages should be commonly in evidence among members of the species from birth to maturity.

A Research Review

Most of the research which tests Piagetian stage claims for Kohlberg's moral-judgment orientations has focused upon the four orientations described above, which will be the referents for the following review.

1. *Underlying generality.* Kohlberg (1973a) expressed this criterion in his assertion that "a given stage-response on a task does not just represent a specific response determined by knowledge and familiarity with that task or tasks similar to it; rather, it represents an underlying thought-organization" (p. 181). The suggestion

that stage features are profoundly interrelated or of a piece implies that the various features of a given stage would emerge somewhat concurrently in the course of development. There is some question as to how strict a concurrence is required by a Piagetian developmental model (Flavell, 1970, 1971; Turiel, 1969). The finding that even in high-growth periods a preponderant or modal moral-judgment orientation can be identified for an individual suggests that different features of an orientation emerge at about the same time (Turiel, 1969).

Further evidence of consistency is provided by Rest (1973), who presented subjects with a series of statements of moral judgment pertinent to a moral dilemma and asked subjects to restate the points made in the statements. The order in which statements were presented was balanced for orientation and pro or con attitude. The subject's ability to recapitulate the statements was taken as a measure of comprehension. By analyzing the comprehension data in terms of the orientations, Rest found that subjects were much more likely to comprehend a few or most of the statements of a given orientation than they were to understand some intermediate percentage.

The criterion of underlying generality usually refers to the features of a stage in a particular domain. The frame of reference can be extended, however, to the question of whether the given stage sequence shows a consistent relation in development to analogous stage sequences in other domains. Moral-judgment orientations have been conceptually related to stages in other domains, such as social perspective-taking and logical operations, and the possibility of correspondence has been empirically investigated, with a review of six recent studies reporting evidence of such correspondence (Colby & Kohlberg, in press).

2. *Upward directionality and stability.* An experimental test of the "upward-tendency" criterion involves providing statements pertinent to a moral dilemma at orientations below as well as above each subject's own orientation to see whether subjects' subsequent orientation shifts, if any, are in the upward or the downward direction in relation to an uninfluenced control group. Bandura and McDonald (1963) were the first to explore this question, operationalizing "higher" moral judgment as the frequent selection of mischievous but inconsequential acts as "naughtier" than acts which were well-intentioned but caused damage (Piaget, 1932/1965). Bandura and McDonald found that children were markedly amenable to change not only in the upward direction, toward bad intentions, but also in the downward direction, toward bad consequences. Cowan, Langer, Heavenrich, and Nathanson (1969) replicated this finding but in a follow-up posttest two weeks later found stable changes only for the upward shifts. Crowley (1968), also using intentionality as a measure of both moral and nonmoral judgment, posited that response shifts he obtained probably reflected the learning of superficial labeling responses and not authentic structural changes (cf. Graham, 1972, p. 212; Kohlberg, 1969, p. 408).

Other experiments that test whether orientation changes tend to be upward and stable have used Kohlberg's stage typology (typically his first four orientations) as their moral-judgment measure. Turiel (1966) found greater change in the upward direction for the experimental group among subjects exposed to statements both above and below their own orientations. Using a similar design, Rest, Turiel, and Kohlberg (1969) found significant upward change and no downward change. Other studies using the Kohlberg typology have found, after discussion sessions on moral dilemmas, upward change by lower-orientation participants (Blatt & Kohlberg, 1975; Maitland & Goldman, 1974). Also relevant to the criterion of upward directionality are findings that subjects reject moral judgments at orientations beneath their own and prefer higher-orientation reasoning on grounds of cogency, reasonableness, and general appeal (Rest, 1973; Rest, Turiel, & Kohlberg, 1969).

3. *Facilitated stage development in a socially "rich" environment.* Piaget (1932/1965) suggested that good social environments for moral growth are those which enable a child to interact with others on a perceived equal footing. He emphasized peer interaction as a prime vehicle for such experiences: "As the child grows up the prestige of older children diminishes . . . he can discuss matters more and more as an equal and has increasing opportunities (beyond the scope of suggestion, opportunism, or negativism) of freely contrasting his point of view with that of others" (pp. 95–96). Piaget further suggested that in childrearing "one must place oneself on the child's own level, and give him a feeling of equality by laying stress on one's own obligations . . . one's own needs, one's own difficulties, even one's own blunders, and [pointing] out their consequences, thus creating an atmosphere of mutual help and understanding" (pp. 133–134). This advice is similar to Hoffman's (1970) study of inductive discipline which stressed explaining to the children how their transgressions had hurt or distressed themselves or others. Kohlberg (1969) has argued for a broad view of the social environment as "a total social world in which perceptions of the law, of the peer group, and of parental teachings all influence one another" (p. 402). He has suggested that the influence of various social settings on moral development can be understood in terms of the "role-taking opportunities" offered by them (p. 402).

Research results have generally been consistent with the expectation of a relation between role-taking opportunities and moral-judgment maturity. Keasy (1971) and Kohlberg (1958) found positive correlations between measures of social participation and conventional moral-judgment maturity. Surveying the results from a dozen correlational studies, Hoffman (1970) found consistently positive correlations between inductive discipline and various indices of moral maturity. Holstein (1972) found a greater percentage of orientation 3 children among parents rated as "taking the child's opinion seriously and discussing it" in an experimentally structured situation.

4. *Consecutive sequence.* Research on Kohlberg's first four moral-judgment orientations has generally supported the hypothesis that the orientations satisfy the stage criterion of consecutive sequence. In several studies (Turiel, 1966; Rest, Turiel, & Kohlberg, 1969), statements presented to each subject were at one or two orientations above or one orientation below the subject's own dominant orientation. Virtually all of the upward change on the posttest was accounted for by "+1" gains (one orientation) rather than "+2." The Blatt and Kohlberg (1975) discussion-group studies also provide support for the consecutive-sequence criterion: on

the follow-up posttest one year later, +1 gains were still in evidence while +2 changes were gone. Rest (1973) provides other evidence pertinent to the criterion of consecutive sequence. About half of his subjects were able to understand statements one orientation above their own, and most of these subjects also showed "substantial" (at least 20 percent) usage of the +1 orientation on the pretest. In other words, subjects generally did not understand the orientation above their own unless they were already using that orientation in some instances.

The demonstration of consecutive sequence in longitudinal data is crucial to satisfying this criterion. Kohlberg is completing a twenty-year longitudinal study of his 1958 dissertation sample of subjects, and the results so far seem to support the consecutive-sequence criterion. Kohlberg's longitudinal results to date are discussed by Brown and Herrnstein (1975, pp. 315–318). In other longitudinal studies Kuhn (1976) found support for consecutive sequence of the first three orientations, and Holstein (1976) found partial support in a study with several acknowledged methodological defects.

5. *Species-wide existence of stages.* The final stage criterion in Piagetian usage is whether or not the orientational sequence is commonly in evidence throughout humanity. Kohlberg (1969, pp. 384–385) has conducted studies of his orientations in Taiwan, Turkey, and Mexico, and schematic representations of his data suggest that at least the first four orientations are widely found. The four orientations have also been found in cross-sectional studies in Kenya (Edwards, 1975) and India (Parikh, 1975). White's (1975) cross-sectional study in the Bahamas provided evidence of the first three orientations among subjects aged seven to fourteen.

Summary

The research reviewed above suggests that Kohlberg's first four moral-judgment orientations define a Piagetian stage sequence. Consistent with the criterion of underlying generality is the following evidence: a preponderance of moral-judgment scores fall within the same orientation for a given subject; subjects' attempts to comprehend statements deriving from a given orientation tend to be either altogether correct or altogether incorrect; and there is some correspondence between moral-judgment orientations and stages in other developmental domains. An upward tendency in orientation change is suggested by findings that potentially two-way orientational shifts under experimental conditions tend to be upward rather than downward, and that subjects reject orientations lower than their own as inadequate, preferring higher orientations. Findings of positive correlations between role-taking opportunities and moral-judgment development are consistent with the expectation that facilitated development of moral judgment should be found in rich social environments. Conclusions in several experimental and longitudinal studies support the notion that the stage advances are gradual and consecutive. Finally, the cross-cultural research available suggests that the first four orientations are found in other cultures. The evidence seems rather impressive that the four candidates define a stage sequence in the Piagetian sense.

Relation of Kohlberg's Stage Theory to Piaget's Naturalistic Theme

Kohlberg can be described as a Piagetian to the extent that his work is based on Piaget's empirical criteria and theoretical conceptions, but Kohlberg does not explicitly adopt all of Piaget's stage criteria, nor does his use of the naturalistic theme fully reflect the naturalistic suppositions basic to the Piagetian approach. The five empirical criteria outlined relate to the four basic features of Piaget's genetic or developmental-structuralist theory: holism, constructivism, interactionism, and naturalism. While the first three of these features are used in Kohlberg's work, it will be shown that the most fundamental feature—naturalism—is not fully used.

Holism

The criterion that developmental stages are underlying generalities corresponds to Piaget's important concept of organizational wholeness or *structure d'ensemble*. In philosophy and psychology "holism" refers to the view that the living organism has a reality distinct from and greater than its constituent parts. Coined by Jan Smuts in 1926, the term was associated with the vitalism movement in biology, with gestaltism in psychology, and with the concepts of "superorganism" and "oversoul" in popular philosophy. In Piagetian theory, holism refers to the existence of structures or organizations at all levels of functioning in the organism: cellular, epigenetic, neurophysiological, and behavioral. It also refers to the existence of genetic and even social population systems in species (cf. Wilson, 1975). "All manifestations of life, whatever they are, and at whatever level, give evidence of the existence of organizations" (Piaget, 1971a, p. 147). For example, at the organic level, one can see the apparent organization of a cellular or respiratory system. At the evolutionary level of human intelligence, structures are to be found which are no less existent because their referents are behavioral or psychological rather than material.

In the context of moral-judgment development, the view that ethical justifications and sentiments relate holistically can be contrasted with more traditional views of moral judgment as deriving from a quantitative total of discrete virtues. For example, Darwin (1936) saw ethical sentiments and habits as a set of "social instincts" which were functionally adaptive and part of man's genetic heritage (pp. 471–501). In contrast, Campbell (1975) argues that social culture is the source of "inhibitory" and prosocial "moral norms." Generally, however, both Darwin and Campbell view moral judgment in terms of collections of elements, while Piaget views moral judgment in terms of organizational wholeness.

Constructivism

In Piagetian theory holism cannot be understood without also considering the "constructivistic" thesis. In Piaget's view (1971a), mental behavior consists "above all in the . . . elaboration of new structures and new lines of conduct in the course of a constantly constructive development." The general constructivistic assumption is that "life, at whatever level, shows a continual 'tendency' to extend itself (dissemination of seeds, movement in animals, etc.)" (p. 204). Piaget has used constructivism to characterize his position against preformationism in biology, gestaltist and Chomskian views in psychology, and Platonism in philosophy. Piaget's constructivism reflects his more general philosophical perspective. His view of the evolution of intelligence is that human intelligence extends, but does not reduce to, organic regulatory processes and structures. His philosophy of science includes the premise that the scale of biological phenomena is not reducible to the scale of physicochemical phenomena. His view of the history of science implies that progress in physics, for example, is not arbitrary but is instead in the direction "of a relational objectivity of increasing efficacy" (1970b, p. 58).

Interactionism

The constructive tendency in life processes is evidenced as the organism interacts with the environment. Piaget uses the term "equilibration" to characterize the organism's coordinations and compensations during the course of exchanges with the environment. The perpetual compensations which regulate and control embryonic growth, for example, reflect equilibration as much as the perpetual coordinations entailed in the growth of understanding, discovering, and inventing during childhood. At the level of cognitive growth, social as well as physical conditions affect the rate of development. The importance of social role-taking opportunities can be understood in this light.

Many theorists posit a transmittance conception of the acquisition of knowledge. They see knowledge as being transmitted from the genetic pool or from environmental influences such as social teaching, and interaction as the means for actualizing this transmission. For example, Darwin's theory of development of the "moral sense" allows for the view that social instincts and the intellectual faculty interact with negative experiences of transgression and positive experiences of social approval. According to Campbell, cultural norms interact with innately selfish inclinations through "reward and punishment . . . identification, imitation . . . indoctrination . . . linguistic meaning systems, conformity pressures, social authority systems, and the like" (Campbell, 1975, p. 1107).

Piagetian epistemology posits *interaction itself* as the generative origin of the acquisition of knowledge (Piaget, 1971a). This interactionist position is reflected in a discussion between Piaget (1971b) and several Soviet psychologists and philosophers:

> The philosopher Kedrov opened the discussion by asking me the question, "Do you believe that the object exists before knowledge?" I replied "As a psychologist I know nothing of this, for I only know the object in acting on it and I can say nothing about it before this action." Rubinstein then proposed the conciliatory formula: "For us the object is a part of the world. Do you believe that the world exists before knowledge?" I then said . . . "This is another matter. In order to act on the object it is necessary for there to be an organism and this organism is also part of the world. I therefore evidently believe that the world exists before all knowledge, but that we only divide it up into individual objects through our ac-

tions and as a result of an interaction between the organism and the environment." At this moment a discussion in Russian occurred . . . Rubinstein . . . said: "We have decided that Piaget is not a Platonist." (pp. 203–204)

Naturalism

We have referred to the organism's developmental tendency to construct implicit or underlying structures. These references point to perhaps the most fundamental feature of Piaget's theory, that is, its *naturalism*. Naturalism as a philosophic doctrine emanated from early Greek theology, which identified deities with nature and natural processes. Rousseau and other Romantics used naturalism as a theory of the good and located the intrinsic goodness of man in the presocialized heart and experience of the young child. In the context of Piaget's theory, naturalism emphasizes a continuity between the human species and other forms of life. Normative human behavior has a "deep biological significance" (Piaget, 1970a, p. 705), and the structural development of human behavior in any human culture takes place in a necessarily gradual manner. This biological basis for the gradual character of development makes the stage criterion of consecutive sequence substantive and not tautological. This point is not recognized in critiques by Phillips and Kelly (1975) and by Satterly (1975).

The naturalistic orientation in Piagetian theory also leads to an emphasis upon the implicit or unreflective character of "theories-in-action" which direct conscious behavior (Karmiloff-Smith and Inhelder, 1975; Piaget, 1976). Noting an analogy between psychoanalytic notions of an affective unconscious and his own notion of a cognitive unconscious, Piaget (1973) writes:

> In the case of cognitive structures the situation is remarkably comparable: some (but rather limited) consciousness of the result and almost entire (or initially entire) unconsciousness of the intimate mechanism leading to the result. . . . The intimate functioning remains entirely unknown to the subject . . . [except] at very superior levels. (p. 33)

Conclusion

At the heart of Piaget's theory is a naturalistic theme that human mental development reflects a deep biological significance. Building upon this theme are the assumptions of holism, constructivism, and interactionism. The empirical criteria specific to naturalism indicate that sequential stage development is: (a) necessarily gradual; (b) widely found among members of the species; and (c) achieved through processes which are spontaneous and essentially unconscious. Kohlberg's first four moral-judgment orientations meet all of these criteria, in addition to underlying generality, upward tendency, and facilitated development, and may therefore be considered natural stages in the Piagetian sense.

The Principled Stage Candidates

The four moral-judgment stages reviewed do not capture the full story of the development of moral judgment. Certainly, Andrei Sakharov's continuing appeal to all governments to recognize fundamental human rights and principles of justice has a significance not reducible to stages 3 or 4. And in the great works of social, political, and ethical philosophers there is clearly something beyond the scope of these stages. Partly out of such considerations, Kohlberg has suggested higher moral-judgment stages. While Kohlberg has rightly called our attention to these higher levels of moral reasoning, his attempt to interpret them as developmental stages may be fundamentally misdirected. We must turn, then, to an examination of Kohlberg's "post-conventional" and "principled" orientations as candidates for naturalistic stages.

Moral thought which is "post-conventional" may emerge as the individual turns upon his ethical sentiments, wondering about their origin, their function, and their validity. Keniston (1969) suggests that disengaging from the workaday adult society (Erikson's "moratorium"), confronting alternative moral viewpoints, and discovering hypocrisy and societal corruption are experiences which promote a post-conventional frame of mind about one's moral values. To ask "What is morality?" or "Why be moral?" at this level is to shed the moral identity derived from family, friends, and job and to take "a standpoint outside that of a member of a constituted society" (Kohlberg, 1973a, p. 192). The existential crisis which sometimes results can occur at any time in adulthood and may relate to the concerns of the introspective adolescent (Kohlberg & Gilligan, 1971). In the context of post-conventional moral judgment, the principled orientations can now be reviewed.

Principled Moral-Judgment Stage Candidates

First principled orientation (Kohlberg's "stage 5"): Justifying moral prescriptions or evaluations by appeal to social-contract rights, values, and principles. The justification for Heinz's stealing the drug offered by one of the subjects in Kohlberg's longitudinal study, a male in his twenties, suggests the social-contract orientation: "Yes . . . there was a human life at stake. I think that transcends any right the druggist had to the drug." Subsequently the subject was asked, "What does morality mean to you?" He replied, "I think it's basically to preserve the human being's right to existence . . . secondly, the human being's right to do as he pleases without interfering with somebody else's rights" (Kohlberg et al., 1976). The subject's justification for stealing the drug seems to derive from an appreciation of the rational priority of life over property in any society and of the right to liberty insofar as its exercise is compatible with the same rights of others. This social-contract reasoning is the hallmark of "stage-5" ethical thought (Kohlberg, 1971).

Second principled orientation (Kohlberg's "stage 6"): Justifying moral prescriptions or evaluations by appeal to the results of ideal role taking. Kohlberg's (1971) classic example of stage-6 moral thinking, embodied in a justification for Heinz's stealing the drug, is excerpted below:

> One can appeal to reason as well as to intuition. First of all, recognition of the moral duty to save a human life whenever possible must be assumed. If someone claims not to recognize this duty, then one can only point out that he is failing to make his decision both reversible and universalizable, i.e., that he is not viewing the situation from the role of the person whose life is being saved as well as the

person who can save the life, or from the point of view of anyone filling these two roles. Then one can point out that . . . [since] all property has only relative value and only persons can have unconditional value, it would be irrational to act in such a manner as to make human life—or the loss of it—a means to the preservation of property rights. (pp. 208–209)

Kohlberg (1975) characterizes the role taking appealed to in such a justification as "ideal" or "systematic" (p. 13). It entails "role-taking the claim of each actor (in a moral conflict) under the assumption that all other actors' claims are also governed by the Golden Rule and accommodated accordingly" (Kohlberg, 1973b, p. 643). Moral judgments reached through ideal role taking are seen as valid in that they are justifiable from all conflicting perspectives in the situation. The "stage-6" ideal role-taking appeal is related to the suggestion made in the philosophical writings of Adam Smith, Frances Hutcheson, Roderick Firth, and especially Kurt Baier (1965), that valid ethical decisions require the perspective of an "impartial spectator" or "ideal observer."

Are Kohlberg's Principled Orientations Stages in the Piagetian Sense?

We can now consider whether Kohlberg's principled orientations conform to Piagetian stage criteria. If they do, the characteristics of each orientation should emerge concurrently and in correspondence with other structural domains of cognitive development. There should be a tendency to move sequentially and progressively from orientation 5 to orientation 6, and there should be facilitated movement in rich social environments. Finally, both orientations should be in evidence in various cultures and social classes.

Whether Kohlberg's principled orientations are stages is rendered problematic by the fact that they are rarely found (Kohlberg, 1973a). Moreover, criteria for identifying orientation 6 are now so stringent that the orientation is not even scored in Kohlberg's forthcoming Standard Form Scoring Manual (Kohlberg, Colby, Gibbs, Speicher-Dubin, & Power, 1976). These points render moot the significance of even the relatively few studies of past years that have been concerned with orientations 5 and 6 (e.g., Haan, Smith, & Block, 1968). As Kohlberg (1973a) notes, "No real data exist on movement to this highest moral stage" (p. 197).

The apparent rarity of the principled orientations is evidence against their significance as part of a Piagetian stage sequence. Stages in human development which are natural in the Piagetian sense are presumably common throughout humanity. In addition, Kohlberg's (1973b) designation of these orientations as natural stages seems improbable in light of the essential role played by reflective meta-ethical thought in their construction, since natural stages are theories-in-action presumably constructed through implicit interactive processes.

The Existential Theme

An existential theme underlies the post-conventional and meta-ethical reflection which are the presumed bases for principled ethical constructions. Post-conventionality is the existential experience of disembedding oneself from an implicit worldview and adopting a detached and questioning posture. More broadly, existential post-conventionality entails "the great anxiety (peculiar to man) of a consciousness wakening up to reflection in a dark universe" (Teilhard de Chardin, 1959, p. 312). Existential psychologists view the existential experience as an antecedent to much of human psychopathology as well as human maturity. Fromm (1947) wrote: "Man is the only animal for whom his own existence is a problem which he has to solve and from which he cannot escape." Others assert that the human problem is to achieve meaning or authenticity (Frankl, 1957; May, 1953) and that man's highest challenge is self-actualization (Maslow, 1968).

As noted, Kohlberg treats the principled orientations as stages in a naturalistic sense. A more plausible interpretation of the principled orientations may derive from a fuller consideration of the existential theme in human development. Earlier it was noted that Piaget views the underlying functioning of intelligence as unknown to the individual except at superior levels. One may also say that theories-in-action are fundamentally unknown until one detachedly reflects upon them and attempts to formalize a philosophy. The distinction between implicit systems of thought and reflective philosophies is found in Piaget's (1971b) attempt to understand the human conception of number. He suggests that insight into the significance of mathematical philosophers' explicit theories can be gained from a recognition of the intuitive starting points in their implicit childhood conceptions of number.

By analogy, the principled orientations may be better understood by looking at their earlier, implicit stages of moral judgment. The social-contract ethic of orientation 5 is highly formal theory which seems to be informed by pragmatic intuitions about human social nature. The perspective-taking demands of this view are not inordinate; *a priori* rational people must simply temper their desires with the recognition that others want their lives and freedom as they themselves want theirs. The social perspective-taking involved does not seem to go beyond that necessary for the natural moral stage 2. In other words, the meta-ethics of orientation 5 are those of the stage-2 rational person. The social perspective taking required in the ideal role taking of orientation 6 meta-ethics is more advanced. Here *a priori* rational people must be capable of moderating their immediate interests by reconstructing them into ideal or mutual sentiments. Third-person perspective-taking is the achievement underlying natural moral stage 3. The meta-ethics of orientation 6, then, is that of the stage-3 rational person.

The principled orientations may be understood, then, as formalizations which are based on implicit achievements of the natural stages and which proceed on a reflective and philosophical plane of discourse. Kohlberg (1973b) has suggested that theories of ethics are interpretable as "constructive systematizations of . . . natural structures" (p. 634). By "natural structures" he does not mean the early moral-judgment stages but instead the principled orientations. Kohlberg contends that "notions of natural rights, social contract, and utility are 'natural structures' emerging in nonphilosophers" (p. 634). However, persons who introduce this complex of notions into their thinking may no longer be nonphilosophers. If the position is accepted that anyone who constructs a social-contract theory of ethics is in effect a philosopher, then it is more reasonable to understand the principled orientations themselves as "constructive systematizations" starting from natural intuitions about morality and human nature.

Formal ethical philosophies may override but do not eliminate the relevance of the natural stages of moral judgment. This point is made in Unger's (1975) suggestion that a formal political philosophy can "act as a signpost for" practical social judgment but "cannot replace it" (p. 259). In natural moral-stage development, succeeding stages in a sequence subsume and become dominant over preceding ones. Once an individual has constructed a stage-3 interpersonal morality, for example, the stage-3 perspective displaces the stage-2 understanding of interpersonal values. It is not clear that a principled ethical philosophy broadly subordinates stage 4 or stage 3 in the same way that stage 3 subordinates stage 2. Nonetheless, a principled orientation may require its holder to *override* the norms of a theory-in-action, as when one's natural norms are operating in the context of fundamentally unjust social institutions or practices. Consider, for example, the principled defiance of otherwise patriotic scientists and artists in the Soviet Union, newspaper editors and judges in India, doctors and teachers in South Africa, and so on. Such individuals have experienced a dissonance between ethical presuppositions and the demands of their social situations. This conflict may provoke considerable meta-ethical reflection in the effort to formulate a defensible ethic. The fundamental insight to emerge is that human life is logically prior to—and therefore supersedes in case of conflict—derivative considerations such as property rights, legal requirements, and so on. It is interesting that this insight appears to be contained in both the social contractarianism of orientation 5 and the systematic or ideal role taking of orientation 6.

It should be noted that all reflective ethical formalizations need not be considered equally valid or adequate. For example, the historically recurrent doctrine that "might makes right" is post-conventional and reflective. The doctrine can even amount to a formal, universalist philosophy, drawing its intuitive inspiration from the fusion of moral with physical superiority evident at natural stage 1. When we compare such a position to the ideal-observer philosophy of Roderick Firth (1952), however, we are struck by the severe limitations of the might-makes-right position. Similarly, an ideal-observer ethic seems superior even to classical social-contract ethics.

The judgment that classical social-contract theory does not draw upon the fullest moral and social perspective-taking capacities of human nature is evident in the works of several contemporary political thinkers. Unger (1975) analyzes what he terms liberal theory, with its atomistic and pragmatic assumptions, as a paradigm of reflective social thought which has arisen in the last three centuries in conjunction with the advent of the industrial age (p. 151). Unger's suggestion that "the liberal doctrine is not powerful enough to subjugate the full range of our feelings and ideas" (p. 28) can be understood in the context of our thesis that classical social contractarianism makes assumptions about human nature which, although valid as far as they go, are primitive in relation to the highest achievements of human moral and social development. Rawls's (1971) formal incorporation of equity into classical social-contract theory may be seen as an effort to enrich liberal theory by expanding its assumptions about the social capacities of rational man.

Conclusion

Greater attention must be accorded to the distinction between natural and existential human development in Kohlberg's theory of moral-judgment development. Human ethical constructions, whether natural or existential, are uniformly treated as stages in Kohlbergian theory. This claim may fail on two counts. First, it implies that even the principled orientations conform to stage criteria. The second objection is more fundamental: a uniform claim for all the constructions as stages fails to take into account the crucial distinction between implicit theories-in-action and detached reflections upon one's theories-in-action. Stages 3 and 4 constitute in their own right a maturity that is important in the everyday conduct of human affairs. This thesis is not incompatible with the recognition that humanistic leaders, ethical philosophers, and moral statesmen go beyond these theories-in-action with the working out of reflective and formal ethics. Explicitly distinguishing the existential and naturalistic themes in Kohlberg's theory permits each theme to assume an important role in his work on the development of moral judgment.

References

Adelson, J., Green, B., & O'Neil, R. Growth of the idea of law in adolescence. *Developmental Psychology*, 1969, 1, 327–332.

Baier, K. *The moral point of view: A rational basis of ethics.* New York: Random House, 1965.

Bandura, A., & McDonald, F. The influence of social reinforcement and the behavior of models in shaping children's moral judgments. *Journal of Abnormal and Social Psychology*, 1963, 67, 274–281.

Bergcross, L. G. Intentionality, degree of damage, and moral judgments. *Child Development*, 1975, 46, 970–974.

Blatt, M., & Kohlberg, L. Effects of classroom moral discussions upon children's levels of moral judgment. *Journal of Moral Education*, 1975, 4, 129–162.

Broughton, J. The cognitive-developmental approach to morality: A reply to Kurtines and Greif. Unpublished manuscript, Columbia University, 1976.

Brown, R., & Herrnstein, R. J. *Psychology.* Boston: Little, Brown, 1975.

Campbell, D. T. On the conflicts between biological and social evolution and between psychology and moral tradition. *American Psychologist*, 1975, 30, 1103–1126.

Caruso, I. H. La notion de responsabilité et du justice immanente chez l'enfant. *Archives de Psychologie*, 1943, 29, 114–169.

Chandler, M. J. Egocentrism and anti-social behavior: The assessment and training of social perspective-taking skills. *Developmental Psychology*, 1973, 9, 326–332.

Coie, J. D., & Pennington, B. F. Children's perceptions of deviance and disorder. *Child Development*, 1976, 47, 407–413.

Colby, A., & Kohlberg, L. The relation between logical and moral development. In D. Bush and S. Feldman (Eds.), *Cognitive development and social development: Relationships and implications.* New York: Lawrence Erlbaum Associates, in press.

Cowan, P. A., Langer, J., Heavenrich, J., & Nathanson, M. Social learning and Piaget's cognitive theory of moral development. *Journal of Personality and Social Psychology,* 1969, **11**, 261–274.

Crowley, P. M. Effect of training upon objectivity of moral judgment in grade-school children. *Journal of Personality and Social Psychology,* 1968, **8**, 228–233.

Darwin, C. *The origin of species and the descent of man.* New York: Modern Library, 1936.

Edwards, C. P. Societal complexity and moral development: A Kenyan study. *Ethos,* 1975, **3**, 505–527.

Feffer, M. H. The cognitive implications of role-taking behavior. *Journal of Personality,* 1959, **27**, 152–158.

Firth, R. Ethical absolutism and the ideal observer. *Philosophy and Phenomenological Research,* 1952, **12**, 317–345.

Flavell, J. Concept development. In P. H. Mussen (Ed.), *Carmichael's manual of child psychology* (Vol. 1, 3rd ed.). New York: Wiley, 1970.

Flavell, J. Stage-related properties of cognitive development. *Cognitive Psychology,* 1971, **2**, 421–453.

Flavell, J., Botkin, P. T., Fry, C. L., Wright, J. W., & Jarvis, P. E. *The development of role-taking and communication skills in children.* New York: Wiley, 1968.

Frankena, W. *Ethics* (2nd ed.). Englewood Cliffs, N.J.: Prentice-Hall, 1973.

Frankl, V. E. *The doctor and the soul: An introduction to logotherapy.* New York: Knopf, 1957.

Fromm, E. *Man for himself: An inquiry into the psychology of ethics.* Greenwich, Conn.: Fawcett, 1947.

Gibbs, J., Kohlberg, L., Colby, A., & Speicher-Dubin, B. The domain and development of moral judgment: A theory and method of assessment. In J. Meyer (Ed.), *Reflections on values education.* Waterloo, Ont.: Wilfrid Laurier University Press, 1976.

Graham, D. *Moral learning and development: Theory and research.* New York: Wiley, 1972.

Haan, N., Smith, M. B., & Block, J. Moral reasoning of young adults: Political-social behavior, family background, and personality correlates. *Journal of Personality and Social Psychology,* 1968, **10**, 183–201.

Hoffman, M. L. Moral development. In P. H. Mussen (Ed.), *Carmichael's manual of child psychology* (Vol. 2, 3rd ed.). New York: Wiley, 1970.

Holstein, C. B. The relation of children's moral judgment level to that of their parents and to communication patterns in the family. In R. D. Smart & M. S. Smart (Eds.), *Readings in child development and relationships.* New York: Macmillan, 1972.

Holstein, C. B. Irreversible, stepwise sequence in development of moral judgment: Longitudinal study of males and females. *Child Development,* 1976, **47**, 51–61.

Inhelder, B., & Piaget, J. *The growth of logical thinking from childhood to adolescence.* New York: Basic Books, 1958.

Karmiloff-Smith, A., & Inhelder, B. If you want to get ahead, get a theory. *Cognition,* 1975, **3**, 195–212.

Keasy, C. B. Social participation as a factor in the moral development of children. *Developmental Psychology,* 1971, **5**, 216–220.

Keniston, K. Moral development, youthful activism, and modern society. *Youth and Society,* 1969, 110–127.

Kohlberg, L. *The development of modes of moral thinking and choice in the years two to sixteen.* Unpublished doctoral dissertation, University of Chicago, 1958.

Kohlberg, L. A cognitive-developmental analysis of children's sex-role concepts and attitudes. In E. E. Maccoby (Ed.), *The development of sex differences.* Stanford, Calif.: Stanford University Press, 1966.

Kohlberg, L. Stage and sequence: The cognitive-developmental approach to socialization. In D. A. Goslin (Ed.), *Handbook of socialization theory and research.* Chicago: Rand McNally, 1969.

Kohlberg, L. From is to ought: How to commit the naturalistic fallacy and get away with it in the study of moral development. In T. Mischel (Ed.), *Cognitive development and epistemology.* New York: Academic Press, 1971.

Kohlberg, L. Continuities in childhood and adult moral development revisited. In P. B. Baltes & L. R. Goulet (Eds.), *Lifespan developmental psychology* (2nd ed.). New York: Academic Press, 1973. (a)

Kohlberg, L. The claim to moral adequacy of a highest stage of moral judgment. *Journal of Philosophy,* 1973, **70,** 630–646. (b)

Kohlberg, L. Why a higher stage is a better stage. In L. Kohlberg (Ed.), *Collected papers on moral development and moral education* (Vol. 2). Unpublished manuscript, 1975. (Available from Harvard University, Center for Moral Education, Cambridge, Mass. 02138.)

Kohlberg, L., Colby, A., Gibbs, J. C., Speicher-Dubin, D., & Power, C. *Identifying moral stages: A manual* (5 sections). Unpublished manuscript, 1976. (Available from Harvard University, Center for Moral Education, Cambridge, Mass. 02138.)

Kohlberg, L., & Gilligan, C. The adolescent as a philosopher: The discovery of the self in a postconventional world. *Daedalus,* 1971, **100,** 1051–1086.

Kohlberg, L., & Kramer, R. Continuities and discontinuities in childhood and adult moral development. *Human Development,* 1969, **12,** 93–120.

Kuhn, D. Short-term longitudinal evidence for sequentiality of Kohlberg's early stages of moral judgment. *Developmental Psychology,* 1976, **12,** 162–166.

Kurtines, W., & Greif, E. G. The development of moral thought: Review and evaluation of Kohlberg's approach. *Psychological Bulletin,* 1974, **81,** 453–470.

Maitland, K. A., & Goldman, J. R. Moral judgment as a function of peer group interaction. *Journal of Personality and Social Psychology,* 1974, **30,** 699–704.

Maslow, A. H. *Toward a psychology of being* (2nd ed.). Princeton, N.J.: Van Nostrand. 1968.

May, R. *Man's search for himself.* New York: Norton, 1953.

Medinnus, G. R. Objective responsibility in children: A comparison with the Piaget data. *Journal of Genetic Psychology,* 1962, **101,** 127–133.

Parikh, B. S. *Moral judgment and its relation to family environmental factors in Indian and American urban upper middle class families.* Unpublished doctoral dissertation, Boston University, 1975.

Phillips, D. C., & Kelly, M. E. Hierarchical theories of development in education and psychology. *Harvard Educational Review,* 1975, **45,** 351–375.

Piaget, J. *The moral judgment of the child.* New York: Free Press, 1965 (Originally published: London: Kegan Paul, 1932).

Piaget, J. Piaget's theory. In P. H. Mussen (Ed.), *Carmichael's manual of child psychology* (Vol. 1, 3rd ed.). New York: Wiley, 1970. (a)

Piaget, J. *The place of the sciences of man in the system of sciences.* New York: Harper & Row, 1970. (b)

Piaget, J. *Biology and knowledge: An essay on the relations between organic regulations and cognitive processes.* Chicago: University of Chicago Press, 1971. (a)

Piaget, J. *Insights and illusions of philosophy.* New York: World, 1971. (b)

Piaget, J. *Psychology and epistemology: Towards a theory of knowledge.* New York: Viking Press, 1971. (c)

Piaget, J. *The child and reality.* New York: Grossman, 1973.

Piaget, J. *The grasp of consciousness.* Cambridge, Mass.: Harvard University Press, 1976.

Rawls, J. *A theory of justice.* Cambridge, Mass.: Harvard University Press, 1971.

Rest, J. The hierarchical nature of moral judgment: A study of patterns of comprehension and preference of moral stages. *Journal of Personality,* 1973, **41,** 86–109.

Rest, J., Turiel, E., & Kohlberg, L. Level of moral development as a determinant of preference and comprehension of moral judgments made by others. *Journal of Personality,* 1969, **37,** 225–252.

Rushton, J. P. Socialization and the altruistic behavior of children. *Psychological Bulletin,* 1976, **83**, 898–913.

Satterly, D. Stages of development: Help or hindrance in educating young children? *Universities Quarterly,* 1975, **29**, 379–388.

Selman, R. L. Taking another's perspective: Role-taking in early childhood. *Child Development,* 1971, **42**, 1721–1734.

Selman, R., & Byrne, D. *Manual for scoring social role-taking stages in moral and social dilemmas.* Unpublished manuscript, 1972. (Available from Harvard University, Social Reasoning Project, Cambridge, Mass. 02138.)

Selman, R. L., & Byrne, D. *Manual for scoring social role taking in social dilemmas.* Unpublished manuscript, 1973. (Available from Harvard University, Social Reasoning Project, Cambridge, Mass. 02138.)

Selman, R. L., & Byrne, D. A structural-development analysis of levels of role taking in middle childhood. *Child Development,* 1974, **45**, 803–806.

Simpson, E. L. Moral development research: A case study of scientific cultural bias. *Human Development,* 1974, **17**, 81–106.

Teilhard de Chardin, P. *The phenomenon of man.* New York: Harper & Row, 1959.

Turiel, E. An experimental test of the sequentiality of developmental stages in the child's moral judgments. *Journal of Personality and Social Psychology,* 1966, **3**, 611–618.

Turiel, E. Developmental processes in the child's moral thinking. In P. H. Mussen, J. Langer, & M. Corington (Eds.), *Trends and issues in developmental psychology.* New York: Holt, Rinehart & Winston, 1969.

Unger, R. M. *Knowledge and politics.* New York: Free Press, 1975.

White, C. B. Moral development in Bahamian school children: Cross-cultural examination of Kohlberg's stages of moral reasoning. *Developmental Psychology,* 1975, **11**, 535–536.

Wilson, E. O. *Sociobiology: The new synthesis.* Cambridge: Harvard University Press, 1975.

Zarncke, L. *Enfance et conscience morale.* Paris: Editions de Cerf, 1955.

In a Different Voice: Women's Conceptions of Self and of Morality

CAROL GILLIGAN
Harvard University

As theories of developmental psychology continue to define educational goals and practice, it has become imperative for educators and researchers to scrutinize not only the underlying assumptions of such theories but also the model of adulthood toward which they point. Carol Gilligan examines the limitations of several theories, most notably Kohlberg's stage theory of moral development, and concludes that developmental theory has not given adequate expression to the concerns and experience of women. Through a review of psychological and literary sources, she illustrates the feminine construction of reality. From her own research data, interviews with women contemplating abortion, she then derives an alternative sequence for the development of women's moral judgments. Finally, she argues for an expanded conception of adulthood that would result from the integration of the "feminine voice" into developmental theory.

The arc of developmental theory leads from infantile dependence to adult autonomy, tracing a path characterized by an increasing differentiation of self from other and a progressive freeing of thought from contextual constraints. The vision of Luther, journeying from the rejection of a self defined by others to the assertive boldness of "Here I stand" and the image of Plato's allegorical man in the cave, separating at last the shadows from the sun, have taken powerful hold on the psychological understanding of what constitutes development. Thus, the individual, meeting fully the developmental challenges of adolescence as set for him by Piaget, Erikson, and Kohlberg, thinks formally, proceeding from theory to fact, and defines both the self and the moral autonomously, that is, apart from the identifications and conventions that had comprised the particulars of his childhood world. So

The research reported here was partially supported by a grant from the Spencer Foundation. I wish to thank Mary Belenky for her collaboration and colleagueship in the abortion decision study and Michael Murphy for his comments and help in preparing this manuscript.

Harvard Educational Review   Vol. 47   No. 4   November 1977, 481–517.

equipped, he is presumed ready to live as an adult, to love and work in a way that is both intimate and generative, to develop an ethical sense of caring and a genital mode of relating in which giving and taking fuse in the ultimate reconciliation of the tension between self and other.

Yet the men whose theories have largely informed this understanding of development have all been plagued by the same problem, the problem of women, whose sexuality remains more diffuse, whose perception of self is so much more tenaciously embedded in relationships with others and whose moral dilemmas hold them in a mode of judgment that is insistently contextual. The solution has been to consider women as either deviant or deficient in their development.

That there is a discrepancy between concepts of womanhood and adulthood is nowhere more clearly evident than in the series of studies on sex-role stereotypes reported by Broverman, Vogel, Broverman, Clarkson, and Rosenkrantz (1972). The repeated finding of these studies is that the qualities deemed necessary for adulthood—the capacity for autonomous thinking, clear decision making, and responsible action—are those associated with masculinity but considered undesirable as attributes of the feminine self. The stereotypes suggest a splitting of love and work that relegates the expressive capacities requisite for the former to women while the instrumental abilities necessary for the latter reside in the masculine domain. Yet, looked at from a different perspective, these stereotypes reflect a conception of adulthood that is itself out of balance, favoring the separateness of the individual self over its connection to others and leaning more toward an autonomous life of work than toward the interdependence of love and care.

This difference in point of view is the subject of this essay, which seeks to identify in the feminine experience and construction of social reality a distinctive voice, recognizable in the different perspective it brings to bear on the construction and resolution of moral problems. The first section begins with the repeated observation of difference in women's concepts of self and of morality. This difference is identified in previous psychological descriptions of women's moral judgments and described as it again appears in current research data. Examples drawn from interviews with women in and around a university community are used to illustrate the characteristics of the feminine voice. The relational bias in women's thinking that has, in the past, been seen to compromise their moral judgment and impede their development now begins to emerge in a new developmental light. Instead of being seen as a developmental deficiency, this bias appears to reflect a different social and moral understanding.

This alternative conception is enlarged in the second section through consideration of research interviews with women facing the moral dilemma of whether to continue or abort a pregnancy. Since the research design allowed women to define as well as resolve the moral problem, developmental distinctions could be derived directly from the categories of women's thought. The responses of women to structured interview questions regarding the pregnancy decision formed the basis for describing a developmental sequence that traces progressive differentiations in their understanding and judgment of conflicts between self and other. While the sequence of women's moral development follows the three-level progression of all social developmental theory, from an egocentric through a societal to a universal perspective, this progression takes place within a distinct moral conception. This conception differs from that derived by Kohlberg from his all-male longitudinal research data.

This difference then becomes the basis in the third section for challenging the current assessement of women's moral judgment at the same time that it brings to bear a new perspective on developmental assessment in general. The inclusion in the overall conception of development of those categories derived from the study of women's moral judgment enlarges developmental understanding, enabling it to encompass better the thinking of both sexes. This is particularly true with respect to the construction and resolution of the dilemmas of adult life. Since the conception of adulthood retrospectively shapes the theoretical understanding of the development that precedes it, the changes in that conception that follow from the more central inclusion of women's judgments recast developmental understanding and lead to a reconsideration of the substance of social and moral development.

Characteristics of the Feminine Voice

The revolutionary contribution of Piaget's work is the experimental confirmation and refinement of Kant's assertion that knowledge is actively constructed rather than passively received. Time, space, self, and other, as well as the categories of developmental theory, all arise out of the active interchange between the individual and the physical and social world in which he lives and of which he strives to make sense. The development of cognition is the process of reappropriating reality at progressively more complex levels of apprehension, as the structures of thinking expand to encompass the increasing richness and intricacy of experience.

Moral development, in the work of Piaget and Kohlberg, refers specifically to the expanding conception of the social world as it is reflected in the understanding and resolution of the inevitable conflicts that arise in the relations between self and others. The moral judgment is a statement of priority, an attempt at rational resolution in a situation where, from a different point of view, the choice itself seems to do violence to justice.

Kohlberg (1969), in his extension of the early work of Piaget, discovered six stages of moral judgment, which he claimed formed an invariant sequence, each successive stage representing a more adequate construction of the moral problem, which in turn provides the basis for its more just resolution. The stages divide into three levels, each of which denotes a significant expansion of the moral point of view from an egocentric through a societal to a universal ethical conception. With this expansion in perspective comes the capacity to free moral judgment from the individual needs and social conventions with which it had earlier been confused and anchor it instead in principles of justice that are universal in application. These principles provide criteria upon which both individual and societal claims can be impartially assessed. In Kohlberg's view, at the highest stages of development morality is freed from both psychological and historical constraints, and the individual can judge independently of his own particular needs and of the values of those around him.

That the moral sensibility of women differs from that of men was noted by Freud (1925/1961) in the following by now well-quoted statement:

> I cannot evade the notion (though I hesitate to give it expression) that for women the level of what is ethically normal is different from what it is in man. Their superego is never so inexorable, so impersonal, so independent of its emotional origins as we require it to be in men. Character-traits which critics of every epoch have brought up against women—that they show less sense of justice than men, that they are less ready to submit to the great exigencies of life, that they are more often influenced in their judgments by feelings of affection or hostility—all these would be amply accounted for by the modification in the formation of their super-ego which we have inferred above. (pp. 257–258)

While Freud's explanation lies in the deviation of female from male development around the construction and resolution of the Oedipal problem, the same observations about the nature of morality in women emerge from the work of Piaget and Kohlberg. Piaget (1932/1965), in his study of the rules of children's games, observed that, in the games they played, girls were "less explicit about agreement [than boys] and less concerned with legal elaboration" (p. 93). In contrast to the boys' interest in the codification of rules, the girls adopted a more pragmatic attitude, regarding "a rule as good so long as the game repays it" (p. 83). As a result, in comparison to boys, girls were found to be "more tolerant and more easily reconciled to innovations" (p. 52).

Kohlberg (1971) also identifies a strong interpersonal bias in the moral judgments of women, which leads them to be considered as typically at the third of his six-stage developmental sequence. At that stage, the good is identified with "what pleases or helps others and is approved of by them" (p. 164). This mode of judgment is conventional in its conformity to generally held notions of the good but also psychological in its concern with intention and consequence as the basis for judging the morality of action.

That women fall largely into this level of moral judgment is hardly surprising when we read from the Broverman et al. (1972) list that prominent among the twelve attributes considered to be desirable for women are tact, gentleness, awareness of the feelings of others, strong need for security, and easy expression of tender feelings. And yet, herein lies the paradox, for the very traits that have traditionally defined the "goodness" of women, their care for and sensitivity to the needs of others, are those that mark them as deficient in moral development. The infusion of feeling into their judgments keeps them from developing a more independent and abstract ethical conception in which concern for others derives from principles of justice rather than from compassion and care. Kohlberg, however, is less pessimistic than Freud in his assessment, for he sees the development of women as extending beyond the interpersonal level, following the same path toward independent, principled judgment that he discovered in the research on men from which his stages were derived. In Kohlberg's view, women's development will proceed beyond Stage Three when they are challenged to solve moral problems that require them to see beyond the relationships that have in the past generally bound their moral experience.

What then do women say when asked to construct the moral domain; how do we identify the characteristically "feminine" voice? A Radcliffe undergraduate, responding to the question, "If you had to say what morality meant to you, how would you sum it up?," replies:

> When I think of the word morality, I think of obligations. I usually think of it as conflicts between personal desires and social things, social considerations, or personal desires of yourself versus personal desires of another person or people or whatever. Morality is that whole realm of how you decide these conflicts. A moral person is one who would decide, like by placing themselves more often than not as equals, a truly moral person would always consider another person as their equal . . . in a situation of social interaction, something is morally wrong where the individual ends up screwing a lot of people. And it is morally right when everyone comes out better of.[1]

Yet when asked if she can think of someone whom she would consider a genuinely moral person, she replies, "Well, immediately I think of Albert Schweitzer because he has obviously given his life to help others." Obligation and sacrifice override the ideal of equality, setting up a basic contradiction in her thinking.

Another undergraduate responds to the question, "What does it mean to say something is morally right or wrong?," by also speaking first of responsibilities and obligations:

> Just that it has to do with responsibilties and obligations and values, mainly values. . . . In my life situation I relate morality with interpersonal relationships that have to do with respect for the other person and myself. [Why respect other people?] Because they have a consciousness or feelings that can be hurt, an awareness that can be hurt.

The concern about hurting others persists as a major theme in the responses of two other Radcliffe students:

> [Why be moral?] Millions of people have to live together peacefully. I personally don't want to hurt other people. That's a real criterion, a main criterion for me. It underlies my sense of justice. It isn't nice to inflict pain. I empathize with anyone in pain. Not hurting others is important in my own private morals. Years ago, I would have jumped out of a window not to hurt my boyfriend. That was pathological. Even today though, I want approval and love and I don't want enemies. Maybe that's why there is morality—so people can win approval, love and friendship.

> My main moral principle is not hurting other people as long as you aren't going against your own conscience and as long as you remain true to yourself. . . . There are many moral issues such as abortion, the draft, killing, stealing, monogamy, etc. If something is a controversial issue like these, then I always say it is up to the individual. The individual has to decide and then follow his own con-

---

[1] The Radcliffe women whose responses are cited were interviewed as part of a pilot study on undergraduate moral development conducted by the author in 1970.

science. There are no moral absolutes. . . . Laws are pragmatic instruments, but they are not absolutes. A viable society can't make exceptions all the time, but I would personally. . . . I'm afraid I'm heading for some big crisis with my boyfriend someday, and someone will get hurt, and he'll get more hurt than I will. I feel an obligation to not hurt him, but also an obligation to not lie. I don't know if it is possible to not lie and not hurt.

The common thread that runs through these statements, the wish not to hurt others and the hope that in morality lies a way of solving conflicts so that no one will get hurt, is striking in that it is independently introduced by each of the four women as the most specific item in their response to a most general question. The moral person is one who helps others; goodness is service, meeting one's obligations and responsibilities to others, if possible, without sacrificing oneself. While the first of the four women ends by denying the conflict she initially introduced, the last woman anticipates a conflict between remaining true to herself and adhering to her principle of not hurting others. The dilemma that would test the limits of this judgment would be one where helping others is seen to be at the price of hurting the self.

The reticence about taking stands on "controversial issues," the willingness to "make exceptions all the time" expressed in the final example above, is echoed repeatedly by other Radcliffe students, as in the following two examples:

I never feel that I can condemn anyone else. I have a very relativistic position. The basic idea that I cling to is the sanctity of human life. I am inhibited about impressing my beliefs on others.

I could never argue that my belief on a moral question is anything that another person should accept. I don't believe in absolutes. . . . If there is an absolute for moral decisions, it is human life.

Or as a thirty-one-year-old Wellesley graduate says, in explaining why she would find it difficult to steal a drug to save her own life despite her belief that it would be right to steal for another: "It's just very hard to defend yourself against the rules. I mean, we live by consensus, and you take an action simply for yourself, by yourself, there's no consensus there, and that is relatively indefensible in this society now."

What begins to emerge is a sense of vulnerability that impedes these women from taking a stand, what George Eliot (1860/1965) regards as the girl's "susceptibility" to adverse judgments of others, which stems from her lack of power and consequent inability to do something in the world. While relativism in men, the unwillingness to make moral judgments that Kohlberg and Kramer (1969) and Kohlberg and Gilligan (1971) have associated with the adolescent crisis of identity and belief, takes the form of calling into question the concept of morality itself, the women's reluctance to judge stems rather from their uncertainty about their right to make moral statements or, perhaps, the price for them that such judgment seems to entail. This contrast echoes that made by Matina Horner (1972), who differentiated the ideological fear of success expressed by men from the personal conflicts about succeeding that riddled the women's responses to stories of competitive achievement.

> Most of the men who responded with the expectation of negative consequences because of success were not concerned about their masculinity but were instead likely to have expressed existential concerns about finding a "non-materialistic happiness and satisfaction in life." These concerns, which reflect changing attitudes toward traditional kinds of success or achievement in our society, played little, if any, part in the female stories. Most of the women who were high in fear of success imagery continued to be concerned about the discrepancy between success in the situation described and feminine identity. (pp. 163–164)

When women feel excluded from direct participation in society, they see themselves as subject to a consensus or judgment made and enforced by the men on whose protection and support they depend and by whose names they are known. A divorced middle-aged woman, mother of adolescent daughters, resident of a sophisticated university community, tells the story as follows:

> As a woman, I feel I never understood that I was a person, that I can make decisions and I have a right to make decisions. I always felt that that belonged to my father or my husband in some way or church which was always represented by a male clergyman. They were the three men in my life: father, husband, and clergyman, and they had much more to say about what I should or shouldn't do. They were really authority figures which I accepted. I didn't rebel against that. It only has lately occurred to me that I never even rebelled against it, and my girls are much more conscious of this, not in the militant sense, but just in the recognizing sense. . . . I still let things happen to me rather than make them happen, than to make choices, although I know all about choices. I know the procedures and the steps and all. [Do you have any clues about why this might be true?] Well, I think in one sense, there is less responsibility involved. Because if you make a dumb decision, you have to take the rap. If it happens to you, well, you can complain about it. I think that if you don't grow up feeling that you ever had any choices, you don't either have the sense that you have emotional responsibility. With this sense of choice comes this sense of responsibility.

The essence of the moral decision is the exercise of choice and the willingness to accept responsibility for that choice. To the extent that women perceive themselves as having no choice, they correspondingly excuse themselves from the responsibility that decision entails. Childlike in the vulnerability of their dependence and consequent fear of abandonment, they claim to wish only to please but in return for their goodness they expect to be loved and cared for. This, then, is an "altruism" always at risk, for it presupposes an innocence constantly in danger of being compromised by an awareness of the trade-off that has been made. Asked to describe herself, a Radcliffe senior responds:

> I have heard of the onion skin theory. I see myself as an onion, as a block of different layers, the external layers for people that I don't know that well, the agreeable, the social, and as you go inward there are more sides for people I know that I show. I am not sure about the innermost, whether there is a core, or whether I have just picked up everything as I was growing up, these different influences. I think I have a neutral attitude towards myself, but I do think in terms of good and bad. . . . Good—I try to be considerate and thoughtful of other people and I try to be fair in situations and be tolerant. I use the words but I try and work

them out practically. . . . Bad things—I am not sure if they are bad, if they are altruistic or I am doing them basically for approval of other people. [Which things are these?] The values I have when I try to act them out. They deal mostly with interpersonal type relations. . . . If I were doing it for approval, it would be a very tenuous thing. If I didn't get the right feedback, there might go all my values.

Ibsen's play, *A Doll House* (1879/1965), depicts the explosion of just such a world through the eruption of a moral dilemma that calls into question the notion of goodness that lies at its center. Nora, the "squirrel wife," living with her husband as she had lived with her father, puts into action this conception of goodness as sacrifice and, with the best of intentions, takes the law into her own hands. The crisis that ensues, most painfully for her in the repudiation of that goodness by the very person who was its recipient and beneficiary, causes her to reject the suicide that she had initially seen as its ultimate expression and chose instead to seek new and firmer answers to the adolescent questions of identity and belief.

The availability of choice and with it the onus of responsibility has now invaded the most private sector of the woman's domain and threatens a similar explosion. For centuries, women's sexuality anchored them in passivity, in a receptive rather than active stance, where the events of conception and childbirth could be controlled only by a withholding in which their own sexual needs were either denied or sacrificed. That such a sacrifice entailed a cost to their intelligence as well was seen by Freud (1908/1959) when he tied the "undoubted intellectual inferiority of so many women" to "the inhibition of thought necessitated by sexual suppression" (p. 199). The strategies of withholding and denial that women have employed in the politics of sexual relations appear similar to their evasion or withholding of judgment in the moral realm. The hesitance expressed in the previous examples to impose even a belief in the value of human life on others, like the reluctance to claim one's sexuality, bespeaks a self uncertain of its strength, unwilling to deal with consequence, and thus avoiding confrontation.

Thus women have traditionally deferred to the judgment of men, although often while intimating a sensibility of their own which is at variance with that judgment. Maggie Tulliver, in *The Mill on the Floss* (Eliot, 1860/1965) responds to the accusations that ensue from the discovery of her secretly continued relationship with Phillip Wakeham by acceding to her brother's moral judgment while at the same time asserting a different set of standards by which she attests her own superiority:

I don't want to defend myself. . . . I know I've been wrong—often continually. But yet, sometimes when I have done wrong, it has been because I have feelings that you would be the better for if you had them. If *you* were in fault ever, if you had done anything very wrong, I should be sorry for the pain it brought you; I should not want punishment to be heaped on you. (p. 188)

An eloquent defense, Kohlberg would argue, of a Stage Three moral position, an assertion of the age-old split between thinking and feeling, justice and mercy, that underlies many of the clichés and stereotypes concerning the difference between the sexes. But considered from another point of view, it is a moment of confrontation, replacing a former evasion, between two modes of judging, two differing constructions of the moral domain—one traditionally associated with masculinity and the public world of social power, the other with femininity and the privacy of domestic interchange. While the developmental ordering of these two points of view has been to consider the masculine as the more adequate and thus as replacing the feminine as the individual moves toward higher stages, their reconciliation remains unclear.

The Development of Women's Moral Judgment

Recent evidence for a divergence in moral development between men and women comes from the research of Haan (Note 1) and Holstein (1976) whose findings lead them to question the possibility of a "sex-related bias" in Kolhberg's scoring system. This system is based on Kohlberg's six-stage description of moral development. Kohlberg's stages divide into three levels, which he designates as preconventional, conventional, and postconventional, thus denoting the major shifts in moral perspective around a center of moral understanding that equates justice with the maintenance of existing social systems. While the preconventional conception of justice is based on the needs of the self, the conventional judgment derives from an understanding of society. This understanding is in turn superseded by a postconventional or principled conception of justice where the good is formulated in universal terms. The quarrel with Kohlberg's stage scoring does not pertain to the structural differentiation of his levels but rather to questions of stage and sequence. Kohlberg's stages begin with an obedience and punishment orientation (Stage One), and go from there in invariant order to instrumental hedonism (Stage Two), interpersonal concordance (Stage Three), law and order (Stage Four), social contract (Stage Five), and universal ethical principles (Stage Six).

The bias that Haan and Holstein question in this scoring system has to do with the subordination of the interpersonal to the societal definition of the good in the transition from Stage Three to Stage Four. This is the transition that has repeatedly been found to be problematic for women. In 1969, Kohlberg and Kramer identified Stage Three as the characteristic mode of women's moral judgments, claiming that, since women's lives were interpersonally based, this stage was not only "functional" for them but also adequate for resolving the moral conflicts that they faced. Turiel (1973) reported that while girls reached Stage Three sooner than did boys, their judgments tended to remain at that stage while the boys' development continued further along Kohlberg's scale. Gilligan, Kohlberg, Lerner, and Belenky (1971) found a similar association between sex and moral-judgment stage in a study of high-school students, with the girls' responses being scored predominantly at Stage Three while the boys' responses were more often scored at Stage Four.

This repeated finding of developmental inferiority in women may, however, have more to do with the standard by which development has been measured than with the quality of women's thinking per se. Haan's data (Note 1) on the Berkeley

Free Speech Movement and Holstein's (1976) three-year longitudinal study of adolescents and their parents indicate that the moral judgments of women differ from those of men in the greater extent to which women's judgments are tied to feelings of empathy and compassion and are concerned more with the resolution of "real-life" as opposed to hypothetical dilemmas (Note 1, p. 34). However, as long as the categories by which development is assessed are derived within a male perspective from male research data, divergence from the masculine standard can be seen only as a failure of development. As a result, the thinking of women is often classified with that of children. The systematic exclusion from consideration of alternative criteria that might better encompass the development of women indicates not only the limitations of a theory framed by men and validated by research samples disproportionately male and adolescent but also the effects of the diffidence prevalent among women, their reluctance to speak publicly in their own voice, given the constraints imposed on them by the politics of differential power between the sexes.

In order to go beyond the question, "How much like men do women think, how capable are they of engaging in the abstract and hypothetical construction of reality?" it is necessary to identify and define in formal terms developmental criteria that encompass the categories of women's thinking. Such criteria would include the progressive differentiations, comprehensiveness, and adequacy that characterize higher-stage resolution of the "more frequently occurring, real-life moral dilemmas of interpersonal, empathic, fellow-feeling concerns" (Haan, Note 1, p. 34), which have long been the center of women's moral judgments and experience. To ascertain whether the feminine construction of the moral domain relies on a language different from that of men, but one which deserves equal credence in the definition of what constitutes development, it is necessary first to find the places where women have the power to choose and thus are willing to speak in their own voice.

When birth control and abortion provide women with effective means for controlling their fertility, the dilemma of choice enters the center of women's lives. Then the relationships that have traditionally defined women's identities and framed their moral judgments no longer flow inevitably from their reproductive capacity but become matters of decision over which they have control. Released from the passivity and reticence of a sexuality that binds them in dependence, it becomes possible for women to question with Freud what it is that they want and to assert their own answers to that question. However, while society may affirm publicly the woman's right to choose for herself, the exercise of such choice brings her privately into conflict with the conventions of femininity, particularly the moral equation of goodness with self-sacrifice. While independent assertion in judgment and action is considered the hallmark of adulthood and constitutes as well the standard of masculine development, it is rather in their care and concern for others that women have both judged themselves and been judged.

The conflict between self and other thus constitutes the central moral problem for women, posing a dilemma whose resolution requires a reconciliation between femininity and adulthood. In the absence of such a reconciliation, the moral problem cannot be resolved. The "good woman" masks assertion in evasion, denying responsibility by claiming only to meet the needs of others, while the "bad woman" forgoes or renounces the commitments that bind her in self-deception and betrayal. It is precisely this dilemma—the conflict between compassion and autonomy, between virtue and power—which the feminine voice struggles to resolve in its effort to reclaim the self and to solve the moral problem in such a way that no one is hurt.

When a woman considers whether to continue or abort a pregnancy, she contemplates a decision that affects both self and others and engages directly the critical moral issue of hurting. Since the choice is ultimately hers and therefore one for which she is responsible, it raises precisely those questions of judgment that have been most problematic for women. Now she is asked whether she wishes to interrupt that stream of life which has for centuries immersed her in the passivity of dependence while at the same time imposing on her the responsibility for care. Thus the abortion decision brings to the core of feminine apprehension, to what Joan Didion (1972) calls "the irreconcilable difference of it—that sense of living one's deepest life underwater, that dark involvement with blood and birth and death" (p. 14), the adult questions of responsibility and choice.

How women deal with such choices has been the subject of my research, designed to clarify, through considering the ways in which women construct and resolve the abortion decision, the nature and development of women's moral judgment. Twenty-nine women, diverse in age, race, and social class, were referred by abortion and pregnancy counseling services and participated in the study for a variety of reasons. Some came to gain further clarification with respect to a decision about which they were in conflict, some in response to a counselor's concern about repeated abortions, and others out of an interest in and/or willingness to contribute to ongoing research. Although the pregnancies occurred under a variety of circumstances in the lives of these women, certain commonalities could be discerned. The adolescents often failed to use birth control because they denied or discredited their capacity to bear children. Some of the older women attributed the pregnancy to the omission of contraceptive measures in circumstances where intercourse had not been anticipated. Since the pregnancies often coincided with efforts on the part of the women to end a relationship, they may be seen as a manifestation of ambivalence or as a way of putting the relationship to the ultimate test of commitment. For these women, the pregnancy appeared to be a way of testing truth, making the baby an ally in the search for male support and protection or, that failing, a companion victim of his rejection. There were, finally, some women who became pregnant either as a result of a failure of birth control or intentionally as part of a joint decision that later was reconsidered. Of the twenty-nine women, four decided to have the baby, one miscarried, twenty-one chose abortion, and three remained in doubt about the decision.

In the initial part of the interview, the women were asked to discuss the decision that confronted them, how they were dealing with it, the alternatives they were considering, their reasons for and against each option, the people involved, the conflicts entailed, and the ways in which making this decision affected their self-concepts and their relationships with others. Then, in the second part of the interview, moral judgment was assessed in the hypothetical mode by presenting for resolution three of Kohlberg's standard research dilemmas.

While the structural progression from a preconventional through a conventional to a postconventional moral perspective can readily be discerned in the women's responses to both actual and hypothetical dilemmas, the conventions that shape women's moral judgments differ from those that apply to men. The construction of the abortion dilemma, in particular, reveals the existence of a distinct moral language whose evolution informs the sequence of women's development. This is the language of selfishness and responsibility, which defines the moral problem as one of obligation to exercise care and avoid hurt. The infliction of hurt is considered selfish and immoral in its reflection of unconcern, while the expression of care is seen as the fulfillment of moral responsibility. The reiterative use of the language of selfishness and responsibility and the underlying moral orientation it reflects sets the women apart from the men whom Kohlberg studied and may be seen as the critical reason for their failure to develop within the constraints of his system.

In the developmental sequence that follows, women's moral judgments proceed from an initial focus on the self at the *first level* to the discovery, in the transition to the *second level,* of the concept of responsibility as the basis for a new equilibrium between self and others. The elaboration of this concept of responsibility and its fusion with a maternal concept of morality, which seeks to ensure protection for the dependent and unequal, characterizes the *second level* of judgment. At this level the good is equated with caring for others. However, when the conventions of feminine goodness legitimize only others as the recipients of moral care, the logical inequality between self and other and the psychological violence that it engenders create the disequilibrium that initiates the *second* transition. The relationship between self and others is then reconsidered in an effort to sort out the confusion between conformity and care inherent in the conventional definition of feminine goodness and to establish a new equilibrium, which dissipates the tension between selfishness and responsibility. At the *third level,* the self becomes the arbiter of an independent judgment that now subsumes both conventions and individual needs under the moral principle of nonviolence. Judgment remains psychological in its concern with the intention and consequences of action, but it now becomes universal in its condemnation of exploitation and hurt.

Level I: Orientation to Individual Survival

In its initial and simplest construction, the abortion decision centers on the self. The concern is pragmatic, and the issue is individual survival. At this level, "should" is undifferentiated from "would," and others influence the decision only through their power to affect its consequences. An eighteen-year-old, asked what she thought when she found herself pregnant, replies: "I really didn't think anything except that I didn't want it. [Why was that?] I didn't want it, I wasn't ready for it, and next year will be my last year and I want to go to school."

Asked if there was a right decision, she says, "There is no right decision. [Why?]

I didn't want it." For her the question of right decision would emerge only if her own needs were in conflict; then she would have to decide which needs should take precedence. This was the dilemma of another eighteen-year-old, who saw having a baby as a way of increasing her freedom by providing "the perfect chance to get married and move away from home," but also as restricting her freedom "to do a lot of things."

At this first level, the self, which is the sole object of concern, is constrained by lack of power; the wish "to do a lot of things" is constantly belied by the limitations of what, in fact, is being done. Relationships are, for the most part, disappointing: "The only thing you are ever going to get out of going with a guy is to get hurt." As a result, women may in some instances deliberately choose isolation to protect themselves against hurt. When asked how she would describe herself to herself, a nineteen-year-old, who held herself responsible for the accidental death of a younger brother, answers as follows:

> I really don't know. I never thought about it. I don't know. I know basically the outline of a character. I am very independent. I don't really want to have to ask anybody for anything and I am a loner in life. I prefer to be by myself than around anybody else. I manage to keep my friends at a limited number with the point that I have very few friends. I don't know what else there is. I am a loner and I enjoy it. Here today and gone tomorrow.

The primacy of the concern with survival is explicitly acknowledged by a sixteen-year-old delinquent in response to Kohlberg's Heinz dilemma, which asks if it is right for a desperate husband to steal an outrageously overpriced drug to save the life of his dying wife:

> I think survival is one of the first things in life and that people fight for. I think it is the most important thing, more important than stealing. Stealing might be wrong, but if you have to steal to survive yourself or even kill, that is what you should do. . . . Preservation of oneself, I think, is the most important thing; it comes before anything in life.

The First Transition: From Selfishness to Responsibility

In the transition which follows and criticizes this level of judgment, the words selfishness and responsibility first appear. Their reference initially is to the self in a redefinition of the self-interest which has thus far served as the basis for judgment. The transitional issue is one of attachment or connection to others. The pregnancy catches up the issue not only by representing an immediate, literal connection, but also by affirming, in the most concrete and physical way, the capacity to assume adult feminine roles. However, while having a baby seems at first to offer respite from the loneliness of adolescence and to solve conflicts over dependence and independence, in reality the continuation of an adolescent pregnancy generally compounds these problems, increasing social isolation and precluding further steps toward independence.

To be a mother in the societal as well as the physical sense requires the assumption of parental responsibility for the care and protection of a child. However, in order to be able to care for another, one must first be able to care responsibly for oneself. The growth from childhood to adulthood, conceived as a move from selfishness to responsibility, is articulated explicitly in these terms by a seventeen-year-old who describes her response to her pregnancy as follows:

> I started feeling really good about being pregnant instead of feeling really bad, because I wasn't looking at the situation realistically. I was looking at it from my own sort of selfish needs because I was lonely and felt lonely and stuff. . . . Things weren't really going good for me, so I was looking at it that I could have a baby that I could take care of or something that was part of me, and that made me feel good . . . but I wasn't looking at the realistic side . . . about the responsibility I would have to take on . . . I came to this decision that I was going to have an abortion [because] I realized how much responsibility goes with having a child. Like you have to be there, you can't be out of the house all the time which is one thing I like to do . . . and I decided that I have to take on responsibility for myself and I have to work out a lot of things.

Stating her former mode of judgment, the wish to have a baby as a way of combating loneliness and feeling connected, she now criticizes that judgment as both "selfish" and "unrealistic." The contradiction between wishes for a baby and for the freedom to be "out of the house all the time"—that is, for connection and also for independence—is resolved in terms of a new priority, as the criterion for judgment changes. The dilemma now assumes moral definition as the emergent conflict between wish and necessity is seen as a disparity between "would" and "should." In this construction the "selfishness" of willful decision is counterposed to the "responsibility" of moral choice:

> What I want to do is to have the baby, but what I feel I should do which is what I need to do, is have an abortion right now, because sometimes what you want isn't right. Sometimes what is necessary comes before what you want, because it might not always lead to the right thing.

While the pregnancy itself confirms femininity—"I started feeling really good; it sort of made me feel, like being pregnant, I started feeling like a woman"—the abortion decision becomes an opportunity for the adult exercise of responsible choice.

> [How would you describe yourself to yourself?] I am looking at myself differently in the way that I have had a really heavy decision put upon me, and I have never really had too many hard decisions in my life, and I have made it. It has taken some responsibility to do this. I have changed in that way, that I have made a hard decision. And that has been good. Because before, I would not have looked at it realistically, in my opinion. I would have gone by what I wanted to do, and I wanted it, and even if it wasn't right. So I see myself as I'm becoming more mature in ways of making decisions and taking care of myself, doing something for myself. I think it is going to help me in other ways, if I have other decisions to make put upon me, which would take some responsibility. And I would know that I could make them.

In the epiphany of this cognitive reconstruction, the old becomes transformed in terms of the new. The wish to "do something for myself" remains, but the terms of its fulfillment change as the decision affirms both femininity and adulthood in its integration of responsibility and care. Morality, says another adolescent, "is the way you think about yourself . . . sooner or later you have to make up your mind to start taking care of yourself. Abortion, if you do it for the right reasons, is helping yourself to start over and do different things."

Since this transition signals an enhancement in self-worth, it requires a conception of self which includes the possibility for doing "the right thing," the ability to see in oneself the potential for social acceptance. When such confidence is seriously in doubt, the transitional questions may be raised but development is impeded. The failure to make this first transition, despite an understanding of the issues involved, is illustrated by a woman in her late twenties Her struggle with the conflict between selfishness and responsibility pervades but fails to resolve her dilemma of whether or not to have a third abortion.

> I think you have to think about the people who are involved, including yourself. You have responsibilities to yourself . . . and to make a right, whatever that is, decision in this depends on your knowledge and awareness of the responsibilities that you have and whether you can survive with a child and what it will do to your relationship with the father or how it will affect him emotionally.

Rejecting the idea of selling the baby and making "a lot of money in a black market kind of thing . . . because mostly I operate on principles and it would just rub me the wrong way to think I would be selling my own child," she struggles with a concept of responsibility which repeatedly turns back on the question of her own survival. Transition seems blocked by a self-image which is insistently contradictory:

> [How would you describe yourself to yourself?] I see myself as impulsive, practical—that is a contradiction—and moral and amoral, a contradiction. Actually the only thing that is consistent and not contradictory is the fact that I am very lazy which everyone has always told me is really a symptom of something else which I have never been able to put my finger on exactly. It has taken me a long time to like myself. In fact there are times when I don't, which I think is healthy to a point and sometimes I think I like myself too much and I probably evade myself too much, which avoids responsibility to myself and to other people who like me. I am pretty unfaithful to myself. . . I have a hard time even thinking that I am a human being, simply because so much rotten stuff goes on and people are so crummy and insensitive.

Seeing herself as avoiding responsibility, she can find no basis upon which to resolve the pregnancy dilemma. Instead, her inability to arrive at any clear sense of decision only contributes further to her overall sense of failure. Criticizing her parents for having betrayed her during adolescence by coercing her to have an abortion she did not want, she now betrays herself and criticizes that as well. In this light, it is less surprising that she considered selling her child, since she felt herself to have, in effect, been sold by her parents for the sake of maintaining their social status.

The Second Level: Goodness as Self-Sacrifice

The transition from selfishness to responsibility is a move toward social participation. Whereas at the first level, morality is seen as a matter of sanctions imposed by a society of which one is more subject than citizen, at the second level, moral judgment comes to rely on shared norms and expectations. The woman at this level validates her claim to social membership through the adoption of societal values. Consensual judgment becomes paramount and goodness the overriding concern as survival is now seen to depend on acceptance by others.

Here the conventional feminine voice emerges with great clarity, defining the self and proclaiming its worth on the basis of the ability to care for and protect others. The woman now constructs the world perfused with the assumptions about feminine goodness reflected in the stereotypes of the Broverman et al. (1972) studies. There the attributes considered desirable for women all presume an other, a recipient of the "tact, gentleness and easy expression of feeling" which allow the woman to respond sensitively while evoking in return the care which meets her own "very strong need for security" (p. 63). The strength of this position lies in its capacity for caring; its limitation is the restriction it imposes on direct expression. Both qualities are elucidated by a nineteen-year-old who contrasts her reluctance to criticize with her boyfriend's straightforwardness:

> I never want to hurt anyone, and I tell them in a very nice way, and I have respect for their own opinions, and they can do the things the way that they want, and he usually tells people right off the bat. . . . He does a lot of things out in public which I do in private. . . . it is better, the other [his way], but I just could never do it.

While her judgment clearly exists, it is not expressed, at least not in public. Concern for the feelings of others imposes a deference which she nevertheless criticizes in an awareness that, under the name of consideration, a vulnerability and a duplicity are concealed.

At the second level of judgment, it is specifically over the issue of hurting that conflict arises with respect to the abortion decision. When no option exists that can be construed as being in the best interest of everyone, when responsibilities conflict and decision entails the sacrifice of somebody's needs, then the woman confronts the seemingly impossible task of choosing the victim. A nineteen-year-old, fearing the consequences for herself of a second abortion but facing the opposition of both her family and her lover to the continuation of the pregnancy, describes the dilemma as follows:

> I don't know what choices are open to me; it is either to have it or the abortion; these are the choices open to me. It is just that either way I don't . . . I think what confuses me is it is a choice of either hurting myself or hurting other people around me. What is more important? If there could be a happy medium, it would be fine, but there isn't. It is either hurting someone on this side or hurting myself.

While the feminine identification of goodness with self-sacrifice seems clearly to dictate the "right" resolution of this dilemma, the stakes may be high for the woman herself, and the sacrifice of the fetus, in any event, compromises the altruism of an abortion motivated by a concern for others. Since femininity itself is in conflict in an abortion intended as an expression of love and care, this is a resolution which readily explodes in its own contradiction.

"I don't think anyone should have to choose between two things that they love," says a twenty-five-year-old woman who assumed responsibility not only for her lover but also for his wife and children in having an abortion she did not want:

> I just wanted the child and I really don't believe in abortions. Who can say when life begins. I think that life begins at conception and . . . I felt like there were changes happening in my body and I felt very protective . . . [but] I felt a responsibility, my responsibility if anything ever happened to her [his wife]. He made me feel that I had to make a choice and there was only one choice to make and that was to have an abortion and I could always have children another time and he made me feel if I didn't have it that it would drive us apart.

The abortion decision was, in her mind, a choice not to choose with respect to the pregnancy—"That was my choice, I had to do it." Instead, it was a decision to subordinate the pregnancy to the continuation of a relationship that she saw as encompassing her life—"Since I met him, he has been my life. I do everything for him; my life sort of revolves around him." Since she wanted to have the baby and also to continue the relationship, either choice could be construed as selfish. Furthermore, since both alternatives entailed hurting someone, neither could be considered moral. Faced with a decision which, in her own terms, was untenable, she sought to avoid responsibility for the choice she made, construing the decision as a sacrifice of her own needs to those of her lover. However, this public sacrifice in the name of responsibility engendered a private resentment that erupted in anger, compromising the very relationship that it had been intended to sustain.

> Afterwards we went through a bad time because I hate to say it and I was wrong, but I blamed him. I gave in to him. But when it came down to it, I made the decision. I could have said, 'I am going to have this child whether you want me to or not,' and I just didn't do it.

Pregnant again by the same man, she recognizes in retrospect that the choice in fact had been hers, as she returns once again to what now appears to have been missed opportunity for growth. Seeking, this time, to make rather than abdicate the decision, she sees the issue as one of "strength" as she struggles to free herself from the powerlessness of her own dependence:

> I think that right now I think of myself as someone who can become a lot stronger. Because of the circumstances, I just go along like with the tide. I never really had anything of my own before . . . [this time] I hope to come on strong and make a big decision, whether it is right or wrong.

Because the morality of self-sacrifice had justified the previous abortion, she now must suspend that judgment if she is to claim her own voice and accept responsibility for choice.

She thereby calls into question the underlying assumption of Level Two, which leads the woman to consider herself responsible for the actions of others, while holding others responsible for the choices she makes. This notion of reciprocity, backwards in its assumptions about control, disguises assertion as response. By reversing responsibility, it generates a series of indirect actions, which leave everyone feeling manipulated and betrayed. The logic of this position is confused in that the morality of mutual care is embedded in the psychology of dependence. Assertion becomes personally dangerous in its risk of criticism and abandonment, as well as potentially immoral in its power to hurt. This confusion is captured by Kohlberg's (1969) definition of Stage Three moral judgment, which joins the need for approval with the wish to care for and help others.

When thus caught between the passivity of dependence and the activity of care, the woman becomes suspended in an immobility of both judgment and action. "If I were drowning, I couldn't reach out a hand to save myself, so unwilling am I to set myself up against fate" (p. 7), begins the central character of Margaret Drabble's novel, *The Waterfall* (1971), in an effort to absolve herself of responsibility as she at the same time relinquishes control. Facing the same moral conflict which George Eliot depicted in *The Mill on the Floss,* Drabble's heroine proceeds to relive Maggie Tulliver's dilemma but turns inward in her search for the way in which to retell that story. What is initially suspended and then called into question is the judgment which "had in the past made it seem better to renounce myself than them" (Drabble, p. 50).

The Second Transition: From Goodness to Truth

The second transition begins with the reconsideration of the relationship between self and other, as the woman starts to scrutinize the logic of self-sacrifice in the service of a morality of care. In the interview data, this transition is announced by the reappearance of the word selfish. Retrieving the judgmental initiative, the woman begins to ask whether it is selfish or responsible, moral or immoral, to include her own needs within the compass of her care and concern. This question leads her to reexamine the concept of responsibility, juxtaposing the outward concern with what other people think with a new inner judgment.

In separating the voice of the self from those of others, the woman asks if it is possible to be responsible to herself as well as to others and thus to reconcile the disparity between hurt and care. The exercise of such responsibility, however, requires a new kind of judgment whose first demand is for honesty. To be responsible, it is necessary first to acknowledge what it is that one is doing. The criterion for judgment thus shifts from "goodness" to "truth" as the morality of action comes to be assessed not on the basis of its appearance in the eyes of others, but in terms of the realities of its intention and consequence.

A twenty-four-year-old married Catholic woman, pregnant again two months following the birth of her first child, identifies her dilemma as one of choice: "You have to now decide; because it is now available, you have to make a decision. And if it wasn't available, there was no choice open; you just do what you have to do." In the absence of legal abortion, a morality of self-sacrifice was necessary in order to insure protection and care for the dependent child. However, when such sacrifice becomes optional, the entire problem is recast.

The abortion decision is framed by this woman first in terms of her responsibilities to others: having a second child at this time would be contrary to medical advice and would strain both the emotional and financial resources of the family. However, there is, she says, a third reason for having an abortion, "sort of an emotional reason. I don't know if it is selfish or not, but it would really be tying myself down and right now I am not ready to be tied down with two."

Against this combination of selfish and responsible reasons for abortion is her Catholic belief that

> . . . it is taking a life, and it is. Even though it is not formed, it is the potential, and to me it is still taking a life. But I have to think of mine, my son's and my husband's, to think about, and at first I think that I thought it was for selfish reasons, but it is not. I believe that too, some of it is selfish. I don't want another one right now; I am not ready for it.

The dilemma arises over the issue of justification for taking a life: "I can't cover it over, because I believe this and if I do try to cover it over, I know that I am going to be in a mess. It will be denying what I am really doing." Asking "Am I doing the right thing; is it moral?," she counterposes to her belief against abortion her concern with the consequences of continuing the pregnancy. While concluding that "I can't be so morally strict as to hurt three other people with a decision just because of my moral beliefs," the issue of goodness still remains critical to her resolution of the dilemma:

> The moral factor is there. To me it is taking a life, and I am going to take that upon myself, that decision upon myself and I have feelings about it, and talked to a priest . . . but he said it is there and it will be from now on, and it is up to the person if they can live with the idea and still believe they are good.

The criteria for goodness, however, move inward as the ability to have an abortion and still consider herself good comes to hinge on the issue of selfishness with which she struggles to come to terms. Asked if acting morally is acting according to what is best for the self or whether it is a matter of self-sacrifice, she replies:

> I don't know if I really understand the question. . . . Like in my situation where I want to have the abortion and if I didn't it would be self-sacrificing, I am really in the middle of both those ways . . . but I think that my morality is strong and if these reasons—financial, physical reality and also for the whole family involved— were not here, that I wouldn't have to do it, and then it would be a self-sacrifice.

The importance of clarifying her own participation in the decision is evident in her attempt to ascertain her feelings in order to determine whether or not she was "putting them under" in deciding to end the pregnancy. Whereas in the first transition, from selfishness to responsibility, women made lists in order to bring to their consideration needs other than their own, now, in the second transition, it is the needs of the self which have to be deliberately uncovered. Confronting the reality of her own wish for an abortion, she now must deal with the problem of selfishness and the qualification that she feels it imposes on the "goodness" of her decision. The primacy of this concern is apparent in her description of herself:

> I think in a way I am selfish for one thing, and very emotional, very . . . and I think that I am a very real person and an understanding person and I can handle life situations fairly well, so I am basing a lot of it on my ability to do the things that I feel are right and best for me and whoever I am involved with. I think I was very fair to myself about the decision, and I really think that I have been truthful, not hiding anything, bringing out all the feelings involved. I feel it is a good decision and an honest one, a real decision.

Thus she strives to encompass the needs of both self and others, to be responsible to others and thus to be "good" but also to be responsible to herself and thus to be "honest" and "real."

While from one point of view, attention to one's own needs is considered selfish, when looked at from a different perspective, it is a matter of honesty and fairness. This is the essence of the transitional shift toward a new conception of goodness which turns inward in an acknowledgement of the self and an acceptance of responsibility for decision. While outward justification, the concern with "good reasons," remains critical for this particular woman: "I still think abortion is wrong, and it will be unless the situation can justify what you are doing." But the search for justification has produced a change in her thinking, "not drastically, but a little bit." She realizes that in continuing the pregnancy she would punish not only herself but also her husband, toward whom she had begun to feel "turned off and irritated." This leads her to consider the consequences self-sacrifice can have both for the self and for others. "God," she says, "can punish, but He can also forgive." What remains in question is whether her claim to forgiveness is compromised by a decision that not only meets the needs of others but that also is "right and best for me."

The concern with selfishness and its equation with immorality recur in an interview with another Catholic woman whose arrival for an abortion was punctuated by the statement, "I have always thought abortion was a fancy word for murder." Initially explaining this murder as one of lesser degree—"I am doing it because I have to do it. I am not doing it the least bit because I want to," she judges it "not quite as bad. You can rationalize that it is not quite the same." Since "keeping the child for lots and lots of reasons was just sort of impractical and out," she considers her options to be either abortion or adoption. However, having previously given up one child for adoption, she says: "I knew that psychologically there was no way that I could hack another adoption. It took me about four-and-a-half years to get my head on straight; there was just no way I was going to go through it again." The decision thus reduces in her eyes to a choice between murdering the fetus or damaging herself. The choice is further complicated by the fact that by continuing the pregnancy she would hurt not only herself but also her parents, with whom she lived. In the face of these manifold moral contradictions, the psychological demand for honesty that arises in counseling finally allows decision:

> On my own, I was doing it not so much for myself; I was doing it for my parents. I was doing it because the doctor told me to do it, but I had never resolved in my mind that I was doing it for me. Because it goes right back to the fact that I never believed in abortions. . . . Actually, I had to sit down and admit, no, I really don't want to go the mother route now. I honestly don't feel that I want to be a mother, and that is not really such a bad thing to say after all. But that is not how I felt up until talking to Maureen [her counselor]. It was just a horrible way to feel, so I just wasn't going to feel it, and I just blocked it right out.

As long as her consideration remains "moral," abortion can be justified only as an act of sacrifice, a submission to necessity where the absence of choice precludes responsibility. In this way, she can avoid self-condemnation, since, "When you get into moral stuff then you are getting into self-respect and that stuff, and at least if I do something that I feel is morally wrong, then I tend to lose some of my self-respect as a person." Her evasion of responsibility, critical to maintaining the innocence necessary for self-respect, contradicts the reality of her own participation in the abortion decision. The dishonesty in her plea of victimization creates the conflict that generates the need for a more inclusive understanding. She must now resolve the emerging contradiction in her thinking between two uses of the term right: "I am saying that abortion is morally wrong, but the situation is right, and I am going to do it. But the thing is that eventually they are going to have to go together, and I am going to have to put them together somehow." Asked how this could be done, she replies:

> I would have to change morally wrong to morally right. [How?] I have no idea. I don't think you can take something that you feel is morally wrong because the situation makes it right and put the two together. They are not together, they are opposite. They don't go together. Something is wrong, but all of a sudden because you are doing it, it is right.

This discrepancy recalls a similar conflict she faced over the question of euthanasia, also considered by her to be morally wrong until she "took care of a couple of patients who had flat EEGs and saw the job that it was doing on their families." Recalling that experience, she says:

> You really don't know your black and whites until you really get into them and are being confronted with it. If you stop and think about my feelings on euthanasia until I got into it, and then my feelings about abortion until I got into it, I thought both of them were murder. Right and wrong and no middle but there is a gray.

In discovering the gray and questioning the moral judgments which formerly she considered to be absolute, she confronts the moral crisis of the second transition. Now the conventions which in the past had guided her moral judgment become subject to a new criticism, as she questions not only the justification for hurting others in the name of morality but also the "rightness" of hurting herself. However, to sustain such criticism in the face of conventions that equate goodness with self-sacrifice, the woman must verify her capacity for independent judgment and the legitimacy of her own point of view.

Once again transition hinges on self-concept. When uncertainty about her own worth prevents a woman from claiming equality, self-assertion falls prey to the old criticism of selfishness. Then the morality that condones self-destruction in the name of responsible care is not repudiated as inadequate but rather is abandoned in the face of its threat to survival. Moral obligation, rather than expanding to include the self, is rejected completely as the failure of conventional reciprocity leaves the woman unwilling any longer to protect others at what is now seen to be her own expense. In the absence of morality, survival, however "selfish" or "immoral," returns as the paramount concern.

A musician in her late twenties illustrates this transitional impasse. Having led an independent life which centered on her work, she considered herself "fairly strong-willed, fairly in control, fairly rational and objective" until she became involved in an intense love affair and discovered in her capacity to love "an entirely new dimension" in herself. Admitting in retrospect to "tremendous naiveté and idealism," she had entertained "some vague ideas that some day I would like a child to concretize our relationship . . . having always associated having a child with all the creative aspects of my life." Abjuring, with her lover, the use of contraceptives because, "as the relationship was sort of an ideal relationship in our minds, we liked the idea of not using foreign objects or anything artificial," she saw herself as having relinquished control, becoming instead "just simply vague and allowing events to just carry me along." Just as she began in her own thinking to confront "the realities of that situation"—the possibility of pregnancy and the fact that her lover was married—she found herself pregnant. "Caught" between her wish to end a relationship that "seemed more and more defeating" and her wish for a baby, which "would be a connection that would last a long time," she is paralyzed by her inability to resolve the dilemma which her ambivalence creates.

The pregnancy poses a conflict between her "moral" belief that "once a certain life has begun, it shouldn't be stopped artificially" and her "amazing" discovery that to have the baby she would "need much more [support] than I thought." Despite her moral conviction that she "should" have the child, she doubts that she could psychologically deal with "having the child alone and taking the responsibility for it." Thus a conflict erupts between what she considers to be her moral obligation to protect life and her inability to do so under the circumstances of this pregnancy. Seeing it as "my decision and my responsibility for making the decision whether to have or have not the child," she struggles to find a viable basis on which to resolve the dilemma.

Capable of arguing either for or against abortion "with a philosophical logic," she says, on the one hand, that in an overpopulated world one should have children only under ideal conditions for care but, on the other, that one should end a life only when it is impossible to sustain it. She describes her impasse in response to the question of whether there is a difference between what she wants to do and what she thinks she should do:

Yes, and there always has. I have always been confronted with that precise situation in a lot of my choices, and I have been trying to figure out what are the things that make me believe that these are things I should do as opposed to what I feel I want to do. [In this situation?] It is not that clear cut. I both want the child and feel I should have it, and I also think I should have the abortion and want it, but I would say it is my stronger feeling, and that I don't have enough confidence in my work yet and that is really where it is all hinged, I think . . . [the abortion] would solve the problem and I know I can't handle the pregnancy.

Characterizing this solution as "emotional and pragmatic" and attributing it to her lack of confidence in her work, she contrasts it with the "better thought out and more logical and more correct" resolution of her lover who thinks that she should have the child and raise it without either his presence or financial support. Confronted with this reflected image of herself as ultimately giving and good, as self-sustaining in her own creativity and thus able to meet the needs of others while imposing no demands of her own in return, she questions not the image itself but her own adequacy in filling it. Concluding that she is not yet capable of doing so, she is reduced in her own eyes to what she sees as a selfish and highly compromised fight

for my survival. But in one way or another, I am going to suffer. Maybe I am going to suffer mentally and emotionally having the abortion, or I would suffer what I think is possibly something worse. So I suppose it is the lesser of two evils. I think it is a matter of choosing which one I know that I can survive through. It is really. I think it is selfish, I suppose, because it does have to do with that. I just realized that. I guess it does have to do with whether I would survive or not. [Why is this selfish?] Well, you know, it is. Because I am concerned with my survival first, as opposed to the survival of the relationship or the survival of the child, another human being . . . I guess I am setting priorities, and I guess I am setting my needs to survive first. . . . I guess I see it in negative terms a lot . . . but I do think of other positive things; that I am still going to have some life left, maybe. I don't know.

In the face of this failure of reciprocity of care, in the disappointment of abandonment where connection was sought, survival is seen to hinge on her work which is "where I derive the meaning of what I am. That's the known factor." While uncertainty about her work makes this survival precarious, the choice for abortion is also distressing in that she considers it to be "highly introverted—that in this one respect, having an abortion would be going a step backward; going outside to love someone else and having a child would be a step forward." The sense of retrenchment that the severing of connection signifies is apparent in her anticipation of the cost which abortion would entail:

Probably what I will do is I will cut off my feelings, and when they will return or what would happen to them after that, I don't know. So that I don't feel anything at all, and I would probably just be very cold and go through it very coldly. . . . The more you do that to yourself, the more difficult it becomes to love again or to trust again or to feel again. . . . Each time I move away from that, it becomes easier, not more difficult, but easier to avoid committing myself to a relationship. And I am really concerned about cutting off that whole feeling aspect.

Caught between selfishness and responsibility, unable to find in the circumstances of this choice a way of caring which does not at the same time destroy, she confronts a dilemma which reduces to a conflict between morality and survival. Adulthood and femininity fly apart in the failure of this attempt at integration as the choice to work becomes a decision not only to renounce this particular relationship and child but also to obliterate the vulnerability that love and care engender.

The Third Level: The Morality of Nonviolence

In contrast, a twenty-five-year-old woman, facing a similar disappointment, finds a way to reconcile the initially disparate concepts of selfishness and responsibility through a transformed understanding of self and a corresponding redefinition of morality. Examining the assumptions underlying the conventions of feminine self-abnegation and moral self-sacrifice, she comes to reject these conventions as immoral in their power to hurt. By elevating nonviolence—the injunction against hurting—to a principle governing all moral judgment and action, she is able to assert a moral equality between self and other. Care then becomes a universal obligation, the self-chosen ethic of a postconventional judgment that reconstructs the dilemma in a way that allows the assumption of responsibility for choice.

In this woman's life, the current pregnancy brings to the surface the unfinished business of an earlier pregnancy and of the relationship in which both pregnancies occurred. The first pregnancy was discovered after her lover had left and was terminated by an abortion experienced as a purging expression of her anger at having been rejected. Remembering the abortion only as a relief, she nevertheless describes that time in her life as one in which she "hit rock bottom." Having hoped then to "take control of my life," she instead resumed the relationship when the man reappeared. Now, two years later, having once again "left my diaphragm in the drawer," she again becomes pregnant. Although initially "ecstatic" at the news, her elation dissipates when her lover tells her that he will leave if she chooses to have the child. Under these circumstances, she considers a second abortion but is unable to keep the repeated appointments she makes because of her reluctance to accept the responsibility for that choice. While the first abortion seemed an "honest mistake," she says that a second would make her feel "like a walking slaughter-house." Since she would need financial support to raise the child, her initial strategy was to take the matter to "the welfare people" in the hope that they would refuse to provide the necessary funds and thus resolve her dilemma:

> In that way, you know, the responsibility would be off my shoulders, and I could say, it's not my fault, you know, the state denied me the money that I would need to do it. But it turned out that it was possible to do it, and so I was, you know, right back where I started. And I had an appointment for an abortion, and I kept calling and cancelling it and then remaking the appointment and cancelling it, and I just couldn't make up my mind.

Confronting the need to choose between the two evils of hurting herself or ending the incipient life of the child, she finds, in a reconstruction of the dilemma itself, a basis for a new priority that allows decision. In doing so, she comes to see the conflict as arising from a faulty construction of reality. Her thinking recapitulates the developmental sequence, as she considers but rejects as inadequate the components of earlier-stage resolutions. An expanded conception of responsibility now reshapes moral judgment and guides resolution of the dilemma, whose pros and cons she considers as follows:

> Well, the pros for having the baby are all the admiration that you would get from, you know, being a single woman, alone, martyr, struggling, having the adoring love of this beautiful Gerber baby . . . just more of a home life than I have had in a long time, and that basically was it, which is pretty fantasyland; it is not very realistic. . . . Cons against having the baby: it was going to hasten what is looking to be the inevitable end of the relationship with the man I am presently with. . . . I was going to have to go on welfare, my parents were going to hate me for the rest of my life, I was going to lose a really good job that I have, I would lose a lot of independence . . . solitude . . . and I would have to be put in a position of asking help from a lot of people a lot of the time. Cons against having the abortion is having to face up to the guilt . . . and pros for having the abortion are I would be able to handle my deteriorating relation with S. with a lot more capability and a lot more responsibility for him and for myself . . . and I would not have to go through the realization that for the next twenty-five years of my life I would be punishing myself for being foolish enough to get pregnant again and forcing myself to bring up a kid just because I did this. Having to face the guilt of a second abortion seemed like, not exactly, well, exactly the lesser of the two evils but also the one that would pay off for me personally in the long run because by looking at why I am pregnant again and subsequently have decided to have a second abortion, I have to face up to some things about myself.

Although she doesn't "feel good about having a second abortion," she nevertheless concludes,

> I would not be doing myself or the child or the world any kind of favor having this child. . . . I don't need to pay off my imaginary debts to the world through this child, and I don't think that it is right to bring a child into the world and use it for that purpose.

Asked to describe herself, she indicates how closely her transformed moral understanding is tied to a changing self-concept:

> I have been thinking about that a lot lately, and it comes up different than what my usual subconscious perception of myself is. Usually paying off some sort of debt, going around serving people who are not really worthy of my attentions because somewhere in my life I think I got the impression that my needs are really secondary to other people's, and that if I feel, if I make any demands on other people to fulfill my needs, I'd feel guilty for it and submerge my own in favor of other people's, which later backfires on me, and I feel a great deal of resentment for other people that I am doing things for, which causes friction and the eventual

deterioration of the relationship. And then I start all over again. How would I describe myself to myself? Pretty frustrated and a lot angrier than I admit, a lot more aggressive than I admit.

Reflecting on the virtues which comprise the conventional definition of the feminine self, a definition which she hears articulated in her mother's voice, she says, "I am beginning to think that all these virtues are really not getting me anywhere. I have begun to notice." Tied to this recognition is an acknowledgement of her power and worth, both previously excluded from the image she projected:

> I am suddenly beginning to realize that the things that I like to do, the things I am interested in, and the things that I believe and the kind of person I am is not so bad that I have to constantly be sitting on the shelf and letting it gather dust. I am a lot more worthwhile than what my past actions have led other people to believe.

Her notion of a "good person," which previously was limited to her mother's example of hard work, patience and self-sacrifice, now changes to include the value that she herself places on directness and honesty. Although she believes that this new self-assertion will lead her "to feel a lot better about myself" she recognizes that it will also expose her to criticism:

> Other people may say, 'Boy, she's aggressive, and I don't like that,' but at least, you know, they will know that they don't like that. They are not going to say, 'I like the way she manipulates herself to fit right around me.' . . . What I want to do is just be a more self-determined person and a more singular person.

While within her old framework abortion had seemed a way of "copping out" instead of being a "responsible person [who] pays for his mistakes and pays and pays and is always there when she says she will be there and even when she doesn't say she will be there is there," now, her "conception of what I think is right for myself and my conception of self-worth is changing." She can consider this emergent self "also a good person," as her concept of goodness expands to encompass "the feeling of self-worth; you are not going to sell yourself short and you are not going to make yourself do things that, you know, are really stupid and that you don't want to do." This reorientation centers on the awareness that:

> I have a responsibility to myself, and you know, for once I am beginning to realize that that really matters to me . . . instead of doing what I want for myself and feeling guilty over how selfish I am, you realize that that is a very usual way for people to live . . . doing what you want to do because you feel that your wants and your needs are important, if to no one else, then to you, and that's reason enough to do something that you want to do.

Once obligation extends to include the self as well as others, the disparity between selfishness and responsibility is reconciled. Although the conflict between self and other remains, the moral problem is restructured in an awareness that the occurrence of the dilemma itself precludes non-violent resolution. The abortion decision is now seen to be a "serious" choice affecting both self and others: "This is a life that I have taken, a conscious decision to terminate, and that is just very heavy, a very heavy thing." While accepting the necessity of abortion as a highly compromised resolution, she turns her attention to the pregnancy itself, which she now considers to denote a failure of responsibility, a failure to care for and protect both self and other.

As in the first transition, although now in different terms, the conflict precipitated by the pregnancy catches up the issues critical to development. These issues now concern the worth of the self in relation to others, the claiming of the power to choose, and the acceptance of responsibility for choice. By provoking a confrontation with these issues, the crisis can become "a very auspicious time; you can use the pregnancy as sort of a learning, teeing-off point, which makes it useful in a way." This possibility for growth inherent in a crisis which allows confrontation with a construction of reality whose acceptance previously had impeded development was first identified by Coles (1964) in his study of the children of Little Rock. This same sense of possibility is expressed by the women who see, in their resolution of the abortion dilemma, a reconstructed understanding which creates the opportunity for "a new beginning," a chance "to take control of my life."

For this woman, the first step in taking control was to end the relationship in which she had considered herself "reduced to a nonentity," but to do so in a responsible way. Recognizing hurt as the inevitable concomitant of rejection, she strives to minimize that hurt "by dealing with [his] needs as best I can without compromising my own . . . that's a big point for me, because the thing in my life to this point has been always compromising, and I am not willing to do that any more." Instead, she seeks to act in a "decent, human kind of way . . . one that leaves maybe a slightly shook but not totally destroyed person." Thus the "nonentity" confronts her power to destroy which formerly had impeded any assertion, as she consider the possibility for a new kind of action that leaves both self and other intact.

The moral concern remains a concern with hurting as she considers Kohlberg's Heinz dilemma in terms of the question, "who is going to be hurt more, the druggist who loses some money or the person who loses their life?" The right to property and right to life are weighed not in the abstract, in terms of their logical priority, but rather in the particular, in terms of the actual consequences that the violation of these rights would have in the lives of the people involved. Thinking remains contextual and admixed with feelings of care, as the moral imperative to avoid hurt begins to be informed by a psychological understanding of the meaning of nonviolence.

Thus, release from the intimidation of inequality finally allows the expression of a judgment that previously had been withheld. What women then enunciate is not a new morality, but a moral conception disentangled from the constraints that formerly had confused its perception and impeded its articulation. The willingness to express and take responsibility for judgment stems from the recognition of the psychological and moral necessity for an equation of worth between self and other. Responsibility for care then includes both self and other, and the obligation not to hurt, freed from conventional constraints, is reconstructed as a universal guide to moral choice.

The reality of hurt centers the judgment of a twenty-nine-year-old woman, married and the mother of a preschool child, as she struggles with the dilemma posed by a second pregnancy whose timing conflicts with her completion of an advanced degree. Saying that "I cannot deliberately do something that is bad or would hurt another person because I can't live with having done that," she nevertheless confronts a situation in which hurt has become inevitable. Seeking that solution which would best protect both herself and others, she indicates, in her definition of morality, the ineluctable sense of connection which infuses and colors all of her thinking:

> [Morality is] doing what is appropriate and what is just within your circumstances, but ideally it is not going to affect—I was going to say, ideally it wouldn't negatively affect another person, but that is ridiculous, because decisions are always going to affect another person. But you see, what I am trying to say is that it is the person that is the center of the decision making, of that decision making about what's right and what's wrong.

The person who is the center of this decision making begins by denying, but then goes on to acknowledge, the conflicting nature both of her own needs and of her various responsibilities. Seeing the pregnancy as a manifestation of the inner conflict between her wish, on the one hand, "to be a college president" and, on the other, "to be making pottery and flowers and having kids and staying at home," she struggles with contradiction between femininity and adulthood. Considering abortion as the "better" choice—because "in the end, meaning this time next year or this time two weeks from now, it will be less of a personal strain on us individually and on us as a family for me not to be pregnant at this time," she concludes that the decision has

> got to be, first of all, something that the woman can live with—a decision that the woman can live with, one way or another, or at least try to live with, and that it be based on where she is at and other people, significant people in her life, are at.

At the beginning of the interview she had presented the dilemma in its conventional feminine construction, as a conflict between her own wish to have a baby and the wish of others for her to complete her education. On the basis of this construction she deemed it "selfish" to continue the pregnancy because it was something "I want to do." However, as she begins to examine her thinking, she comes to abandon as false this conceptualization of the problem, acknowledging the truth of her own internal conflict and elaborating the tension which she feels between her femininity and the adulthood of her work life. She describes herself as "going in two directions" and values that part of herself which is "incredibly passionate and sensitive"—her capacity to recognize and meet, often with anticipation, the needs of others. Seeing her "compassion" as "something I don't want to lose" she regards it as endangered by her pursuit of professional advancement. Thus the self-deception of her initial presentation, its attempt to sustain the fiction of her own innocence, stems from her fear that to say that *she* does not want to have another baby at this time would be

> an acknowledgement to me that I am an ambitious person and that I want to

have power and responsibility for others and that I want to live a life that extends from 9 to 5 every day and into the evenings and on weekends, because that is what the power and responsibility means. It means that my family would necessarily come second . . . there would be such an incredible conflict about which is tops, and I don't want that for myself.

Asked about her concept of "an ambitious person" she says that to be ambitious means to be

power hungry [and] insensitive. [Why insensitive?] Because people are stomped on in the process. A person on the way up stomps on people, whether it is family or other colleagues or clientele, on the way up. [Inevitably?] Not always, but I have seen it so often in my limited years of working that it is scary to me. It is scary because I don't want to change like that.

Because the acquisition of adult power is seen to entail the loss of feminine sensitivity and compassion, the conflict between femininity and adulthood becomes construed as a moral problem. The discovery of the principle of nonviolence begins to direct attention to the moral dilemma itself and initiates the search for a resolution that can encompass both femininity and adulthood.

Developmental Theory Reconsidered

The developmental conception delineated at the outset, which has so consistently found the development of women to be either aberrant or incomplete, has been limited insofar as it has been predominantly a male conception, giving lip-service, a place on the chart, to the interdependence of intimacy and care but constantly stressing, at their expense, the importance and value of autonomous judgment and action. To admit to this conception the truth of the feminine perspective is to recognize for both sexes the central importance in adult life of the connection between self and other, the universality of the need for compassion and care. The concept of the separate self and of the moral principle uncompromised by the constraints of reality is an adolescent ideal, the elaborately wrought philosophy of a Stephen Daedalus, whose flight we know to be in jeopardy. Erikson (1964), in contrasting the ideological morality of the adolescent with the ethics of adult care, attempts to grapple with this problem of integration, but is impeded by the limitations of his own previous developmental conception. When his developmental stages chart a path where the sole precursor to the intimacy of adult relationships is the trust established in infancy and all intervening experience is marked only as steps toward greater independence, then separation itself becomes the model and the measure of growth. The observation that for women, identity has as much to do with connection as with separation led Erikson into trouble largely because of his failure to integrate this insight into the mainstream of his developmental theory (Erikson, 1968).

The morality of responsibility which women describe stands apart from the morality of rights which underlies Kohlberg's conception of the highest stages of moral judgment. Kohlberg (Note 3) sees the progression toward these stages as resulting from the generalization of the self-centered adolescent rejection of societal morality into a principled conception of individual natural rights. To illustrate this progression, he cites as an example of integrated Stage Five judgment, "possibly moving to Stage Six," the following response of a twenty-five-year-old subject from his male longitudinal sample:

> [What does the word morality mean to you?] Nobody in the world knows the answer. I think it is recognizing the right of the individual, the rights of other individuals, not interfering with those rights. Act as fairly as you would have them treat you. I think it is basically to preserve the human being's right to existence. I think that is the most important. Secondly, the human being's right to do as he pleases, again without interfering with somebody else's rights. (p. 29)

Another version of the same conception is evident in the following interview response of a male college senior whose moral judgment also was scored by Kohlberg (Note 4) as at Stage Five or Six:

> [Morality] is a prescription, it is a thing to follow, and the idea of having a concept of morality is to try to figure out what it is that people can do in order to make life with each other livable, make for a kind of balance, a kind of equilibrium, a harmony in which everybody feels he has a place and an equal share in things, and it's doing that—doing that is kind of contributing to a state of affairs that go beyond the individual in the absence of which, the individual has no chance for self-fulfillment of any kind. Fairness; morality is kind of essential, it seems to me, for creating the kind of environment, interaction between people, that is prerequisite to this fulfillment of most individual goals and so on. If you want other people to not interfere with your pursuit of whatever you are into, you have to play the game.

In contrast, a woman in her late twenties responds to a similar question by defining a morality not of rights but of responsibility:

> [What makes something a moral issue?] Some sense of trying to uncover a right path in which to live, and always in my mind is that the world is full of real and recognizable trouble, and is it heading for some sort of doom and is it right to bring children into this world when we currently have an overpopulation problem, and is it right to spend money on a pair of shoes when I have a pair of shoes and other people are shoeless. . . . It is part of a self-critical view, part of saying, how am I spending my time and in what sense am I working? I think I have a real drive to, I have a real maternal drive to take care of someone. To take care of my mother, to take care of children, to take care of other people's children, to take care of my own children, to take care of the world. I think that goes back to your other question, and when I am dealing with moral issues, I am sort of saying to myself constantly, are you taking care of all the things that you think are important and in what ways are you wasting yourself and wasting those issues?

While the postconventional nature of this woman's perspective seems clear, her judgments of Kohlberg's hypothetical moral dilemmas do not meet his criteria for scoring at the principled level. Kohlberg regards this as a disparity between normative and metaethical judgments which he sees as indicative of the transition

81

between conventional and principled thinking. From another perspective, however, this judgment represents a different moral conception, disentangled from societal conventions and raised to the principled level. In this conception, moral judgment is oriented toward issues of responsibility. The way in which the responsibility orientation guides moral decision at the postconventional level is described by the following woman in her thirties:

> [Is there a right way to make moral decisions?] The only way I know is to try to be as awake as possible, to try to know the range of what you feel, to try to consider all that's involved, to be as aware as you can be to what's going on, as conscious as you can of where you're walking. [Are there principles that guide you?] The principle would have something to do with responsibility, responsibility and caring about yourself and others. . . . But it's not that on the one hand you choose to be responsible and on the other hand you choose to be irresponsible—both ways you can be responsible. That's why there's not just a principle that once you take hold of you settle—the principle put into practice here is still going to leave you with conflict.

The moral imperative that emerges repeatedly in the women's interviews is an injunction to care, a responsibility to discern and alleviate the "real and recognizable trouble" of this world. For the men Kohlberg studied, the moral imperative appeared rather as an injunction to respect the rights of others and thus to protect from interference the right to life and self-fulfillment. Women's insistence on care is at first self-critical rather than self-protective, while men initially conceive obligation to others negatively in terms of noninterference. Development for both sexes then would seem to entail an integration of rights and responsibilities through the discovery of the complementarity of these disparate views. For the women I have studied, this integration between rights and responsibilities appears to take place through a principled understanding of equity and reciprocity. This understanding tempers the self-destructive potential of a self-critical morality by asserting the equal right of all persons to care. For the men in Kohlberg's sample as well as for those in a longitudinal study of Harvard undergraduates (Gilligan & Murphy, Note 5) it appears to be the recognition through experience of the need for a more active responsibility in taking care that corrects the potential indifference of a morality of noninterference and turns attention from the logic to the consequences of choice. In the development of a postconventional ethic understanding, women come to see the violence generated by inequitable relationships, while men come to realize the limitations of a conception of justice blinded to the real inequities of human life.

Kohlberg's dilemmas, in the hypothetical abstraction of their presentation, divest the moral actors from the history and psychology of their individual lives and separate the moral problem from the social contingencies of its possible occurrence. In doing so, the dilemmas are useful for the distillation and refinement of the "objective principles of justice" toward which Kohlberg's stages strive. However, the reconstruction of the dilemma in its contextual particularity allows the understanding of cause and consequence which engages the compassion and tolerance considered by previous theorists to qualify the feminine sense of justice. Only when substance is given to the skeletal lives of hypothetical people is it possible to consider the social injustices which their moral problems may reflect and to imagine the individual suffering their occurrence may signify or their resolution engender.

The proclivity of women to reconstruct hypothetical dilemmas in terms of the real, to request or supply the information missing about the nature of the people and the places where they live, shifts their judgment away from the hierarchical ordering of principles and the formal procedures of decision making that are critical for scoring at Kohlberg's highest stages. This insistence on the particular signifies an orientation to the dilemma and to moral problems in general that differs from any of Kohlberg's stage descriptions. Given the constraints of Kohlberg's system and the biases in his research sample, this different orientation can only be construed as a failure in development. While several of the women in the research sample clearly articulated what Kohlberg regarded as a postconventional metaethical position, none of them were considered by Kohlberg to be principled in their normative moral judgments of his hypothetical moral dilemmas (Note 4). Instead, the women's judgments pointed toward an identification of the violence inherent in the dilemma itself which was seen to compromise the justice of any of its possible resolutions. This construction of the dilemma led the women to recast the moral judgment from a consideration of the good to a choice between evils.

The woman whose judgment of the abortion dilemma concluded the developmental sequence presented in the preceding section saw Kohlberg's Heinz dilemma in these terms and judged Heinz's action in terms of a choice between selfishness and sacrifice. For Heinz to steal the drug, given the circumstances of his life (which she inferred from his inability to pay two thousand dollars), he would have "to do something which is not in his best interest, in that he is going to get sent away, and that is a supreme sacrifice, a sacrifice which I would say a person truly in love might be willing to make." However, not to steal the drug "would be selfish on his part . . . he would just have to feel guilty about not allowing her a chance to live longer." Heinz's decision to steal is considered not in terms of the logical priority of life over property which justifies its rightness, but rather in terms of the actual consequences that stealing would have for a man of limited means and little social power.

Considered in the light of its probable outcomes—his wife dead, or Heinz in jail, brutalized by the violence of that experience and his life compromised by a record of felony—the dilemma itself changes. Its resolution has less to do with the relative weights of life and property in an abstract moral conception than with the collision it has produced between two lives, formerly conjoined but now in opposition, where the continuation of one life can now occur only at the expense of the other. Given this construction, it becomes clear why consideration revolves around the issue of sacrifice and why guilt becomes the inevitable concomitant of either resolution.

Demonstrating the reticence noted in the first section about making moral judgments, this woman explains her reluctance to judge in terms of her belief that everybody's existence is so different that I kind of say to myself, that might be something that I wouldn't do, but I can't say that it is right or wrong for that person. I can only deal with what is appropriate for me to do when I am faced with specific problems.

Asked if she would apply to others her own injunction against hurting, she says:

See, I can't say that it is wrong. I can't say that it is right or that it's wrong because I don't know what the person did that the other person did something to hurt him . . . so it is not right that the person got hurt, but it is right that the person who just lost the job has got to get that anger up and out. It doesn't put any bread on his table, but it is released. I don't mean to be copping out. I really am trying to see how to answer these questions for you.

Her difficulty in answering Kohlberg's questions, her sense of strain with the construction which they impose on the dilemma, stems from their divergence from her own frame of reference:

I don't even think I use the words right and wrong anymore, and I know I don't use the word moral, because I am not sure I know what it means. . . . We are talking about an unjust society, we are talking about a whole lot of things that are not right, that are truly wrong, to use the word that I don't use very often, and I have no control to change that. If I could change it, I certainly would, but I can only make my small contribution from day to day, and if I don't intentionally hurt somebody, that is my contribution to a better society. And so a chunk of that contribution is also not to pass judgment on other people, particularly when I don't know the circumstances of why they are doing certain things.

The reluctance to judge remains a reluctance to hurt, but one that stems now not from a sense of personal vulnerability but rather from a recognition of the limitations of judgment itself. The deference of the conventional feminine perspective can thus be seen to continue at the postconventional level, not as moral relativism but rather as part of a reconstructed moral understanding. Moral judgment is renounced in an awareness of the psychological and social determinism of all human behavior at the same time as moral concern is reaffirmed in recognition of the reality of human pain and suffering.

I have a real thing about hurting people and always have, and that gets a little complicated at times, because, for example, you don't want to hurt your child. I don't want to hurt my child but if I don't hurt her sometimes, then that's hurting her more, you see, and so that was a terrible dilemma for me.

Moral dilemmas are terrible in that they entail hurt; she sees Heinz's decision as "the result of anguish, who am I hurting, why do I have to hurt them." While the morality of Heinz's theft is not in question, given the circumstances which necessitated it, what is at issue is his willingness to substitute himself for his wife and become, in her stead, the victim of exploitation by a society which breeds and legitimizes the druggist's irresponsibility and whose injustice is thus manifest in the very occurrence of the dilemma.

The same sense that the wrong questions are being asked is evident in the response of another woman who justified Heinz's action on a similar basis, saying "I don't think that exploitation should really be a right." When women begin to make direct moral statements, the issues they repeatedly address are those of exploitation and hurt. In doing so, they raise the issue of nonviolence in precisely the same psychological context that brought Erikson (1969) to pause in his consideration of the truth of Gandhi's life.

In the pivotal letter, around which the judgment of his book turns, Erikson confronts the contradiction between the philosophy of nonviolence that informed Gandhi's dealing with the British and the psychology of violence that marred his relationships with his family and with the children of the ashram. It was this contradiction, Erikson confesses,

> which almost brought *me* to the point where I felt unable to continue writing *this* book because I seemed to sense the presence of a kind of untruth in the very protestation of truth; of something unclean when all the words spelled out an unreal purity; and, above all, of displaced violence where nonviolence was the professed issue. (p. 231)

In an effort to untangle the relationship between the spiritual truth of Satyagraha and the truth of his own psychoanalytic understanding, Erikson reminds Gandhi that "Truth, you once said, 'excludes the use of violence because man is not capable of knowing the absolute truth and therefore is not competent to punish' " (p. 241). The affinity between Satyagraha and psychoanalysis lies in their shared commitment to seeing life as an "experiment in truth," in their being

> somehow joined in a universal "therapeutics," committed to the Hippocratic principle that one can test truth (or the healing power inherent in a sick situation) only by action which avoids harm—or better, by action which maximizes mutuality and minimizes the violence caused by unilateral coercion or threat. (p. 247)

Erikson takes Gandhi to task for his failure to acknowledge the relativity of truth. This failure is manifest in the coercion of Gandhi's claim to exclusive possession of the truth, his "unwillingness to learn from *anybody anything* except what was approved by the 'inner voice' " (p. 236). This claim led Gandhi, in the guise of love, to impose his truth on others without awareness or regard for the extent to which he thereby did violence to their integrity.

The moral dilemma, arising inevitably out of a conflict of truths, is by definition a "sick situation" in that its either/or formulation leaves no room for an outcome that does not do violence. The resolution of such dilemmas, however, lies not in the self-deception of rationalized violence—"I was " said Gandhi, "a cruelly kind husband. I regarded myself as her teacher and so harassed her out of my blind love for her" (p. 233)—but rather in the replacement of the underlying antagonism with a mutuality of respect and care.

Gandhi, whom Kohlberg has mentioned as exemplifying Stage Six moral judgment and whom Erikson sought as a model of an adult ethical sensibility, instead is criticized by a judgment that refuses to look away from or condone the infliction of harm. In denying the validity of his wife's reluctance tc open her home to strangers and in his blindness to the different reality of adolescent sexuality and temptation, Gandhi compromised in his everyday life the ethic of nonviolence to which in principle and in public he was so steadfastly committed.

The blind willingness to sacrifice people to truth, however, has always been the danger of an ethics abstracted from life. This willingness links Gandhi to the biblical Abraham, who prepared to sacrifice the life of his son in order to demonstrate the integrity and supremacy of his faith. Both men, in the limitations of their fatherhood, stand in implicit contrast to the woman who comes before Solomon and verifies her motherhood by relinquishing truth in order to save the life of her child. It is the ethics of an adulthood that has become principled at the expense of care that Erikson comes to criticize in his assessment of Gandhi's life.

This same criticism is dramatized explicitly as a contrast between the sexes in *The Merchant of Venice* (1598/1912), where Shakespeare goes through an extraordinary complication of sexual identity (dressing a male actor as a female character who in turn poses as a male judge) in order to bring into the masculine citadel of justice the feminine plea for mercy. The limitation of the contractual conception of justice is illustrated through the absurdity of its literal execution, while the "need to make exceptions all the time" is demonstrated contrapuntally in the matter of the rings. Portia, in calling for mercy, argues for that resolution in which no one is hurt, and as the men are forgiven for their failure to keep both their rings and their word, Antonio in turn foregoes his "right" to ruin Shylock.

The research findings that have been reported in this essay suggest that women impose a distinctive construction on moral problems, seeing moral dilemmas in terms of conflicting responsibilities. This construction was found to develop through a sequence of three levels and two transitions, each level representing a more complex understanding of the relationship between self and other and each transition involving a critical reinterpretation of the moral conflict between selfishness and responsibility. The development of women's moral judgment appears to proceed from an initial concern with survival, to a focus on goodness, and finally to a principled understanding of nonviolence as the most adequate guide to the just resolution of moral conflicts.

In counterposing to Kohlberg's longitudinal research on the development of hypothetical moral judgment in men a cross-sectional study of women's responses to actual dilemmas of moral conflict and choice, this essay precludes the possibility of generalization in either direction and leaves to further research the task of sorting out the different variables of occasion and sex. Longitudinal studies of women's moral judgments are necessary in order to validate the claims of stage and sequence presented here. Similarly, the contrast drawn between the moral judgments of men and women awaits for its confirmation a more systematic comparison of the responses of both sexes. Kohlberg's research on moral development has confounded the variables of age, sex, type of decision, and type of dilemma by presenting a single configuration (the responses of adolescent males to hypothetical dilemmas of conflicting rights) as the basis for a universal stage sequence. This paper underscores the need for systematic treatment of these variables and points toward their study as a critical task for future moral development research.

For the present, my aim has been to demonstrate the centrality of the concepts of responsibility and care in women's constructions of the moral domain, to indicate the close tie in women's thinking between conceptions of the self and conceptions of morality, and, finally, to argue the need for an expanded developmental theory that would include, rather than rule out from developmental consideration, the difference in the feminine voice. Such an inclusion seems essential, not only for explaining the development of women but also for understanding in both sexes the characteristics and precursors of an adult moral conception.

Reference Notes

1. Haan, N. *Activism as moral protest: Moral judgments of hypothetical dilemmas and an actual situation of civil disobedience.* Unpublished manuscript, University of California at Berkeley, 1971.
2. Turiel, E. *A comparative analysis of moral knowledge and moral judgment in males and females.* Unpublished manuscript, Harvard University, 1973.
3. Kohlberg, L. *Continuities and discontinuities in childhood and adult moral development revisited.* Unpublished paper, Harvard University, 1973.
4. Kohlberg, L. Personal communication, August, 1976.
5. Gilligan, C., & Murphy, M. *The philosopher and the "dilemma of the fact": Moral development in late adolescence and adulthood.* Unpublished manuscript, Harvard University, 1977.

References

Broverman, I., Vogel, S., Broverman, D., Clarkson, F., & Rosenkrantz, P. Sex-role stereotypes: A current appraisal. *Journal of Social Issues,* 1972, **28**, 59–78.
Coles, R. *Children of crisis.* Boston: Little, Brown, 1964.
Didion, J. The women's movement. *New York Times Book Review,* July 30, 1972, pp. 1–2; 14.
Drabble, M. *The waterfall.* Hammondsworth, Eng.: Penguin Books, 1969.
Eliot, G. *The mill on the floss.* New York: New American Library, 1965. (Originally published, 1860.)
Erikson, E. H. *Insight and responsibility.* New York: W. W. Norton, 1964.
Erikson, E. H. *Identity: Youth and crisis.* New York: W. W. Norton, 1968.
Erikson, E. H. *Gandhi's truth.* New York: W. W. Norton, 1969.
Freud, S. "Civilized" sexual morality and modern nervous illness. In J. Strachey (Ed.), *The standard edition of the complete psychological works of Sigmund Freud* (Vol. 9). London: Hogarth Press, 1959. (Originally published, 1908.)
Freud, S. Some psychical consequences of the anatomical distinction between the sexes. In J. Strachey (Ed.), *The standard edition of the complete psychological works of Sigmund Freud* (Vol. 19). London: Hogarth Press, 1961. (Originally published, 1925.)
Gilligan, C., Kohlberg, L., Lerner, J., & Belenky, M. Moral reasoning about sexual dilemmas: The development of an interview and scoring system. *Technical Report of the President's Commission on Obscenity and Pornography* (Vol. 1) [415 060–137]. Washington, D.C.: U.S. Government Printing Office, 1971.
Haan, N. Hypothetical and actual moral reasoning in a situation of civil disobedience. *Journal of Personality and Social Psychology,* 1975, **32**, 255–270.
Holstein, C. Development of moral judgment: A longitudinal study of males and females. *Child Development,* 1976, **47**, 51–61.

Horner, M. Toward an understanding of achievement-related conflicts in women. *Journal of Social Issues,* 1972, **29,** 157–174.

Ibsen, H. *A doll's house.* In *Ibsen plays.* Hammondsworth, Eng.: Penguin Books, 1965. (Originally published, 1879.)

Kohlberg, L. From is to ought: How to commit the naturalistic fallacy and get away with it in the study of moral development. In T. Mischel (Ed.), *Cognitive development and epistemology.* New York: Academic Press, 1971.

Kohlberg, L., & Gilligan, C. The adolescent as a philosopher: The discovery of the self in a postconventional world. *Daedalus,* 1971, **100,** 1051–1056.

Kohlberg, L., & Kramer, R. Continuities and discontinuities in childhood and adult moral development. *Human Development,* 1969, **12,** 93–120.

Piaget, J. *The moral judgment of the child.* New York: The Free Press, 1965. (Originally published, 1932.)

Shakespeare, W. *The merchant of Venice.* In *The comedies of Shakespeare.* London: Oxford University Press, 1912. (Originally published, 1598.)

Piagetian and Psychometric Conceptions of Intelligence

DAVID ELKIND
University of Rochester

Professor Elkind devotes much of his discussion to the concept of intelligence. He finds both similarities and differences when comparing the Piagetian description of intelligence with Jensen's (and the psychometrician's) definition of intelligence. Operating from quite different assumptions than those of J. McV. Hunt (Piaget's Structuralism, rather than neurology) Elkind also finds reason to believe that intelligence is developed in experience. For Piaget and Elkind, intelligence is "an extension of biological adaptation" and is characterized by ability to assimilate (develop in response to internal processes) and accommodate (respond to environmental intrusions).

I have been asked to respond to Professor Jensen's (1969) paper from the standpoint of Piaget's genetic psychology of intelligence. While I clearly cannot speak for Piaget, only the "Patron" can do that, I can react as someone steeped in Piagetian theory and research and as one who looks at cognitive problems from the Genevan perspective. Accordingly, while I hope that what I have to say would be acceptable to Piaget, I cannot guarantee that this is in fact the case, and must take full responsibility for whatever is said below. I plan to discuss, in the first section of the paper, some of the similarities between the Piagetian and psychometric positions. Then, in the second section, some of their differences will be pointed out. Finally, in the third section, I want to consider two related practical issues regarding the modification of intelligence.

Harvard Educational Review Vol. 39 No. 2 Spring 1969, 319–337.

Conceptual Similarities

What struck me in reading Professor Jensen's (1969) paper, and what had not really occurred to me before, were the many parallels and affinities between the psychometric or mental test approach to the problem of intelligence and the developmental approach as represented by Piaget. It brought to mind the fact that Piaget began his career as a developmental psychologist by working in Binet's laboratory where he sought to standardize some of Burt's (1962) reasoning tests on Parisian children. Indeed, Piaget's *method clinique* is a combination of mental test and clinical interview procedures which consists in the use of a standardized situation as a starting point for a flexible interrogation. The affinities, however, between the Piagetian and psychometric approaches to intelligence run more deeply than that. In this section I want to discuss such affinities: the acceptance of genetic and maturational determination in intelligence, the use of non-experimental methodologies and the conception of intelligence as being essentially rational.

Genetic Determination

Implicit and often explicit in both the psychometric and Piagetian positions is the assumption that mental ability is, in part at least, genetically determined. With respect to the psychometric position, it assumes that at least some of the variance in intelligence test performance is attributable to variance in genetic endowment (Burt & Howard, 1957, Jensen). Piaget (1967a) also acknowledges the importance of genetic factors for intellectual ability but qualifies this by pointing out that what may be genetic in one generation may not always have been so and could be the partial result of prior environmental influences. So, for Piaget, as for the biologist Waddington (1962a) there is a certain relativity with respect to what is attributed to genetic endowment because what is genetic now may not always have been genetic. To illustrate, Waddington (1962a) observed that after several generations a strain of the fly grub drosophilia developed enlarged anal papillae when reared on a high salt diet. When the insects were returned to a "normal" low salt diet the anal papillae of successive generations became less large but never returned to their original size. Waddington speaks of this as "genetic assimilation" by which he means that the effects of an altered environment upon the selection process within a species may not be completely reversible even when the environment returned to its unaltered state.

One consequence of their joint acceptance of the partial genetic determination of intellectual ability, is that both psychometricians and Piaget recognize the importance of maturation in human development. To illustrate their commonality in this regard, consider these two passages, one written by Harold Jones in 1954 and the other by Piaget in 1967.

Dubnoff's work, together with other related studies, may lead to the speculative suggestion that between natio-racial groups, as within a given group, a slight tendency exists for early precocity to be associated with a slower mental growth at later ages and perhaps with a lower average intelligence level at maturity. A parallel situation may be noted when we compare different animal species; among the primates, for example, the maturity of performance at a given age in infancy can be used inversely to predict the general level of adaptive ability that will be attained at the end of the growth span. (Jones, 1954, p. 638)

And Piaget writes:

We know that it takes 9 to 12 months before babies develop the notion that an object is still there when a screen is placed in front of it. Now kittens go through the same substages but they do it in three months—so they are six months ahead of the babies. Is this an advantage or isn't it? We can certainly see our answer in one sense. The kitten is not going to go much further. The child has taken longer, but he is capable of going further so it seems to me the nine months were not for nothing. (Piaget, 1967b)

Non-Experimental Methodology

In addition to their shared genetic or maturational emphasis, the Piagetian and psychometric approaches to intelligence have still another characteristic in common. This common feature is their failure, for the most part, to use the experimental method in the strict sense of that term. It seems fair to say that most of the studies which attempt to get at the determinants of test intelligence are correlational in nature. By and large such studies attempt to relate the test scores of parents and their children, of twins or of adopted children and their parents, or of the same children tested at different points in time and so on. Only in rare instances such as the Skeels (1966) study is an attempt made to modify intelligence by active intervention and with the utilization of a control group which does not receive the experimental treatment. While experimental work on human intelligence might well be desirable, such research often raises serious moral and ethical questions.

Piaget, for his part, has not employed the experimental method simply because it was not appropriate for the problems he wished to study. This is true because Piaget has been primarily concerned with the diagnosis of mental contents and abilities and not with their modification. To illustrate, the discovery of what the child means by "more," "less" and "same" number of things requires flexible diagnostic interview procedures and not experimental procedures. Once the concept is diagnosed, then experimental methods are appropriate to determine the effects of various factors on the attainment and modification of the concepts in question. The sequence of events is not unlike the situation in medicine where the discovery or diagnosis of a disease is often the first step to its experimental investigation. In short, Piaget has focused upon the discovery of what and how children think and not with the modification of thinking which is a subsequent and experimental question. In every science there is a natural history stage of enquiry during which relevant phenomena must be carefully observed and classified. American psychology has often tried to bypass this stage in its headlong rush to become an experimental science. In his studies Piaget has revealed a wide range of hitherto unknown and unsuspected facts about children's thinking, which have in America now become the starting points for a great deal of experimental investigation. What is often forgotten, when Piaget is criticized for not using the experimental method, is that such a method would not have revealed the wealth of phenomena which experimental investigators are now so busily studying.

Rationality as the Definition of Intelligence

There is a third and final commonality in the mental test and Piagetian approaches to intelligence which should be mentioned. This commonality resides in what these two positions regard as the nature or essence of intelligence. While there is considerable variability among psychometricians in this regard, many agree in general with the position taken by Jensen (1969). Jensen argues that the g factor which is present in all tests of mental ability appears in its purest forms on tests of generalization and abstraction. Spearman (1923) called these activities the eduction of relations (A is greater than B; B is greater than C; so A is in what relation to C?) and of correlates (Complete the series A AB ABC ———). While intelligence tests contain measures of many different types of mental abilities, including language and perceptual skills, the psychometric approach holds that the most central feature of human intelligence is its rationality, or as Wechsler put it: "Intelligence is the aggregate or global capacity of the individual to act purposefully, to think rationally and to deal effectively with his environment" (Wechsler, 1944, p. 3).

For Piaget, too, the essence of intelligence lies in the individual's reasoning capacities. Piaget, however, is more specific in his description of these abilities and defines them in terms of mental operations which have the properties of mathematical groupings in general and the property of reversibility in particular. An operational grouping is present when in the course of any mental activity one can always get back to the starting point. For example, if the class *boys* and the class *girls* is mentally combined to form the class *children,* it is always possible to recapture the subclass by subtraction. That is to say, the class of children minus the class of boys equals the class of girls. Put differently, the operation of subtraction can be used to undo the operation of addition so that each of the combined classes can be retrieved. Verbal material learned by heart is, however, not rationally organized as is illustrated by the fact that no matter how well a passage is learned, it is impossible, without additional effort, to say it backwards. If an operational system were involved, having learned the passage forward would automatically imply the ability to say it backwards. In Piaget's view, neither perception nor language are truly rational since neither one shows complete reversibility. So, while perception and language play an important part in intellectual activity, they do not epitomize that activity.

The psychometric and Piagetian approaches to intelligence thus agree on its genetic determination (at least in part), and on the use of non-experimental methodology and upon the essentially rational nature of mental ability. After this look at their commonalities, it is perhaps time to look at their differences.

Conceptual Differences

Despite the commonalities noted above, the psychometric and developmental approaches to intelligence also differ in certain respects. These differences, however, derive from the unique ways in which the psychometricians and Piaget approach and view intelligence and not from any fundamental disagreements regarding the nature of intelligence itself. In other words the differences are due to the fact that the two approaches are interested in assessing and describing different facets of intelligent behavior. Accordingly the differences arise with respect to: (a) the type of genetic causality they presuppose; (b) the description of mental growth they provide; and (c) the contributions of nature and nurture which they assess.

Genetic Causality

Although the Piagetian and psychometric approaches to intelligence agree on the importance of genetic determination, at least in part, of human mental ability, each approach emphasizes a somewhat different mode of genetic determination or causality. In order to make these differences clear, it is necessary to recall some of the basic features of evolutionary theory upon which all modern conceptions of intelligence are based.

Within the Darwinian conception of evolution there are two major phenomena that have to be taken into account: within-species variability and natural selection. For any given species of animal or plant one can observe a range of variations in such features as color, shape and size. Among a flock of robins, to illustrate, one can see that some adult birds differ in size, in richness of breast coloration and that some even manifest slight variations in head and wing conformation. Similar variations can be observed among a group of collies, Persian cats and even among tomato plants in the garden. This within-species variability, we know today, is due to the chance pairings of parental genes and to gene complexes which occur because each parent contributes only half of its genetic complement to its offspring. Variations within a given species at a given time are, therefore, primarily due to chance factors: namely the random genetic assortments provided by the parent generation. One determinant of variability among animals and plants is then, simply, chance.

Now in the psychometric conception of intelligence, this random type of variation is just what is presupposed. Test intelligence, it is assumed, is randomly distributed in a given population at a given time and such distributions should resemble the bell shaped curve of the normal probability function. Measurement of human abilities does in fact reveal a tendency for such measurements to fall into normal distributions. In addition evidence such as "regression toward the mean" (children of exceptionally bright or dull parents tend to be less bright and less dull than their parents) is also characteristic of genetic traits which are randomly determined. In short, when the psychometrician speaks of genetic determination, he is speaking of the chance gene combinations which produce a "normal" bell-shaped distribution of abilities within a given population.

Obviously this description of genetic determination is extremely over-simplified; we know that a test score is a phenotype which is determined by many different factors not all of which are genetic. Jensen, to illustrate, breaks down the variance of test intelligence into a large number of components such as genotypic variation, environment, environment genotype interaction, epistasis, error of measurement variance and so on. With the exception, perhaps, of the selective mating variable, however, all of these factors can again be assumed to operate in a random manner so that one might say that the chance distribution of observed test scores is the product of many underlying chance distributions. That the psychometric approach does in general presuppose a random distribution is also shown by the fact that the criterion of a true change in intellectual ability is the demonstration that such a change could *not* be attributed to chance factors.

That variability within a species is in part determined by chance gene and gene complex assortments has of course been demonstrated by Mendel and all of the research which has derived from his theory of genetics. There are, however, other forms of organismic variability which cannot be attributed to chance. Natural selection, the other component of evolution, is never random but always moves in the direction of improved adaptation to the milieu. To illustrate, over the past hundred years there has been a gradual predominance of dark over light colored moths in the industrial sections of England. Kettlewell (1955) demonstrated the survival value of dark coloration by showing that light moths placed on soot darkened bark were more readily eaten by insectivorous birds than were similarly placed dark moths. When variations across generations are considered, the variations are not random but rather show a clear cut direction.

The same holds true within the course of individual development. In the case of individual growth, however, the direction of progress is not determined by mating practices but rather by biochemical mechanisms which are only now in the process of being understood. That these biochemical agents determine the direction of development, however, cannot be doubted. As Waddington (1962b) points out, animals consist of a limited variety of cells such as nerve cells, muscle cells and so on. Likewise the organs of the body are also distinct from one another in form, composition and function. What direction particular cells will take as the egg matures will depend upon the action of chemical agents which Spemann (discussed in Bertalaffny, 1962) called *organizers* with definite loci in the cell material called *organization centers*. It is the organizer which determines whether particular cells will become nerve, muscle or organ tissue. Individual development, therefore, is not determined by random factors but rather by biochemical organizers which specify the nature and direction of organismic differentiation.

Now when Piaget speaks of the genetic determination of intelligence, he has in mind not the random factors which determine gene combinations, but rather the non-random action of biochemical organizers and organization centers. Indeed, this is the kind of determination which Piaget assumes when he argues that the *sequence* in which the child attains the successive components of a concept or in which he acquires systems of mental operations, is invariant. In the formation of body organs the order of differentiation is fixed because each new phase of differentiation produces the organizer for the next stage. In Piaget's view this is equally valid for the growth of cognitive structures because the preceding cognitive structures, say the concrete operations of childhood, are a necessary prerequisite to the elaboration of the more complex formal operational structures of adolescence. For Piaget, then, genetic determination means that there are factors which give development a definite non-random direction.

In pointing out that the Piagetian and psychometric approaches to intelligence postulate different forms of genetic determinism, I want to reiterate that these two positions are not in contradiction one with the other. The mental test approach to intelligence is concerned with inter-individual differences in ability and these are, in so far as we know, largely randomly determined. Piaget, in contrast, is concerned with the intra-individual changes which occur in the course of development and these, to the best of our knowledge, are not random but rather have a direction given them by specific organizing mechanisms. Accordingly, and this is the genius of evolution, human intelligence manifests both determinism *and* freedom.

The Course of Mental Growth

Let us look now at a somewhat different issue, the age-wise course of mental growth. Here again we find a difference in perspective rather than a contradiction in conception as between the two positions. In psychometric terms, the course of mental growth is plotted as a curve which measures the amount of intelligence at some criterion age that can be predicted at any preceding age. As Bloom (1964) has pointed out, when age 17 is taken as the criterion age, some 50% of the total IQ at that age can be predicted at age four, and an additional 30% can be predicted from ages four to eight. Based on correlational data of this sort, curves of mental growth appear to rise rapidly in early childhood and taper off to a plateau in late adolescence. Such curves, it must be noted to avoid a frequent misinterpretation, say nothing as to the *amount* or *quality* of knowledge at given age levels. (See Jensen, 1969, pp. 115-117.)

From the mental test perspective, therefore, intellectual growth is pretty much a statistical concept derived from correlations of test scores obtained at different age levels on the same individuals in the course of longitudinal studies. Such curves can be interpreted as reflecting the rate of mental growth but say nothing as to the nature of what is developing. Indeed, if intelligence is defined in the narrow sense of the abilities to generalize and abstract, then any qualitative differences in these abilities will necessarily be obscured by the curve of mental

growth which suggests merely a quantitative increase in mental ability with increasing age.

Looked at from the standpoint of Piagetian psychology, however, mental growth
involves the formation of new mental structures and consequently the emergence
of new mental abilities. The child, to illustrate, cannot deal with propositional
logic of the following sort, "Helen is shorter than Alice and taller than Ethel, who
is the tallest of the three?" (Glick & Wapner, 1968), nor can children grasp the
metaphorical connotations of satirical cartoons or proverbs (Shaffer, 1930). Adolescents, in contrast, have no trouble with either propositional logic or with metaphor. In the Piagetian view, therefore, mental growth is not a quantitative but
rather a qualitative affair and presupposes significant differences between the
thinking of children and adolescents as well as between preschool and school age
children.

These qualitative differences are, as a matter of fact, built into the items of
mental tests but are masked by the assignment of point scores to successes and
failures. On the Wechsler Intelligence Scale for Children various of the sub-
tests recognize qualitatively different responses only by assigning them additional
points (Wechsler, 1949). For example, a child who says that a peach and a plum
are alike because "they both have pits" is given a single point, whereas a child who
says "they are both fruit" is given two points. On other sub-tests, such as the
arithmetic sub-test, there is no point differential for success on problems which
patently require different levels of mental ability. To illustrate, correct answers
to the following two problems are both given only a single point: "If I cut an
apple in half, how many pieces will I have?" A correct answer to that question
is given the same score as the correct answer to this problem:

Smith and Brown start a card game with $27 each. They agree that at the end of each
deal the loser shall pay the winner one third of what he (the loser) then has in his possession. Smith wins the first three deals. How much does Brown have at the beginning of
the fourth deal?

Clearly, the items on any given sub-test can tap quite different mental processes but these qualitative differences are obscured by assigning equivalent
point scores to the various items regardless of the mental processes involved.

This is not to say that Piaget is right and that the mental test approach
is wrong, or vice versa. The quantitative evaluation of mental growth is necessary
and has considerable practical value in predicting school success. The qualitative
approach is also of value, particularly when diagnosis of learning difficulties and

educational remediation are in question. Which approach to mental growth one adopts will depend upon the purposes of the investigation. The only danger in the quantitative approach is to assume that, because sub-tests include items of the same general type and are scored with equal numerical weights, that they therefore assess only quantitative differences in the ability in question.

The Contributions of Nature and Nurture to Intelligence

Still a third way in which the psychometric and Piagetian views of intelligence differ has to do with the manner in which they treat the contributions of nature and nurture to intellectual ability. In the psychometric approach this contribution is treated substantively, with regard to the amount of variance in intellectual ability that can be attributed to nature and nurture respectively. Piaget, on the contrary, treats these contributions functionally with respect to the regulative role played by the environment or inner forces for any given mental activity. Both positions now need to be described in somewhat more detail.

The psychometric approach is substantive (and static) in the sense that it regards intelligence as capable of being measured and holds that such measures can be used to assess the extent to which nature and nurture contribute to intellectual ability. In the discussion of genetic causality the various components into which test scores could be analyzed were briefly noted. We are indebted to writers such as Burt & Howard (1957) and Jensen for making clear the many and complex determinants into which test performance can be analyzed. Without wishing to minimize these other determinants, the needs of the present discussion will be served if we consider only how the psychometric approach arrives at the contribution of the heredity and environmental factors.

As Jensen points out, heritability is the proportion of variability among observed or phenotypic intelligence (test scores) that can be attributed to genotypic variations. Estimates of heritability are obtained from correlational data for subjects with known kinship relations such as parents and children, siblings, and identical twins. The contribution of the environment is arrived at somewhat differently. Variability in intelligence test scores attributable to the environment is estimated from that variability which cannot be attributed to any other factors. It is, in fact, the residual variance, that which is left after all the other factors contributing to intelligence test performance have been accounted for. For the psychometrician, then, nature and nurture are regarded as substantive and static, and their contributions are assessed quantitatively with the aid of statistical procedures.

When we turn to the work of Piaget, however, we encounter quite a different conception of the contributions of nature and nurture. In Piaget's view, these contributions must be conceived functionally and dynamically with respect to their regulatory control over various mental activities. In this regard Piaget's views are not unlike those of David Rapaport (1958) who spoke of "the relative autonomy of the ego," a conception which may help to introduce Piaget's some-what more difficult formulation. Rapaport argued that we are endowed with some mental processes, such as perception, that are responsive to the environ-ment and so tend to guarantee or insure a certain independence of the mind from the domination of instinctual drives. Other mental processes, such as fantasy, are most responsive to internal forces and these in turn guarantee a certain in-dependence of the mind from the domination of the environment. The presence and activity of both types of processes thus insures that the mind is enslaved neither by the environment nor by drives but retains a "relative autonomy" from both.

Piaget's view (1967c) is roughly similar. He argues that intelligence is an ex-tension of biological adaptation which, in lieu of the instinctive adaptations in animals, permits relatively autonomous adaptations which bear the stamp not only of our genetic endowment, but also of our physical and social experience. On the plane of intelligence we inherit the processes of assimilation (processes responsive to inner promptings) and of accommodation (processes responsive to environmental intrusions). Assimilative processes guarantee that intelligence will not be limited to passively copying reality, while accommodative processes in-sure that intelligence will not construct representations of reality which have no correspondence with the real world. To make this functional conception of the contributions of nature and nurture to intelligence concrete, let us consider sev-eral different mental abilities which are differently regulated by internal and external forces.

If we look at imitation (Piaget, 1951), it is clear that it is largely accommoda-tive in the sense that it is most responsive to environmental influence and is rela-tively independent of inner forces. The vocal mimic, for example, is expert to the extent that he can capture the pitch, timbre and inflections of his model's voice and to the extent to which he can suppress those aspects of his own speech which differ from the model's. Play, in contrast, is largely assimilative in that it is most responsive to inner needs and is relatively independent of environmental influ-ence. The child who uses a stick alternatively as a gun, as an airplane and as a boat has responded to the object largely in terms of his own inner needs and with a relative disregard of its real properties.

Between the two extremes of imitation and play is intelligence which manifests a balance or equilibrium between assimilative and accommodative activities and is thus relatively autonomous both of inner *and* outer forces. To illustrate, suppose we deduce, from the premise that Helen is taller than Jane and that Jane is taller than Mary, that Helen is the taller of three girls. We have in so doing attained a new bit of knowledge, an adaptation, but without altering the elements involved (assimilation without transformation of the objects) and without modifying the reasoning processes (accommodation without alteration of mental structures). Reason, or intelligence, is thus the only system of mental processes which guarantees that the mind and the environment will each retain its integrity in the course of their interaction.

Accordingly, for Piaget as for Rapaport, the question is not how much nature and nurture contribute to mental ability, but rather the *extent to which various mental processes are relatively autonomous from environmental and instinctual influence.* Such a conception is functional and dynamic, rather than substantive and static, because it deals with the regulatory activity of nature and nurture upon various mental processes. Those processes which show the greatest independence from environmental *and* internal regulation, the rational processes, are the most advanced of all human abilities. It is for this reason that Piaget reserves for them, and for them alone, the term intelligence.

In summary then, the psychometric and Piagetian approaches to intelligence differ with respect to: (a) the type of genetic causality which they presuppose; (b) their conceptions of the course of mental growth; and finally (c) the manner in which they conceive the contributions of nature and nurture to intellectual ability. In closing this section on the differences between the two positions I want to say again that the differences arise from differences in perspective and emphasis and are not contradictory but rather complementary. Both the psychometric and the Piagetian approaches to the conceptualization of human intelligence provide useful starting points for the assessment and interpretation of human mental abilities. Let us turn now to a couple of practical issues related to the modification and stimulation of mental abilities.

Practical Issues

In his essay, Jensen has tried to clarify many of the ambiguities regarding the nature and modification of intellectual ability and to put down some of the myths and misinterpretations prevalent with regard to test intelligence. For the most part, I find myself in agreement with Jensen and in this section, I would like to discuss two practical issues related to the modification and stimulation of intellectual abilities which seem to involve some misinterpretation of the Piagetian position. First, Piaget's insistence upon the qualitative differences between the modes of thinking at different age levels has been wrongly taken to suggest the need for preschool instruction in order to move children into concrete operational stage more quickly. Secondly, Piaget's emphasis upon the non-chance or self-directed nature of mental development has mistakenly been taken as justification for the use of methods such as "discovery learning" which supposedly stimulate the child's intrinsic motivations to learn. I would like, therefore, to try in the following section to clarify what seems to me to be the implications of Piaget's conception of intelligence for preschool instruction and for the implementation of intrinsic motivation.

Preschool Instruction

There appears to be increasing pressure these days in both the popular and professional literature for beginning academic instruction in early childhood, i.e., from 3 to 5 years. Bruner's famous statement that "We begin with the hypothesis that any subject can be taught effectively in some intellectually honest form to any child at any stage of development" (Bruner, 1962, p. 33) as well as the work of Hunt (1961), of Bloom (1964), of O. K. Moore (1961), of Fowler (1968), and of Skeels (1966) have all been used in the advocacy of preschool instruction. Indeed Piaget and Montessori have been invoked in this connection as well. The argument essentially is that the preschool period is critical for intellectual growth and that if we leave this period devoted to fun and games, we are lowering the individual's ultimate level of intellectual attainment. Parental anxiety and pressure in this regard have been so aroused that legislation has been passed or is pending for the provision of free preschool education for all parents who wish it for their children in states such as New York, Massachusetts and California.

What is the evidence that preschool instruction has lasting effects upon mental growth and development? The answer is, in brief, that there is none. To prove the point one needs longitudinal data on adults who did not have preschool instruction but who were equal in every other regard to children receiving such instruction. With the exception of the Montessori schools, however, the preschool instruction programs have not been in existence long enough to provide any evidence on the lastingness of their effects. Indeed, most of the earlier work on the effects of nursery school education (see Goodenough, 1940, and Jones, 1954, for reviews of this literature) has shown that significant positive effects are hard to demonstrate when adequate experimental controls are employed. It is interesting that no one, to my knowledge, has done a longitudinal study of adult Montessori graduates. Have they done better in life than children from comparable backgrounds not so trained? In any case, it is such unavailable longitudinal data that are crucial to the proposition that the preschool period is a critical one for intellectual development.

I am sure that someone will object at this point that studies of mental growth such as those of Bloom (1964) suggest that half of the individual's intellectual potential is realized by age four. Does this not mean that the preschool period is important for intellectual growth and that interventions during this period will have lasting effects? Not necessarily, if we look at the facts in a somewhat different way. Bloom writes, "Both types of data suggest that in terms of intelligence measured at age 17, about 50% of the development takes place between conception and age 4, about 30% between ages 4 and 8, and about 20% between 8 and seventeen" (Bloom, 1964, p. 88). Now an equally feasible implication of this statement is quite in contradiction to that of preschool instruction: the child has only 50% of his intellectual ability at age 4 but 80% at age 8, why not delay his education three years so that he can more fully profit from instruction? With 80% of his ability he is likely to learn more quickly and efficiently and is not as likely to learn in ways that he will need to unlearn later. That is to say, without stretching the fact, it is possible to interpret the Bloom statement as implying that instruction should *not* be introduced into the preschool program.

Not only are there no clear-cut longitudinal data to support the claims of the lastingness of preschool instruction, there is evidence in the opposite direction. The work cited by Jones (1954) and by Piaget (1967b) in the quotations given earlier in this paper are cases in point. This evidence, together with more recent data reported in Jensen's paper, suggest a negative correlation between early physical maturation and later intellectual attainments. Animals are capable of achieving early some skills (a dog or a chimp will be housebroken before a child is toilet trained) but perhaps at the expense of not being able to attain other skills at all. These data suggest the hypothesis that *the longer we delay formal instruction, up to certain limits, the greater the period of plasticity and the higher the ultimate level of achievement.* There is at least as much evidence and theory in support of this hypothesis as there is in favor of the early-instruction proposition. Certainly, from the Piagetian perspective, there are "optimal periods" for the growth of particular mental structures which cannot be rushed.

Please understand, I am not arguing against the benefits of preschool enrichment for children. Even preschool instruction may be of value for those disadvantaged children who do not benefit from what Strodtbeck (1967) called the "hidden curriculum of the middle class home." What I am arguing is that there is no evidence for the *long term effects* of either preschool instruction or enrichment. Nursery school experience most assuredly has immediate value for the child to the extent that it helps him to appreciate and enjoy his immediate world to the full and to better prepare him for future social and intellectual activities. Everyone, for example, recognizes the value of a vacation without expecting that it will produce any permanent alterations. Isn't it enough that we lighten the burdens of childhood for even a brief period each day without demanding at the same time that we produce permanent results? The contributions of the nursery school, no less than that of the vacation, do not have to be long-lived to be of value.

In closing the discussion, I would like to emphasize another side to this issue of preschool instruction. This is the consideration that the emphasis on preschool education has obscured the fact that it is the elementary school years which are crucial to later academic achievement. It is during these years that the child learns the basic tool subjects, acquires his conception of himself as a student and develops his attitudes towards formal education. In this connection it might be well to quote a less publicized finding of Bloom's (1964) study:

We may conclude from our results on general achievement, reading comprehension and vocabulary development, that by age 9 (grade 3) at least 50% of the general achievement pattern at age 18 (grade 12) has been developed whereas at least 75% of the pattern has been developed by age 13 (grade 7). (Bloom, 1964, p. 105)

With respect to the intellectual operations of concern to Piaget, similar trends appear to hold true. While children all over the world and across wide ranges of cultural and socioeconomic conditions appear to attain concrete operations at about the age of 6 or 7 (Goodnow, 1969), the attainment and use of formal operations in adolescence, in contrast, appear to be much more subject to socioculturally determined factors such as sex roles and symbolic proficiency (Elkind, 1961; Elkind, Barocas & Rosenthal, 1968; Goodnow & Bethon, 1966). Apparently, therefore, environmental variation during the elementary school period is more significant for later intellectual attainments of the Piagetian variety. In short, there is not much justification for making the preschool the scapegoat for our failures in elementary education. Like it or not, the years from six to twelve are still the crucial ones with respect to later academic achievement.

Motivation and Intellectual Growth

In recent years there has been an increasing recognition among psychologists such as Berlyne (1965), Hunt (1965), and White (1959), that certain mental activities can be self-rewarding and do not have to be externally reinforced. European writers such as Piaget (1954) and Montessori (1964) long ago recognized the existence of "intrinsic motivation" (to use Hunt's apt phrase), and Montessori in particular gave incomparable descriptions of children who suddenly discover they can read and proceed to read everything in sight. Piaget (1967d) too, has argued that needs and interests are simply another aspect of all cognitive activities.

Educators, however, in their efforts to capitalize upon this intrinsic motivation seem to have missed the point of what Montessori and Piaget had in mind. To maximize intrinsic motivation and to accelerate mental growth we have recently had an emphasis upon "learning by discovery" and upon "interesting reading materials" and so on. These approaches miss the point because they assume that intrinsic motivation can be built into materials and procedures which will in turn maximize mental growth. But as Piaget and Montessori pointed out (Elkind, 1967) intrinsic motivation resides in the child and not in methods and procedures. It is the child who must, at any given point in time, choose the method of learning and the materials that are reinforcing *to him*. Without the opportunity for student choice and the provision of large blocks of time in which the child can totally engross himself in an activity, the values of intrinsic motivation will not be realized.

Indeed, I am very much afraid that by the time most children have reached the third or fourth grade a good deal of their intrinsic motivation for learning has been stifled. This is because spontaneous interest follows only the timetable of the child's own growth schedule. We can all remember, I am sure, those periods when we were so totally immersed in an activity that we forgot time, food and rest. During such periods we are at our creative and productive best and afterwards the feeling of exhaustion is coupled with a deep sense of accomplishment. In the school, however, we do not permit children to become totally engrossed in an activity but rather shuttle them from activity to activity on the hour or half hour. The result is what might be called *intellectually burned children*. Just as the burned child shuns the fire so the intellectually burned child shies away from total intellectual involvement.

How is this condition produced? In clinical practice we often see children (and adults) who are unwilling to form any emotional attachment. In the history of such children one always finds a series of broken relationships due to a wide variety of causes including the death of parents or the forced separation from them. Such children have learned that every time they reached out and became emotionally involved, rejection, hurt and misery were the result. Consequently they prefer not to get involved any more because the pain and anguish of still another broken relationship is just too high a price to pay for an emotional attachment. The intellectually burned child is in somewhat the same position. He refuses to become totally involved in intellectual activities because the repeated frustration of being interrupted in the middle is just too much to bear. Our lockstep curricula, thirty minutes for this and an hour for that, have the consequence, I suspect, of producing children who shun the fire of intense mental involvement.

Accordingly, the educational practice which would best foster intrinsically motivated children in the Piagetian and Montessori sense would be the provision of "interest areas" where children could go on their own and for long periods of time. Only when the child can choose an activity and persist at it until he is satiated can we speak of true intrinsically motivated behavior. Where such interest areas and time provisions have been made, as in the World of Inquiry School in Rochester, New York, the results are impressive indeed.[1]

In summary then, the Piagetian conception of intelligence provides no support either for those who advocate formal preschool instruction or for those who argue for new methods and materials to stimulate intrinsic motivation. As we have seen, there is no evidence as yet for the lastingness of preschool instruction. In addition, intrinsic motivation seems best stimulated by allowing the child to engage in the activity of his choice for unbroken periods of time. As Jensen has so rightly pointed out, if we really want to maximize the effects of instruction, it does not pay to blink at the facts whether they have to do with racial or socioeconomic differences in intelligence, the effects of preschool instruction, or the nature of intrinsic motivation.

[1] The results of our preliminary evaluation of this school suggest that World of Inquiry pupils are significantly higher in their need for achievement and more positive in their self evaluations than are their matched controls (children taken from the waiting list) who are attending other schools.

References

Berlyne, D. E. Curiosity and education. In J. D. Krumboltz (Ed.) *Learning and the educational process.* Chicago: Rand McNally, 1965, 67-89.

Bertalaffny, Ludwig von. *Modern theories of development.* New York: Harper & Bros. (Torchbook Ed.), 1962.

Bloom, B. S. *Stability and change in human characteristics.* New York: John Wiley & Sons, Inc., 1964.

Bruner, J. *The process of education.* Cambridge, Mass.: Harvard University Press, 1962.

Burt, C. *Mental and scholastic tests.* London: Staples Press, 1962 (4th edition).

Burt, C., & Howard, M. The relative influence of heredity and environment on assessments of intelligence. *British Journal of Statistics Psychology,* 1957, **10**, 33-63.

Elkind, D. Quantity conceptions in junior and senior high school students. *Child Development,* 1961, **32**, 551-560.

Elkind, D. Piaget and Montessori. *Harvard Educational Review,* 1967 (Fall) 535-545.

Elkind, D., Barocas, R., & Rosenthal, B. Combinatorial thinking in children from graded and ungraded classrooms. *Perceptual and Motor Skills,* 1968, **27**, 1015-1018.

Fowler, W. The effect of early stimulation in the emergence of cognitive processes. In R. D. Hess & Roberta M. Meyers (Eds.) *Early Education.* Chicago: Aldine Press, 1968, 9-36.

Glick, J., & Wapner, S. Development of transitivity: Some findings and problems of analysis. *Child Development,* 1968, **39**, 621-638.

Goodenough, Florence. New evidence on environmental influence on intelligence. *Yearbook of the National Society for the Study of Education,* 1940, **39**, 307-365.

Goodnow, Jacqueline J. Problems in research on culture and thought. In D. Elkind and J. Piaget (Eds.) *Studies in cognitive development.* New York: Oxford University Press, 1969, 439-464.

Goodnow, Jacqueline J., & Bethon, G. Piaget's tasks: The effects of schooling and intelligence. *Child Development,* 1966, **37**, 573-582.

Hunt, J. McV. *Intelligence and experience.* New York: The Ronald Press, 1961.

Hunt, J. McV. Intrinsic motivation and its role in psychological development. In D. Levine (Ed.) *Nebraska symposium on motivation.* Lincoln: University of Nebraska Press, 1965, 189-282.

Jensen, A. How much can we boost IQ and scholastic achievement? *Harvard Educational Review,* 1969 (Winter), 1-123.

Jones, H. E. The environment and mental development. In L. Carmichael (Ed.) *Manual of child psychology.* New York: John Wiley & Sons, Inc., 1954, 631-696.

Kittlewell, H. B. D. Selection experiments on industrial melanism in the lepidoptera. *Heredity,* 1955, **9**, 323-342.

Montessori, Maria. *The Montessori Method.* New York: Schocken, 1964 (first published in English, 1912).

Moore, O. K. Orthographic symbols and the preschool child: A new approach. In E. P. Torrence (Ed.) *Creativity: 1960 proceedings of the 3rd conference on gifted children.* Minneapolis: University of Minnesota, Center for Continuation Studies, 1961.

Piaget, J. *Play, dreams and imitation in childhood.* New York: Norton, 1951.

Piaget, J. *Les relations entre l'affectivité et l'intelligence dans la developpement mental de l'enfant.* Paris: C.D.U., 1954 (mimeographed and bound lectures given at the Sorbonne).

Piaget, J. Genesis and structure in the psychology of intelligence. In D. Elkind (Ed.) *Six Psychological Studies by Jean Piaget.* New York: Random House, 1967a, 143-158.

Piaget, J. *On the nature and nurture of intelligence.* Address delivered at New York University, March, 1967b.

Piaget, J. Intelligence et adaptation biologique. In F. Bresson *et al* (Eds.) *Les Processus d'adaptation,* Paris: Presses Universitaires de France 1967c, 65-82.

Piaget, J. The mental development of the child. In D. Elkind (Ed.) *Six Psychological Studies by Jean Piaget.* New York: Random House, 1967d, pp. 3-73.

Rapaport, D. The theory of ego autonomy. *Bulletin of the Menninger Clinic,* 1958, **22,** 13-35.

Shaffer, L. F. Children's interpretations of cartoons. *Contributions to Education,* No. 429. New York: Teacher's College, Columbia University, 1930.

Skeels, Harold M. Adult status of children with contrasting early life experiences. *Monographs of the Society for Research in Child Development,* 1966, **31,** 3, No. 105.

Spearman, C. *The nature of "intelligence" and the principles of cognition.* London: Macmillan, 1923.

Strodtbeck, F. L. The hidden curriculum of the middle class home. In H. Passow, Miriam Goldberg and E. J. Tannenbaum (Eds.) *Education of the disadvantaged.* New York: Holt, Rinehart & Winston, 1967, 244-259.

Waddington, C. H. *The nature of life.* New York: Atheneum, 1962a.

Waddington, C. H. *How animals develop.* New York: Harper & Bros. (Torchbook Ed.), 1962b.

Wechsler, D. *The measurement of adult intelligence.* Baltimore: Williams & Wilkens, 1944.

Wechsler, D. *Wechsler intelligence scale for children.* New York: Psychological Corporation, 1949.

White, R. W. Motivation reconsidered: The concept of competence. *Psychological Review,* 1959, **66,** 297-333.

The Having of Wonderful Ideas

ELEANOR DUCKWORTH

Atlantic Institute of Education

Explaining that no definitive pedagogy flows from the developmental theory of Jean Piaget, the author explores ways that classroom teachers can nevertheless make powerful use of that theory. For her, the essence of the child's intellectual development lies not in the progressive accomplishment of Piagetian tasks, but in the child's testing out the ideas that she or he finds significant. This process of testing out ideas, she argues, is critical for the child's cognitive growth. Teachers can assist this growth primarily by accepting the child's perspective as the legitimate framework for generating ideas—allowing the child to work out her or his own questions and answers. This approach—and the importance of providing varied settings and materials which suggest ideas to children—is discussed with particular reference to the author's classroom experience and her evaluation of an elementary science program.

Kevin, Stephanie and the Mathematician

The other day I was going over some classic Piaget interviews with a few children to show a friend what they were like. One involved seriation of lengths. I had cut ten cellophane drinking straws at different lengths, and was asking the children to put them in order, from smallest to biggest. The first two seven-year-olds did it with no difficulty and little interest. And then came Kevin. Before I said a word about the straws, he picked them up and said to me, "I know what

Harvard Educational Review   Vol. 42   No. 2   May 1972, 217–231.

I'm going to do," and proceeded, on his own, to seriate them by length. He didn't mean, "I know what you're going to ask me to do." He meant, "I have a wonderful idea about what to do with these straws. You'll be surprised by my wonderful idea."

It wasn't easy for him. He needed a good deal of trial and error as he set about developing his system. But he was so pleased with himself when he accomplished his self-set task that when I decided to offer them to him to keep (ten whole drinking straws!) he glowed with joy, showed them to one or two select friends, and stored them away with other treasures in a shoe box.

The having of wonderful ideas is what I consider to be the essence of intellectual development. And I consider it the essence of pedagogy to give Kevin the occasion to have his wonderful ideas, and to let him feel good about himself for having them. To develop this point of view, and to indicate where Piaget fits in for me, I need to start with some autobiography, and I apologize for that. But it was a struggle of some years' duration for me to see how Piaget was relevant to schools at all.

I had never heard of Piaget when I first sat in one of his classes in Paris in 1957. I was fresh from a B.A. in philosophy, and it was Piaget the philosopher who won me—won me to such an extent that I went on to spend two years in Geneva as a graduate student and research assistant. Then, in 1962, I began to pay attention to schools when, as a Ph.D. drop-out, I accepted a job developing elementary science curriculum. I began the work chiefly because it was a job, but fortunately for me I had happened into an exciting circle of educators, and I got hooked.

The colleagues I admired most got along very well without any special knowledge of psychology. They trusted their own insights about when and how children were learning, and they were right. Their insights were excellent. Moreover, they were especially distrustful of Piaget. He hadn't yet appeared on the cover of the *Saturday Review* or the *New York Times Magazine,* and they had their own picture of him: a severe, humorless intellectual confronting a small child with questions that were surely incomprehensible, while the child tried to tell from the look in his eyes what the answer was supposed to be. No wonder the child couldn't think straight. (More than one of these colleagues first started to pay attention to Piaget when they saw a photo of him. He may be Swiss but he doesn't look like Calvin: maybe he can talk to children after all!)

I myself didn't know what to think. My colleagues did not seem to be any the worse for not taking Piaget seriously. Nor, I had to admit, did I seem any the better. Compared with psychology labs, schools were such complicated places that I couldn't find a way to be of any special help. Not only did Piaget seem to be irrelevant, I was no longer sure he was right. For a couple of years, I scarcely ever mentioned him, and simply went about the business of trying to be helpful, never, as I recall, drawing directly on any of his specific findings.

The lowest point came when one of my colleagues gleefully showed me an essay written in first grade by six-year-old Stephanie. The children had been investigating capillary tubes, looking at the difference in the height of the water as a function of the diameter of the tube. Stephanie's essay went as follows: "I know why it looks like there's more in the skinny tube. Because it's higher. But the other is fatter, so there's the same."

My colleague triumphantly took this as proof that six-year-olds can reason about the compensation of two dimensions. And I didn't know what to say. Of course, it should have been simple. Some six-year-olds *can* reason about compensations. The ages that Piaget mentions are only norms, not universals. Some children develop slower and some develop faster. But I was so unsure of myself at that point that the incident shook me badly, and my explanation only sounded like a lame excuse.

I do have something else to say about that incident, but I'll get to it a little later. For now, I simply want to describe the struggle.

Even if I did believe that Piaget was right, how could he be helpful? If the main thing we take from Piaget is that before certain ages children are unable to understand certain things—conservation, transitivity, spatial coordinates—then what can we do about it? Do we try to teach the children these things? Probably not, because on the one hand Piaget leads us to believe that we probably won't be very successful at it. And on the other hand, if there is one thing we have learned from Piaget, it is that children can be left to their own devices in coming to understand these notions. We don't have to try to furnish them. It took a few months before I straightened that out for myself and concluded that this was not a very good way to make use of Piaget.

Another alternative was to keep in mind the limits on children's abilities to classify, conserve, seriate, and so forth when deciding what to teach them at certain ages. But I found that this was an inadequate criterion for deciding what to teach. There was so much else to keep in mind. The most obvious reason, of course, was that in any class of children there is great diversity of levels. Tailoring to an average level of development is sure to miss a large proportion of the children. In addition, a Piaget psychologist has no monopoly here. When trying to approximate the abilities of a group of children of some given age, able teachers like my colleagues could make as good approximations as I.

I found it appealing that the people with whom I was working judged the merits of any suggestion by how well it worked in classrooms. That is, instead of deciding on *a priori* grounds what children *ought* to know, or what they *ought* to be able to do at a certain age, they found activities, lessons, points of departure which would engage children in ordinary classrooms, with ordinary teachers. In their view, it was easy to devise all-embracing schemes of how science, as it was in this instance, could be organized for children, but making things work pedagogically in classrooms was the difficult part. They started with the difficult part. A theory of intellectual development might have been the basis of a theoretical framework for a curriculum. But in making things work in a classroom, it was but a small part compared with finding ways to interest children, to take into account different children's interests and abilities, to help teachers with no special training in the subject, and so forth. So the burden of this curriculum effort was classroom trials. The criterion was whether or not they worked, and their working depended only in part on their being at the right intellectual level for the children. They might be perfectly all right, from the point of view of intellectual demands, and yet fall short in other ways. Most often, it was a complex combination.

As I was struggling to find some framework within which my knowledge of Piaget would be useful, I found, more or less incidentally, that I was starting to be useful myself. As an observer for some of the pilot teaching of this program, and later as a pilot teacher myself, I found that I did have some good insights into the intellectual difficulties that children encountered. I had a certain skill in being able to watch and listen to children and figure out how they were really seeing a problem. And this led to a certain ability to raise questions that made sense to them and to think of a new orientation for activities which might correspond better to their way of seeing things. I don't want to suggest that I was unique in this. Many of the excellent teachers with whom I was in contact had similar insights. So did many of the mathematicians and scientists among my colleagues, who, from their points of view, could tell when children were seeing things differently from the ways they did. But the question of whether I was unique is not really pertinent. The point is that my experience with Piaget, working closely with one child at a time and trying to figure out what was really in his mind, was a wonderful background for being sensitive to children in classrooms. I feel that a certain amount of this kind of background would be similarly useful for every teacher.

In my own development, it was this sensitivity to children in classrooms which continued to be central. As a framework for thinking about learning, my under-

111

standing of Piaget has been invaluable. This understanding, however, has also been deepened by working with teachers and children on questions of how they can best spend their time together. I may be able to shed some light on that mutual relationship by referring again to six-year-old Stephanie's essay on compensation.

Few of us, looking at water rise in capillary tubes of different diameters, would have bothered to wonder whether the quantities were the same. Nobody had asked Stephanie to make that comparison and in fact it is impossible to tell just by looking. But, on her own, she felt it was a significant thing to comment upon. I take that as an indication that for her it was a wonderful idea. Not long before, she believed that there was more in the tube where the water was higher. She had recently won her own intellectual struggle on that issue, and she wanted to point out her finding to the world for the benefit of those who might be taken in by preliminary appearances.

This incident, once I had figured it out, helped me think about a point that bothered me in one of Piaget's anecdotes. You may recall Piaget's account of a mathematician friend who inspired his studies of the conservation of number. This man told Piaget about an incident from his childhood, where he counted a number of pebbles he had set out in a line. Having counted them from left to right and found there were ten, he decided to see how many there would be if he counted them from right to left. Intrigued to find that there were still ten, he put them in a different arrangement and counted them again. And he kept rearranging and counting them until he decided that, no matter what the arrangement, he was always going to find that there were ten—number is independent of the order of counting.

The problem for me was this: in Piaget's accounts of his subjects, if ten eggs are spread out so they take more space than ten eggcups, a classic non-conserver will maintain that there are more eggs than eggcups, even if he counts and finds that he comes to ten in both cases. Counting is not sufficient to convince him that there are enough egg-cups for all the eggs. How is it, then, that for the mathematician, counting was sufficient? If he was a non-conserver at the time, counting shouldn't have made any difference. If he was a conserver, then he should have known from the start that it would always come out the same.

I think it must be that the whole enterprise was his own wonderful idea. He raised the question for himself, and figured out, for himself, how to try to answer it. In essence, I am saying that he was in a transitional moment, and Stephanie and Kevin were, too. He was at a point where a certain experience fit into certain thoughts and took them a step forward.

I think a powerful pedagogical point can be made from this. These three instances dramatize it, because they deal with children moving ahead with Piaget notions, which are usually difficult to advance with any one experience. The point has two aspects: first, the right question at the right time can move children to peaks in their thinking which result in significant steps forward and real intellectual excitement; and second, although it is almost impossible for an adult to know exactly the right time for a given question for a given child—especially for a teacher who is concerned with thirty or more children—children can raise the right question for themselves when the setting is right. And once the right question is raised, they are moved to tax themselves to the fullest to find an answer. The answers did not come easily in any of these three cases, but the children were prepared to work them through. Having confidence in one's ideas doesn't mean, "I know my ideas are right"; it means, "I am willing to try out my ideas."

As I put together experiences like these and continued to think about them, I started developing some ideas about what education could be, and about the relationships between education and intellectual development.

Hank

It is a truism that all children in their first year or two make incredible intellectual advances. Piaget has documented these advances from his own point of view, but every parent and every psychologist knows this to be the case. One recurring question is why, for such vast numbers of children, does intellectual development slow down so? What happens to children's curiosity and resourcefulness later in their childhood? Why do so few continue to have their own wonderful ideas? I think part of the answer is that intellectual breakthroughs come to be less and less valued. Either they are dismissed as being trivial—as Kevin's or Stephanie's or the mathematician's might have been by some adults. Or else they are discouraged as being unacceptable—like seeing how it feels to wear shoes on the wrong feet (witness Sesame Street), or asking questions that are socially embarrassing, or destroying something to see what it's like inside. The effect is to discourage children from exploring their own ideas, and to make them feel that they have no important ideas of their own—only silly or evil ones.

113

But I think there is at least one other part of the answer, too. Wonderful ideas cannot spring out of nothing. They build on a foundation of other ideas. The following incident may help to clarify what I mean.

Hank was an energetic and not very scholarly fifth-grader. His class had been learning about electric circuits with flashlight batteries, bulbs, and various wires. After the children had developed considerable familiarity with these materials and what they do, the teacher made a number of mystery boxes. Two wires came from each box, but inside, unseen, each box had a different way of making contact between the wires. In one box the wires were attached to a battery; in another box they were attached to a bulb; in another box they were attached to a certain length of resistance wire; in another box they were not attached at all. By trying to complete the circuit on the outside of a box, the children were able to figure out what made the connection inside the box. Like many other children, Hank attached a battery and a bulb to the wire outside the box. Since the bulb lit, he knew at least that the wires inside the box were connected in some way. But since it was somewhat dimmer than usual, he also knew that the wires inside were not connected directly to each other and that they were not connected by another piece of ordinary copper wire. Along with many other children, he knew that the degree of dimness of this bulb meant that the wires inside were connected either by another bulb of the same kind or by a certain kind of resistance wire.

This was as far as the teacher expected them to be able to go. But in order to push the children to think a little further, she asked them if there was any way to tell whether it was bulb or a piece of wire inside the box. She herself thought there was no way to tell. But after some thought, Hank had an idea. He undid the battery and bulb that he had already attached on the outside of the box. In their place, and using additional copper wire, he attached six batteries in a series. He had already experimented enough to know that six batteries would burn out a bulb, if it was a bulb inside the box. And he knew that once a bulb is burnt out, it no longer keeps the circuit complete. So he then attached the original battery and bulb again. This time he found that the bulb on the outside of the box did not light. So he reasoned, with justice, that there had been a bulb inside the box, and now it was burnt out. If there had been a wire inside, it would not have burned through, and the bulb on the outside would still light.

Note that to carry out that idea, Hank had to take the risk of destroying a light bulb. In fact, he did destroy one. In accepting this idea, the teacher had to accept not only the fact that Hank had a good idea which even she did not have, but also accept that it was worthwhile to destroy a small bit of property for the sake of following through an idea. These features almost turn the incident into a parable. Without these kinds of acceptance, Hank would not have been able to pursue his idea. Think of how many times this acceptance is not forthcoming in the life of any child.

But the other important point to be made here is that in order to have that wonderful idea, Hank had to know a lot about batteries, bulbs, and wires. A good deal of previous work and familiarity with those materials were a necessary aspect of this occasion.

David Hawkins has said of curriculum development, "You don't want to cover a subject; you want to uncover it." That, it seems to me, is what schools should be about. They can help to uncover parts of the world which children would not otherwise know how to tackle. Wonderful ideas build on other wonderful ideas. They are not had without content. In Piaget's terms, you have to reach out to the world with your own intellectual tools and grasp it, assimilate it, yourself. All kinds of things are hidden from us—even though they surround us—unless we know how to reach out for them. Schools and teachers can provide materials and questions in ways that suggest things to be done with them; and children, in the doing, cannot help being inventive.

There are two aspects to providing occasions for wonderful ideas, then. One is being prepared to accept children's ideas. The other is providing a setting which suggests wonderful ideas to children—different ideas to different children —as they get caught up in intellectual problems that are real to them.

What Schools Can Do

Recently I had the chance to evaluate an elementary school science program. It happened to be in Africa, but for the purposes of this discussion there is nothing special about the African setting. The program might have been anywhere. This program was by no means a deliberate attempt to apply Piaget, as that is usually understood. But it was, to my mind, an application of Piaget in the best sense. The assumptions that lay behind the work would correspond very well with Piaget's views of the nature of learning and intellectual development. In fact, they correspond with the ideas I have just been developing. The program set out to reveal the world to children. They wanted the children to be familiar with the material world—with biological phenomena, physical phenomena, technological phenomena—flashlights, mosquito larvae, clouds, clay. When I speak of familiarity, I mean feeling at home with these things—knowing what to expect of them and what can be done with them; knowing how they react to various circumstances; what you like about them and what you don't like about them; how they can be changed, avoided, preserved, destroyed, enhanced.

Certainly the material world is too diverse and too complex for anyone to become familiar with all of it in the course of an elementary school career. So the best one can do is to make such knowledge, such familiarity, seem interesting and accessible to the child. That is, one can familiarize children with a few phenomena in such a way as to catch their interest, to let them raise and answer their own questions, to let them realize that what they can do is significant—so that they have the interest, the ability, and the self-confidence to go on by themselves.

Such a program is a curriculum if you will, but a curriculum with a difference. The difference can best be characterized by saying that the unexpected is valued. Instead of expecting teachers and children to do only what was specified in the booklets, without missing anything, the aim of the program is for children and teachers to have so many unanticipated ideas of their own about what to do with the materials that they never even use the booklets. The point of developing materials at all is to get teachers and children started producing their own ideas and following through on their own, and if possible getting beyond needing anybody else's suggestions. This goal is never likely to be completely realized, of course. But as an ideal it represents the orientation of the program. It is a rather radical view of curriculum development.

It is just as necessary for teachers as for children to feel confidence in their own ideas. It is important for them as people, and also important if they are really going to feel free to acknowledge the children's ideas. If teachers feel that their class must do things just as the book says, and that their excellence as a teacher depends upon that, they cannot possibly accept children's divergence and children's creations. A teacher's guide must give enough indications, enough suggestions, so the teacher has ideas to start with and to pursue in some depth. But it must also enable the teacher to feel free to move in directions of her own when other ideas arise.

For instance, the teachers' guides for this program include many examples of things children are likely to do. The risk is that teachers may see these as things that the children in their classes must do—whether or not the children do them becomes a measure of successful or unsuccessful teaching. Sometimes the writers of the teachers' guides intentionally omit mention of some of the most exciting activities because they almost always happen even when they are not arranged. If the teacher expected them, often they would be forced, and they would no longer happen with the excitement of wonderful ideas. Often the writers include extreme examples, so extreme that teachers wouldn't really expect them to happen in their own classes. These examples are meant to convey the message that "even if the children do this it's OK! Look, in one class they even did that!" This often seems more fruitful than putting in more common examples, whose message is more likely to be "this is what ought to happen in your class."

The teachers' guides dealt with materials which were readily available in or out of schools, and suggested activities that could be done with these materials so that children became interested in them and started asking their own questions. For instance, there are common substances all around us which provide the essential basis of chemistry knowledge. They interact together in all sorts of interesting ways, accessible to all of us if only we know how to reach out for them. This is a good instance of a part of the world which is waiting to be uncovered. How can it be uncovered for children in a way which gives them an interest in continuing to find out about it, a way which gives them the occasion to take their own initiatives, and to feel at home in this part of the world?

The teachers' guide suggested starting with salt, sugar, cassava starch, alum, lemon juice, and water. Some of these when mixed together cause bubbles. Which combinations cause bubbles? How long does the bubbling last? How can it be kept going longer? What other substances might cause bubbles? If a combination is bubbling, what else could be added that would stop the bubbling? Other things change colour when they are mixed together, and the same sorts of questions can be asked of them.

Written teachers' guides, however, cannot bear the burden alone, where this kind of teaching is totally new. To get this program started, a great deal of teacher education was necessary as well. I will not try to go into any detail, but there seemed to be three major aspects to such teacher education. One is that teachers themselves learn the same way that children in their classes will be learning. Almost any one of the units developed in this program is as effective with adults as with children, so the teachers learn through some of the units themselves, and they can see what it feels like to learn in this way. Another major aspect seems to be working with one or two children at a time, so that teachers can observe children closely enough to realize what is involved for the children. The third major aspect is seeing films or live demonstrations of a class of children, so teachers can start to feel that it really is possible to conduct their class in this way.

There is a fourth aspect of a slightly different nature. Except for the rare teacher who will take this leap entirely on her own, on the basis of a single course and some written teachers' guides, it is important to provide most teachers with the support of at least some others nearby trying to do the same thing, with whom they can share notes. It is even better when there is somebody experienced whom they can consult when problems arise.

An Evaluation Study

What children do in one of these classrooms may be lively and interesting, but it would be nice to be able to know what difference it makes to them in the long run. I thought it would be important to compare in some way the children who had been in this program with children who hadn't, and to try to show in some standard situation that they now act differently.

I had two thoughts about ways in which these children might be different. The first was based on the following fact: many teachers had told us that when they taught this way, children improved in generating their own ideas of what to do, at raising questions, and at answering their own questions. That is, they improved at having their own ideas and being confident about their own ideas. My first thought, then, was to see whether this was really the case.

My second idea was more ambitious. If these children had really become more intellectually alert, so that their minds were alive and working not only in school but outside school, they might, over a long enough period of time, make significant headway in their operational thinking as compared to other children.

In sum, these two aspects would put to the test my notion that the development of intelligence is a matter of having wonderful ideas and feeling confident enough to try them out; and my idea that schools can have an effect on the continuing development of wonderful ideas. The study has been written up elsewhere, but let me give a summary of it here.[1]

The evaluation study had two phases. The procedures for the first phase were inspired in part by a physics examination that was given to students at M.I.T. by Philip Morrison, in which each student was given the same set of materials but was given no specific problem. Instead, the problem was to *find* a problem, and then to work on it. For Professor Morrison the essential task was finding the question, just as it was for Kevin, Stephanie, and the mathematician. In this examination clear differences emerged in the extent of knowledge and inventiveness revealed in the problems the students set themselves, and the work they did was only as good as their problems.

---

[1] For a full report, see Eleanor Duckworth, "A Comparison Study for Evaluating Primary School Science in Africa," African Primary Science Program of Education Development Center, Newton, Mass., October, 1971.

In our evaluation study we had to modify this procedure somewhat to make it appropriate for children as young as six years of age. We wanted to see what children with a year or more of experience in our program would do with materials when they were left on their own, without any teacher at all. We wanted to see whether children who had been in this program in fact had more ideas about what to do with materials than other children.

The materials we chose were not, of course, those which children in the program had spent time studying. We chose materials of two sorts. On the one hand, there were imported materials which none of the children had ever seen before —plastic color filters, geometric pattern blocks, folding mirrors, commercial building sets, for example. On the other hand, we chose some materials that were familiar to all the children whether or not they had been in the program—cigarette foil, match boxes, rubber rings from inner tubes, scraps of wire and wood and metal, empty spools, and so forth.

From each class we chose a dozen children at random, and told them—in their own vernacular—to go into the room and do whatever they wanted with the materials they found there. We told them they could move around the room, talk to each other, and work with their friends. By way of brief—and inadequate—summary of this phase, let me say that we found that the children who had been in the program did indeed have more ideas about how to work with these materials. Typically, the children in these classes would take a first look at what was offered, try a few things, and then settle down to work at something, with involvement and concentration. Children sometimes worked alone and sometimes collaborated. They carried materials from table to table, using them in ways we had not anticipated. As time went on, there was no sign that they were running out of ideas. On the contrary, their work became more and more interesting, so that it was always a disappointment to have to stop them after forty minutes.

By contrast, the other children had a much smaller range of ideas about what to do with the materials. They tended to copy a few leaders and tended to leave one piece of work fairly soon and switch to something else. There were few instances of elaborate work where a child spent much time and effort to overcome difficulties. In some of these classes, after thirty or thirty-five minutes, all the children had run out of ideas and had nothing left to do.

We looked at two things: diversity of ideas in a class, and depth to which the ideas were pursued. The experimental classes were clearly ahead in each of these two dimensions.

Our procedure was actually a substitute for what we would have liked to do. Ideally, we wanted to know whether the experience of these children in the program had the effect of making them more alert and aware of the possibilities in ordinary things around them, questioning and exploring, during the time they spent outside school hours. This would have been an intriguing question to try to answer directly, but we did not have the time to tackle it. The procedure which we did develop, as just described, may have been too close to the school setting to give rise to any valid conclusions about the children's activity outside school. But if you can accept with me, tentatively, the thought that our results might indicate a greater intellectual alertness in general—a tendency to have wonderful ideas—then the next phase takes on a considerable interest.

I am hypothesizing that this alertness is the motor of development in operational thinking. No doubt there is a continuum. No child would be without any at all. But some would be far more alert than others. I am also hypothesizing that a child's alertness is not fixed. By opening up to children the many fascinating aspects of the world of ordinary things, and by enabling them to feel that their ideas are worth having and following through, I think that their tendency to have wonderful ideas could be affected in significant ways. This program seemed to be doing both those things, and by the time I went to evaluate, some classes of children had been in it for up to three years. It seemed to me that we might—just might—find that the two or three years of increased alertness which this program fostered had made some difference in their intellectual development.

In the second phase, then, we examined the same children individually, on Piaget-type problems, administered by a trained assistant who spoke the language of the children. A statistical analysis revealed that on five of the six problems we studied, the children in the experimental classes did significantly better than the children in the comparison classes.

I find this to be a pretty stunning result on the whole. It is the only program I know of which even suggests that something happening in schools might make a difference to operational development.

But I want to insist on one particular view of the result. I do not, in any way, want to suggest that the important thing for education to be about is acceleration of Piaget stages. I want to make a theoretical point. My thesis at the outset of this paper was that the development of intelligence is a matter of having wonderful ideas. In other words, it is a creative affair. When children are afforded the occasions to be intellectually creative—by being offered matter to be concerned about intellectually and by having their ideas accepted—then not only do they learn about the world, but their general intellectual ability is stimulated as a happy side effect.

Another way of putting this is that I think the distinction made between "divergent" and "convergent" thinking is over-simple. Even to think through a problem to its most appropriate end-point (convergent) one must create various hypotheses to check out (divergent). When Hank came up with a closed end-point to the problem, it was the result of a brilliantly imaginative—divergent—thought. We have to conceive of the possibilities before we can check them out.

Conclusion

I am suggesting, in this paper, that children do not have a built-in pace of intellectual development. Or I would be willing to temper that to say that the built-in aspect of the pace is minimal. The having of wonderful ideas, which I am suggesting is the essence of intellectual development, would depend instead to an overwhelming extent on the occasions for having them. I have already dwelt at some length on how important it is to allow children to accept their own ideas, and work them through. I would like now to consider the intellectual basis for new ideas.

I react strongly against the thought that all we need to provide for children is a set of intellectual processes, a dry, contentless set of tools which they can then go about applying. I believe that the tools cannot help developing, once children have something real to think about. And if they don't have anything real to think about, they won't apply tools anyway. That is, there really is no such thing as a contentless intellectual tool. If you have some knowledge at your disposal then you can try to make sense of new experiences and new information related to it. You fit it into what you have. Let me make it clear that by content I do not mean verbal summaries of somebody else's knowledge. I am not urging a return to textbooks and lectures. I mean a person's own repertoire of thoughts and actions and connections and predictions and feelings. Some of them may have their source in something the child has read or heard. But he has done the work of putting them together for himself, and they give rise to new ways for him to put them together for himself.

The greater the child's repertory of actions and thoughts—in Piaget's terms, *schemes*—the more matter he has for trying to put things together in his head. The essence of the African program I described is to increase children's repertories of actions they might carry out on ordinary things, which in turn gives rise to the need to make more intellectual connections.

Let us think of a child who has had the world of common substances opened to him, as I described earlier. He now has a vastly increased repertory of actions and connections to make. He has seen that when you boil away sea water, a salt residue remains. Would some residue remain if he boiled away beer? If he dissolved this residue in water again, would he have beer again—flat beer? He has seen that he can get a colored liquid from flower petals if he crushes them. Could he get that liquid to dissolve in water and make colored water? Could he make colored coconut oil this way? All these questions and the actions they prompt are based on familiarity he has gained with the possibilities contained in the world of common substances.

I think intelligence cannot develop without content. Making new connections depends on knowing enough about something in the first place to be able to think of other things to do, of other questions to ask, which demand the more complex connections in order to make sense of it all. The more ideas a person already has at his disposal, the more new ideas occur, and the more he can coordinate to build up still more complicated schemes.

Piaget has speculated that some people may reach the level of formal operations in some specific area which they know well—auto mechanics, for example —without reaching the formal level in other areas. That fits into what I am trying to say. In an area you know well, you can think of many possibilities, and working them through often makes demands of a formal nature. If there is no area in which you are familiar enough with the phenomena to have to make sense of complex relationships, then you are not likely to have to develop formal operations. Knowing enough about things is one prerequisite for wonderful ideas.

And one closing remark. The wonderful ideas I am referring to need not necessarily look wonderful to the outside world. I think there is no difference in kind between wonderful ideas which many other people have already had, and wonderful ideas which nobody has happened upon before. That is, the nature of creative intellectual acts remains the same, whether it is an infant who for the first time makes the connection between seeing things and reaching for them, or Kevin who had the idea of putting straws in order of their length, or a cook who conceives of a new combination of herbs, or an astronomer who develops a new theory of the creation of the universe. In each case, it is a matter of making new connections between things already mastered.

The more we can help children to have their own wonderful ideas, and feel good about themselves for having them, the more likely it is that they will some day happen upon ideas that nobody else has happened upon before.

Development as the Aim
of Education

LAWRENCE KOHLBERG and ROCHELLE MAYER

Harvard University

The authors offer an explanation of the psychological and philosophical positions underlying aspects of educational progressivism. They contrast tenets of progressivism, most clearly identified with the work of John Dewey, with two other educational ideologies, the romantic and the cultural transmission conceptions, which historically have competed in the minds of educators as rationales for the choice of educational goals and practices. Kohlberg and Mayer maintain that only progressivism, with its cognitive-developmental psychology, its interactionist epistemology, and its philosophically examined ethics, provides an adequate basis for our understanding of the process of education.

The most important issue confronting educators and educational theorists is the choice of ends for the educational process. Without clear and rational educational goals, it becomes impossible to decide which educational programs achieve objectives of general import and which teach incidental facts and attitudes of dubious worth. While there has been a vast amount of research comparing the effects of various educational methods and programs on various outcome measures, there has been very little empirical research designed to clarify the worth of these outcome

The position presented in this paper was elaborated in a different form in *Proceedings of the Conference on Psychology and the Process of Schooling in the Next Decade: Alternative conceptions.* Washington, D.C.: U. S. Office of Education, 1971. This paper, itself, is an abridged version of a chapter in a forthcoming book by the authors, *Early Education, A Cognitive-Developmental View.* Chicago: Dryden Press (in preparation).

Harvard Educational Review Vol. 42 No. 4 November, 1972, 449–496.

measures themselves. After a deluge of studies in the sixties examining the effects of programs on I.Q. and achievement tests, and drawing policy conclusions, researchers finally began to ask the question, "What is the justification for using I.Q. tests or achievement tests to evaluate programs in the first place?"

The present paper examines such fundamental issues and considers the strategies by which research facts can help generate and substantiate educational objectives and measures of educational outcomes. Three prevalent strategies for defining objectives and relating them to research facts are considered: the desirable trait or "bag of virtues" strategy; the prediction of success or "industrial psychology" strategy; and the "developmental-philosophic" strategy. It will be our claim in this paper that the first two strategies: 1) lack a clear theoretical rationale for defining objectives which can withstand logical and philosophic criticism; and 2) that as currently applied they rest upon assumptions which conflict with research findings. In contrast, we claim that the developmental-philosophic strategy for defining educational objectives, which emerges from the work of Dewey and Piaget, is a theoretical rationale which withstands logical criticism and is consistent with, if not "proved" by, current research findings.

This presentation begins by making explicit how a cognitive-developmental *psychological* theory can be translated into a rational and viable progressive *educational ideology,* i.e., a set of concepts defining desirable aims, content, and methods of education. We contrast the progressive ideology with the "romantic" and the "cultural transmission" schools of thought, with respect to underlying psychological, epistemological, and ethical assumptions. In doing so we focus on two related problems of value theory. The first is the issue of *value-relativity,* the problem of defining some general ends of education whose validity is not relative to the values and needs of each individual child or to the values of each subculture or society. The second is the problem of relating psychological statements about the actual characteristics of children and their development to philosophic statements about desirable characteristics, the problem of relating the natural *is* to the ethical *ought.* We claim that the cognitive-developmental or progressive approach can satisfactorily handle these issues because it combines a psychological theory of development with a rational ethical philosophy of development. In contrast, we claim that other educational ideologies do not stem from psychological theories which can be translated into educational aims free of the philosophic charge that they are arbitrary and relative to the values of the particular educator or school.

Subsequently, we look at the ways in which these ideologies form the basis for contemporary educational policy. We evaluate longitudinal evidence relevant to the "bag of virtues" definition of education objectives favored in maturationist models of education, and the academic achievement definition of objectives favored in environmental learning models. We conclude that the available research lends little support for either of these alternative educational strategies. More specifically:

1. The current prevalent definition of the aims of education, in terms of academic achievement supplemented by a concern for mental health, cannot be justified empirically or logically.
2. The overwhelming emphasis of educational psychology on methods of instruction and tests and measurements which presuppose a "value-neutral" psychology is misplaced.
3. An alternative notion that the aim of the schools should be the stimulation of human development is a scientifically, ethically, and practically viable conception which provides the framework for a new kind of educational psychology.

Three Streams of Educational Ideology

There have been three broad streams in the development of Western educational ideology. While their detailed statements vary from generation to generation, each stream exhibits a continuity based upon particular assumptions of psychological development.

Romanticism

The first stream of thought, the "romantic," commences with Rousseau and is currently represented by Freud's and Gesell's followers. A. S. Neill's Summerhill represents an example of a school based on these principles. Romantics hold that what comes from within the child is the most important aspect of development; therefore the pedagogical environment should be permissive enough to allow the inner "good" (abilities and social virtues) to unfold and the inner "bad" to come under control. Thus teaching the child the ideas and attitudes of others through rote or drill would result in meaningless learning and the suppression of inner spontaneous tendencies of positive value.

Romantics stress the biological metaphors of "health" and "growth" in equating optimal physical development with bodily health and optimal mental development with mental health. Accordingly, early education should allow the child to work through aspects of emotional development not allowed expression at home, such as the formation of social relations with peers and adults other than his parents. It should also allow the expression of intellectual questioning and curiosity. To label this ideology "romantic" is not to accuse it of being unscientific; rather it is to recognize that the nineteenth century discovery of the natural development of the child was part of a larger romantic philosophy, an ethic and epistemology involving a discovery of the natural and the inner self.

With regard to childhood, this philosophy involved not only an awareness that the child possessed an inner self but also a valuing of childhood, to which the origins of the self could be traced. The adult, through taking the child's point of view, could experience otherwise inaccessible elements of truth, goodness, and reality.

As stated by G. H. Mead (1936):

The romantic comes back to the existence of the self as the primary fact. That is what gives the standard to values. What the Romantic period revealed was not simply a past but a past as the point of view from which to come back at the self. . . . It is this self-conscious setting-up of the past again that constitutes the origin of romanticism. (p. 61)

The work of G. Stanley Hall, the founder of American child psychology, contains the core ideas of modern romantic educational thought, including "deschooling."

The guardians of the young should strive first to keep out of nature's way and to prevent harm and should merit the proud title of the defenders of the happiness and rights of children. They should feel profoundly that childhood, as it comes from the hand of God, is not corrupt but illustrates the survival of the most consummate thing in the world; they should be convinced that there is nothing else so worthy of love, reverence and service as the body and soul of the growing child.

Before we let the pedagog loose upon childhood, we must overcome the fetishes of the alphabet, of the multiplication tables, and must reflect that but a few generations ago the ancestors of all of us were illiterate. There are many who ought not to be educated and who would be better in mind, body and morals if they knew no school. What shall it profit a child to gain the world of knowledge and lose his own health? (1901, p. 24)

Cultural Transmission

The origins of the cultural transmission ideology are rooted in the classical academic tradition of Western education. Traditional educators believe that their primary task is the transmission to the present generation of bodies of information and of rules or values collected in the past; they believe that the educator's job is the direct instruction of such information and rules. The important emphasis, however, is not on the sanctity of the past, but on the view that educating consists of transmitting knowledge, skills, and social and moral rules of the culture. Knowledge and rules of the culture may be rapidly changing or they may be static. In either case, however, it is assumed that education is the transmission of the culturally given.

More modern or innovative variations of the cultural transmission view are represented by educational technology and behavior modification.[1] Like traditional education, these approaches assume that knowledge and values—first located in the culture—are afterwards internalized by children through the imitation of adult behavior models, or through explicit instruction and reward and punishment. Accordingly, the educational technologist evaluates the individual's success in terms of his ability to incorporate the responses he has been taught and to respond favorably to the demands of the system. Although the technologist stresses the child as an individual learner, learning at his own pace, he, like the traditionalist, assumes that what is learned and what is valued in education is a culturally given body of knowledge and rules.

There are, of course, a number of contrasts between the traditional academic and the educational technology variations of the cultural-transmission ideology. The traditional academic school has been humanistic in the sense that it has emphasized the transmission of knowledge considered central to the culture of Western man. The educational technology school, in contrast, has emphasized the transmission of skills and habits deemed necessary for adjustment to a technological society. With regard to early education, however, the two variations of the cultural transmission school find an easy rapprochement in stressing such goals as literacy and mathematical skills. The traditionalist sees literacy as the central avenue to the culture of Western man, the technologist sees it as a means to vocational adaptation to a society depending on impersonal information codes. Both approaches, however, emphasize definition of educational goals in terms of fixed knowledge or skills assessed by standards of cultural correctness. Both also stress internalization of basic moral rules of the

[1] The romantic-maturationist position also has "conservative" and "radical" wings. Emphasizing "adaptation to reality," psychoanalytic educators like A. Freud (1937) and Bettelheim (1970) stress mental health as ego-control, while radicals stress spontaneity, creativity, etc.

culture. The clearest and most thoughtful contemporary elaboration of this view in relation to preschool education is to be found in the writing of Bereiter and Engelmann (1966).

In contrast to the child-centered romantic school, the cultural transmission school is society-centered. It defines educational ends as the internalization of the values and knowledge of the culture. The cultural transmission school focuses on the child's need to learn the discipline of the social order, while the romantic stresses the child's freedom. The cultural transmission view emphasizes the common and the established, the romantic view stresses the unique, the novel, and the personal.

Progressivism

The third stream of educational ideology which is still best termed "progressive," following Dewey (1938), developed as part of the pragmatic functional-genetic philosophies of the late nineteenth and early twentieth centuries. As an educational ideology, progressivism holds that education should nourish the child's natural interaction with a developing society or environment. Unlike the romantics, the progressives do not assume that development is the unfolding of an innate pattern or that the primary aim of education is to create an unconflicted environment able to foster healthy development. Instead, they define development as a progression through invariant ordered sequential stages. The educational goal is the eventual attainment of a higher level or stage of development in adulthood, not merely the healthy functioning of the child at a present level. In 1895, Dewey and McLellan suggested the following notion of education for attainment of a higher stage:

Only knowledge of the order and connection of the stages in the development of the psychical functions can insure the full maturing of the psychical powers. Education is the work of supplying the conditions which will enable the psychical functions, as they successively arise, to mature and pass into higher functions in the freest and fullest manner. (p. 207)

In the progressive view, this aim requires an educational environment that actively stimulates development through the presentation of resolvable but genuine problems or conflicts. For progressives, the organizing and developing force in the child's experience is the child's active thinking, and thinking is stimulated by the problematic, by cognitive conflict. Educative experience makes the child think—think in ways which organize both cognition and emotion. Although both the cultural transmission and the progressive views emphasize "knowledge," only the latter sees the acquisition of "knowledge" as *an active change in patterns of thinking* brought about by experiential problem-solving situations. Similarly, both views emphasize "morality," but the progressive sees the acquisition of morality as an active change in patterns of response to problematic social situations rather than the learning of culturally accepted rules.

. The progressive educator stresses the essential links between cognitive and moral development; he assumes that moral development is not purely affective, and that cognitive development is a necessary though not sufficient condition for moral development. The development of logical and critical thought, central to cognitive education, finds its larger meaning in a broad set of moral values. The progressive also points out that moral development arises from social interaction in situations of social conflict. Morality is neither the internalization of established cultural values nor the unfolding of spontaneous impulses and emotions; it is justice, the reciprocity between the individual and others in his social environment.

Psychological Theories Underlying Educational Ideologies

We have described three schools of thought describing the general ends and means of education. Central to each of these educational ideologies is a distinctive educational psychology, a distinctive psychological theory of development (Kohlberg, 1968). Underlying the romantic ideology is a maturationist theory of development; underlying the cultural transmission ideology is an associationistic-learning or environmental-contingency theory of development; and underlying the progressive ideology is a cognitive-developmental or interactionist theory of development.

The three psychological theories described represent three basic metaphors of development (Langer, 1969). The romantic model views the development of the mind through the metaphor of organic growth, the physical growth of a plant or animal. In this metaphor, the environment affects development by providing necessary nourishment for the naturally growing organism. Maturationist psychologists elaborating the romantic metaphor conceive of cognitive development as unfolding through prepatterned stages. They have usually assumed not only that cognitive development unfolds but that individual variations in rate of cognitive development are largely inborn. Emotional development is also believed to unfold through hereditary stages, such as the Freudian psychosexual stages, but is thought to be vulnerable to fixation and frustration by the environment. For the maturationist, although both cognitive and social-emotional development unfold, they are two different things. Since social-emotional development is an unfolding of something biologically given and is not based on knowledge of the social world, it does not depend upon cognitive growth.

The cultural transmission model views the development of the mind through the metaphor of the machine. The machine may be the wax on which the environment transcribes its markings, it may be the telephone switchboard through which environmental stimulus-energies are transmitted, or it may be the computer in which bits of information from the environment are stored, retrieved, and recombined. In any case, the environment is seen as "input," as information or energy more or less directly transmitted to, and accumulated in, the organism. The organism in turn emits "output" behavior. Underlying the mechanistic metaphor is the associationistic, stimulus-response or environmentalist psychological theory, which can be traced from John Locke to Thorndike to B. F. Skinner. This psychology views both specific concepts and general cognitive structures as reflections of structures that exist outside the child in the physical and social world. The structure of the child's concepts or of his behavior is viewed as the result of the association of discrete stimuli with one another, with the child's responses, and with his experiences of pleasure and pain. Cognitive development is the result of guided learning and teaching. Consequently, cognitive education requires a careful statement of desirable behavior patterns described in terms of specific responses. Implied here is the idea that the child's behavior can be shaped by immediate repetition and elaboration of the correct response, and by association with feedback or reward.

The cognitive-developmental metaphor is not material, it is dialectical; it is a model of the progression of ideas in discourse and conversation. The dialectical metaphor was first elaborated by Plato, given new meaning by Hegel, and finally stripped of its metaphysical claims by John Dewey and Jean Piaget, to form a psychological method. In the dialectical metaphor, a core of universal ideas are redefined and reorganized as their implications are played out in experience and as they are confronted by their opposites in argument and discourse. These reorganizations define qualitative levels of thought, levels of increased epistemic adequacy. The child is not a plant or a machine; he is a philosopher or a scientist-poet. The dialectical metaphor of progressive education is supported by a cognitive-developmental or interactional psychological theory. Discarding the dichotomy between maturation and environmentally determined learning, Piaget and Dewey claim that mature thought emerges through a process of development that is neither direct biological maturation nor direct learning, but rather a reorganization of psychological structures resulting from organism-environment interactions. Basic mental structure is the product of the patterning of interaction between the organism and the environment, rather than a direct reflection of either innate neurological patterns or external environmental patterns.

To understand this Piaget-Dewey concept of the development of mental pattern, we must first understand its conception of cognition. Cognitions are assumed to be structures, internally organized wholes or systems of internal relations. These structures are *rules* for the processing of information or the connecting of events. Events in the child's experience are organized actively through these cognitive connecting processes, not passively through external association and repetition. Cognitive development, which is defined as change in cognitive structures, is assumed to depend on experience. But the effects of experience are not regarded as learning in the ordinary sense (training, instruction, modeling, or specific response practices). If two events which follow one another in time are cognitively connected in the child's mind, this implies that he relates them by means of a category such as causality; he perceives his operant behavior as causing the reinforcer to occur. A program of reinforcement, then, cannot directly change the child's causal structures since it is assimilated by the child in terms of his present mode of thinking. When a program of reinforcement cannot be assimilated to the child's causal structure, however, the child's structure may be reorganized to obtain a better fit between the two. Cognitive development is a dialogue between the child's cognitive structures and the structures of the environment. Further, the theory emphasizes that the core of development is not the unfolding of instincts, emotions, or sensorimotor patterns, but instead is cognitive change in distinctively human, general patterns of thinking about the self and the world. The child's relation to his social environment is cognitive; it involves thought and symbolic interaction.

Because of its emphasis on ways of perceiving and responding to experience, cognitive-developmental theory discards the traditional dichotomy of social *versus* intellectual development. Rather, cognitive and affective development are parallel aspects of the structural transformations which take place in development. At the core of this interactional or cognitive-developmental theory is the doctrine of cognitive stages. Stages have the following general characteristics:

1. Stages imply distinct or qualitative differences in children's modes of thinking or of solving the same problem.

2. These different modes of thought form an invariant sequence, order, or succession in individual development. While cultural factors may speed up, slow down, or stop development, they do not change its sequence.

3. Each of these different and sequential modes of thought forms a "structural whole." A given stage-response on a task does not just represent a specific response determined by knowledge and familiarity with that task or tasks similar to it; rather, it represents an underlying thought-organization.

4. Cognitive stages are hierarchical integrations. Stages form an order of increasingly differentiated and integrated *structures* to fulfill a common function. (Piaget, 1960, pp. 13-15)

In other words, a series of stages form an invariant developmental sequence; the sequence is invariant because each stage stems from the previous one and prepares the way for the subsequent stage. Of course, children may move through these stages at varying speeds and they may be found to be half in and half out of a particular stage. Individuals may stop at any given stage and at any age, but if they continue to progress they must move in accord with these steps.

The cognitive-developmental conception of stage has a number of features in common with maturational-theory conceptions of stage. The maturational conception of stage, however, is "embryological," while the interactional conception is "structural-hierarchical." For maturational theory, a stage represents the total state of the organism at a given period of time; for example, Gesell's embryological concept of stage equates it with the typical behavior pattern of an age period, e.g., there is a stage of "five-year-olders." While in the theories of Freud and Erikson stages are less directly equated with ages, psychoanalytic stages are still embryological in the sense that age leads to a new stage regardless of experience and regardless of reorganizations at previous stages. As a result, education and experience become valuable not for movement to a new stage but for healthy or successful integration of the concerns of the present stage. Onset of the next stage occurs regardless of experience; only healthy integration of a stage is contingent on experience.

By contrast, in cognitive-developmental theory a stage is a delimited structure of thought, fixed in a sequence of structures but theoretically independent of time and total organismic state (Kohlberg, 1969b; Loevinger *et al.*, 1970). Such stages are hierarchical reorganizations; attainment of a higher stage presupposes attainment of the prior stage and represents a reorganization or transformation of it. Accordingly, attainment of the next stage is a valid aim of educational experience.

For the interactionist, experience is essential to stage progression, and more or richer stimulation leads to faster advance through the series of stages. On the other hand, the maturational theory assumes that extreme deprivation will retard or fixate development, but that enrichment will not necessarily accelerate it. To understand the effects of experience in stimulating stage-development, cognitive-developmental theory holds that one must analyze the relation of the structure of a child's specific experience to behavior structures. The analysis focuses upon discrepancies between the child's action system or expectancies and the events experienced. The hypothesis is that some moderate or optimal degree of conflict or discrepancy constitutes the most effective experience for structural change.

As applied to educational intervention, the theory holds that facilitating the child's movement to the next step of development involves exposure to the next higher level of thought and conflict requiring the active application of the current level of thought to problematic situations. This implies: (1) attention to the child's mode or styles of thought, i.e., stage; (2) match of stimulation to that stage, e.g., exposure to modes of reasoning one stage above the child's own; (3) arousal, among children, of genuine cognitive and social conflict and disagreement about problematic situations (in contrast to traditional education which has stressed adult "right answers" and has reinforced "behaving well"); and (4) exposure to stimuli toward which the child can be active, in which assimilatory response to the stimulus-situation is associated with "natural" feedback.

In summary, the maturationist theory assumes that basic mental structure results from an innate patterning; the environmentalist learning theory assumes that basic mental structure results from the patterning or association of events in the outside world; the cognitive-developmental theory assumes that basic mental structure results from an interaction between organismic structuring tendencies and the structure of the outside world, not reflecting either one directly. This interaction leads to cognitive stages that represent the transformations of early cognitive structures as they are applied to the external world and as they accommodate to it.

Epistemological Components of Educational Ideologies

We have considered the various psychological theories as parts of educational ideologies. Associated with these theories are differing epistemologies or philosophies of science, specifying what is knowledge, i.e. what are observable facts and how can these facts be interpreted. Differences in epistemology, just as differences in actual theory, generate different strategies for defining objectives.

Romantic educational ideology springs not only from a maturational psychology, but from an existentialist or phenomenological epistemology, defining knowledge and reality as referring to the immediate inner experience of the self. Knowledge or truth in the romantic epistemology is self-awareness or self-insight, a form of truth with emotional as well as intellectual components. As this form of truth extends beyond the self, it is through sympathetic understanding of humans and natural beings as other "selves."

In contrast, cultural transmission ideologies of education tend to involve epistemologies which stress knowledge as that which is repetitive and "objective," that which can be pointed to in sense-experience and measurement and which can be culturally shared and tested.

The progressive ideology, in turn, derives from a functional or pragmatic epistemology which equates knowledge with neither inner experience nor outer sense-reality, but with an equilibrated or resolved relationship between an inquiring human actor and a problematic situation. For the progressive epistemology, the immediate or introspective experience of the child does not have ultimate truth or reality. The meaning and truth of the child's experience depends upon its relationship to the situations in which he is acting. At the same time, the progressive epistemology does not attempt to reduce psychological experience to observable responses in reaction to observable stimuli or situations. Rather, it attempts to functionally coordinate the external meaning of the child's experiences as *behavior* with its internal meaning as it appears to the observer.

With regard to educational objectives, these differences in epistemology generate differences with respect to three issues. The first issue concerns whether to focus objectives on internal states or external behavior. In this respect, cultural transmission and romantic ideologies represent opposite poles. The cultural transmission view evaluates educational change from children's performances, not from their feelings or thoughts. Social growth is defined by the conformity of behavior to particular cultural standards such as honesty and industriousness. These skill and trait terms are found in both common-sense evaluations of school grades and report cards, and in "objective" educational psychological measurement. Behaviorist ideologies systematize this focus by rigorously eliminating references to internal or subjective experience as "non-scientific." Skinner (1971) says:

We can follow the path taken by physics and biology by turning directly to the relation between behavior and the environment and neglecting . . . states of mind. . . . We do not need to try to discover what personalities, states of mind, feelings, . . . intentions—or other prerequisites of autonomous man really are in order to get on with a scientific analysis of behavior. (p. 15)

In contrast, the romantic view emphasizes inner feelings and states. Supported by the field of psychotherapy, romantics maintain that skills, achievements, and performances are not satisfying in themselves, but are only a means to inner awareness, happiness, or mental health. They hold that an educator or therapist who ignores the child's inner states in the name of science does so at his peril, since it is these which are most real to the child.

The progressive or cognitive-developmental view attempts to integrate both behavior and internal states in a functional epistemology of mind. It takes inner experience seriously by attempting to observe thought process rather than language behavior and by observing valuing processes rather than reinforced behavior. In doing so, however, it combines interviews, behavioral tests, and naturalistic observation methods in mental assessment. The cognitive-developmental approach stresses the need to examine mental competence or mental structure as opposed to examining only performance, but it employs a functional rather than an introspective approach to the observation of mental structure. An example is Piaget's systematic and reproducible observations of the preverbal infant's thought-structure of space, time, and causality. In short, the cognitive-developmental approach does not select a focus on inner experience or on outer behavior objectives by epistemological fiat, but uses a functional methodology to coordinate the two through empirical study.

A second issue in the definition of educational objectives involves whether to emphasize immediate experience and behavior or long-term consequences in the child's development. The progressive ideology centers on education as it relates to the child's experience, but attempts to observe or assess experience in functional terms rather than by immediate self-projection into the child's place. As a result the progressive distinguishes between *humanitarian* criteria of the quality of the child's experience and *educative* criteria of quality of experience, in terms of long-term developmental consequences. According to Dewey (1938):

Some experiences are miseducative. Any experience is miseducative that has the effect of arresting or distorting the growth of further experience. . . . An experience may be immediately enjoyable and yet promote the formation of a slack and careless attitude . . . (which) operates to modify the quality of subsequent experiences so as to prevent a person from getting out of them what they have to give. . . . Just as no man lives or dies to himself, so no experience lives or dies to itself. Wholly independent of desire or intent, every experience lives on in further experiences. Hence the central problem of an education based on experience is to select the kind of present experiences that live fruitfully and creatively in subsequent experience. (pp. 25-28)

Dewey maintains that an educational experience which stimulates development is one which arouses interest, enjoyment, and challenge in the immediate experience of the student. The reverse is not necessarily the case; immediate interest and enjoyment does not always indicate that an educational experience stimulates long-range development. Interest and involvement is a necessary but not sufficient condition for education as development. For romantics, especially of the "humanistic psychology" variety, having a novel, intense, and complex experience is *self-development* or self-actualization. For progressives, a more objective test of the effects of the experience on later behavior is required before deciding that the experience is developmental. The progressive views the child's enjoyment and interest as a basic and legitimate criterion of education, but views it as a humanitarian rather than an educational criterion. The progressive holds that education must meet humanitarian criteria, but argues that a concern for the enjoyment and liberty of the child is not in itself equivalent to a concern for his development.

Psychologically, the distinction between humanitarian and developmental criteria is the distinction between the short-term value of the child's immediate experience and the long-term value of that experience as it relates to development. According to the progressive view, this question of the relation of the immediate to the long-term is an empirical rather than a philosophic question. As an example, a characteristic behaviorist strategy is to demonstrate the reversibility of learning by performing an experiment in which a preschooler is reinforced for interacting with other children rather than withdrawing in a corner. This is followed by a reversal of the experiment, demonstrating that when the reinforcement is removed the child again becomes withdrawn. From the progressive or cognitive-developmental perspective, if behavior changes are of this reversible character they cannot define genuine educational objectives. The progressive approach maintains that the worth of an educational effect is decided by its effects upon later behavior and development. Thus, in the progressive view, the basic problems of choosing and validating educational ends can only be solved by longitudinal studies of the effects of educational experience.

The third basic issue is whether the aims of education should be universal as opposed to unique or individual. This issue has an epistemological aspect because romantics have often defined educational goals in terms of the expression or development of a unique self or identity; "objectivist" epistemologies deny that such concepts are accessible to clear observation and definition. In contrast, cultural transmission approaches characteristically focus on measures of individual differences in general dimensions of achievement, or social behavior dimensions on which any individual can be ranked. The progressive, like the romantic, questions the significance of defining behavior relative to some population norm external to the individual. Searching for the "objective" in human experience, the progressive seeks universal qualitative states or sequences in development. Movement from one stage to the next is significant because it is a sequence in the individual's own development, not just a population average or norm. At the same time, insofar as the sequence is a universally observed development it is not unique to the individual in question.

In summary, the cognitive-developmental approach derives from a functional or pragmatic epistemology which attempts to integrate the dichotomies of the inner versus the outer, the immediate versus the remote in time, the unique versus the general. The cognitive-developmental approach focuses on an empirical search for continuities between inner states and outer behavior and between immediate reaction and remote outcome. While focusing on the child's experience, the progressive ideology defines such experience in terms of universal and empirically observable sequences of development.

Ethical Value Positions Underlying Educational Ideologies

When psychologists like Dewey, Skinner, Neill and Montessori actually engage in innovative education, they develop a theory which is not a mere statement of psychological principle, it is an ideology. This is not because of the dogmatic, non-scientific attitude they have as psychologists, but because prescription of educational practice cannot be derived from psychological theory or science alone. In addition to theoretical assumptions about how children learn or develop (the psychological theory component), educational ideologies include value assumptions about what is educationally good or worthwhile. To call a pattern of educational thought an ideology is to indicate it is a fairly systematic combination of a theory about psychological and social fact with a set of value principles.

The Fallacy of Value Neutrality

A "value-neutral" position, based only on facts about child development or about methods of education, cannot in itself directly contribute to educational practice. Factual statements about what the processes of learning and development *are* cannot be directly translated into statements about what children's learning and development *ought to be* without introduction of some value-principles.

In "value-neutral" research, learning does not necessarily imply movement to a stage of greater cognitive or ethical adequacy. As an example, acquisition of a cognitively arbitrary or erroneous concept (e.g., it is best to put a marble in the hole) is considered learning in the same general sense as is acquisition of a capacity for logical inference. Such studies do not relate learning to some justifiable notion of knowledge, truth, or cognitive adequacy. Values are defined relative to a particular culture. Thus, morality is equivalent to conformity to, or internalization of, the particular standards of the child's group or culture. As an example, Berkowitz (1964) writes: "Moral values are evaluations of actions generally believed by the members of a given society to be either 'right' or 'wrong' " (p. 44).

Such "value-free" research cannot be translated into prescriptions for practice without importing a set of value-assumptions having no relation to psychology itself. The effort to remain "value-free" or "non-ideological" and yet prescribe educational goals usually has followed the basic model of counselling or consulting. In the *value-free consulting model,* the client (whether student or school) defines educational ends and the psychologist can then advise about means of education without losing his value-neutrality or imposing his values. Outside education, the value-free consulting model not only provides the basic model for counselling and psychotherapy, where the client is an individual, but also for industrial psychology, where the client is a social system. In both therapy and industrial psychology the consultant is paid by the client and the financial contract defines whose values are to be chosen. The educator or educational psychologist, however, has more than one client. What the child wants, what parents want, and what the larger community wants are often at odds with one another.

An even more fundamental problem for the "value-free" consulting model is the logical impossibility of making a dichotomy between value-free means and value-loaded ends. Skinner (1971, p. 17) claims that "a behavior technology is ethically neutral. Both the villain and the saint can use it. There is nothing in a methodology that determines the values governing its use." But consider the use of torture on the rack as a behavior technology for learning which could be used by saint and villain alike. On technological grounds Skinner advises against punishment, but this does not solve the ethical issue.

Dewey's logical analysis and our present historical awareness of the value consequences of adopting new technologies have made us realize that choices of means, in the last analysis, also imply choices of ends. Advice about means and methods involves value considerations and cannot be made purely on a basis of "facts." Concrete, positive reinforcement is not an ethically neutral means. To advise the use of concrete reinforcement is to advise that a certain kind of character, motivated by concrete reinforcement, is the end of education. Not only can advice about means not be separated from choice of ends, but there is no way for an educational consultant to avoid harboring his own criteria for choosing ends. The "value-neutral" consulting model equates value-neutrality with acceptance of value-relativity, i.e., acceptance of whatever the values of the client are. But the educator or educational psychologist cannot be neutral in this sense either.

Values and the Cultural Transmission Ideology

In an effort to cope with the dilemmas inherent in value-neutral prescription, many psychologists tend to move to a cultural transmission ideology, based on the value premise of *social relativity*. Social relativity assumes some consistent set of values characteristic of the culture, nation, or system as a whole. While these values may be arbitrary and may vary from one social system to another, there is at least some consensus about them. This approach says, "Since values are relative and arbitrary, we might as well take the given values of the society as our starting point and advocate 'adjustment' to the culture or achievement in it as the educational end." The social relativist basis of the Bereiter-Engelmann system, for example, is stated as follows:

In order to use the term cultural deprivation, it is necessary to assume some point of reference. . . The standards of the American public schools represent one such point of reference. . . . There are standards of knowledge and ability which are consistently held to be valuable in the schools, and any child in the schools who falls short of these standards by reason of his particular cultural background may be said to be culturally deprived. (1966, p. 24)

The Bereiter-Engelmann preschool model takes as its standard of value "the standard of the American public schools." It recognizes that this standard is arbitrary and that the kinds of learning prized by the American public schools may not be the most worthy; but it accepts this arbitrariness because it assumes that "all values are relative," that there is no ultimate standard of worth for learning and development.

Unlike Bereiter and Engelmann, many social relativist educators do not simply accept the standards of the school and culture and attempt to maximize conformity to them. Rather, they are likely to elaborate or create standards for a school or society based on value premises derived from what we shall call "the psychologist's fallacy." According to many philosophical analysts, the effort to derive statements of *ought* (or value) directly from statements of *is* (or fact) is a logical fallacy termed the "naturalistic fallacy" (Kohlberg, 1971). The psychologist's fallacy is a form of the naturalistic fallacy. As practiced by psychologists, the naturalistic fallacy is the direct derivation of statements about what human nature, human values, and human desires ought to be from psychological statements about what they are. Typically, this derivation slides over the distinction between what is desired and what is desirable.

The following statement from B. F. Skinner (1971) offers a good example of the psychologist's fallacy:

Good things are positive reinforcers. Physics and biology study things without reference to their values, but the reinforcing effects of things are the province of behavioral science, which, to the extent that it concerns itself with operant reinforcement, is a science of values. Things are good (positively reinforcing) presumably because of the contingencies of survival under which the species evolved. It is part of the genetic endowment called 'human nature' to be reinforced in particular ways by particular things. . . . The effective reinforcers are matters of observation and no one can dispute them. (p. 104)

In this statement, Skinner equates or derives a value word (good) from a fact word (positive reinforcement). This equation is questionable; we wonder whether obtaining positive reinforcement really is good. The psychologist's fallacy or the naturalistic fallacy is a fallacy because we can always ask the further question, "Why is that good?" or "By what standard is that good?" Skinner does not attempt to deal with this further question, called the "open question" by philosophers. He also defines good as "cultural survival." The postulation of cultural survival as an ultimate value raises the open question too. We may ask, "Why should the Nazi culture (or the American culture) survive?" The reason Skinner is not concerned with answering the open question about survival is because he is a cultural relativist, believing that any non-factual reasoning about what is good or about the validity of moral principles is meaningless. He says:

> What a given group of people calls good is a fact, it is what members of the group find reinforcing as a result of their genetic endowment and the natural and social contingencies to which they have been exposed. Each culture has its own set of goods, and what is good in one culture may not be good in another. (p. 128)

The Fallacy of Value-Relativism

Behind Skinner's value-relativism, then, lie the related notions that: 1) all valid inferences or principles are factual or scientific; 2) valid statements about values must be statements about facts of valuing; and 3) what people actually value differs. The fact that people do value different things only becomes an argument for the notion that values are relative if one accepts the first two assumptions listed. Both assumptions are believed by many philosophers to be mistaken because they represent forms of the fact-value confusion already described as the naturalistic fallacy. Confusing discourse about fact with discourse about values, the relativist believes that when ethical judgment is not empirical science, it is not rational. This equation of science with rationality arises because the relativist does not correctly understand philosophical modes of inquiry. In modern conceptions, philosophy is the clarification of concepts for the purpose of critical evaluation of beliefs and standards. The kinds of beliefs which primarily concern philosophy are normative beliefs or standards, beliefs about what ought to be rather than about what is. These include standards of the right or good (ethics), of the true (epistemology), and of the beautiful (esthetics). In science, the critical evaluation of factual beliefs is limited to criteria of causal explanation and prediction; a "scientific" critical evaluation of normative beliefs is limited to treating them as a class of facts. Philosophy, by contrast, seeks rational justification and criticism of normative beliefs, based on considerations additional to their predictive or causal explanatory power. There is fairly widespread agreement among philosophers that criteria for the validity of ethical judgments can be established independent of "scientific" or predictive criteria. Since patterns for the rational statement and justification of normative beliefs, or "oughts," are not identical with patterns of scientific statement and justification, philosophers can reject both Skinner's notion of a strictly "scientific" ethics and Skinner's notion that whatever is not "scientific" is relative. The open question, "Why is reinforcement or cultural survival good?," is meaningful because there are patterns of ethical justification which are ignored by Skinner's relativistic science.

Distinguishing criteria of moral judgment from criteria of scientific judgment, most philosophers accept the "methodological non-relativism" of moral judgment just as they accept the methodological non-relativism of scientific judgment (Brandt, 1956). This ethical non-relativism is based on appeal to principles for making moral judgments, just as scientific non-relativism is based on appeal to principles of scientific method or of scientific judgment.

In summary, cultural transmission ideologies rest on the value premise of social relativism—the doctrine that values are relative to, and based upon, the standards of the particular culture and cannot be questioned or further justified. Cultural transmission ideologies of the "scientific" variety, like Skinner's, do not recognize moral principles since they equate what is desirable with what is observable by science, or with what is desired. Philosophers are not in agreement on the exact formulation of valid moral principles though they agree that such formulations center around notions like "the greatest welfare" or "justice as equity." They also do not agree on choice of priorities between principles such as "justice" and "the greatest welfare." Most philosophers do agree, however, that moral evaluations must be rooted in, or justified by, reference to such a realm of principles. Most also maintain that certain values or principles ought to be universal and that these principles are distinct from the rules of any given culture. A principle is a universalizeable, impartial mode of deciding or judging, not a concrete cultural rule. "Thou shalt not commit adultery" is a rule for specific behavior in specific situations in a monogamous society. By contrast, Kant's Categorical Imperative—act only as you would be willing that everyone should act in the same situation—is a principle. It is a guide for choosing among behaviors, not a prescription for behavior. As such it is free from culturally-defined content; it both transcends and subsumes particular social laws. Hence it has universal applicability.

In regard to values, Skinner's cultural transmission ideology is little different from other, older ideologies based on social relativism and on subjective forms of hedonism, e.g., social Darwinism and Benthamite utilitarianism. As an educational ideology, however, Skinner's relativistic behavior technology has one feature which distinguishes it from older forms of social utilitarianism. This is its denial that rational concern for social utility is itself a matter of moral character or moral principle to be transmitted to the young. In Skinner's view, moral character concepts which go beyond responsiveness to social reinforcement and control rely on "prescientific" concepts of free will. Stated in different terms, the concept of moral education is irrelevant to Skinner; he is not concerned with teaching to the children of his society the value-principles which he himself adopts. The culture designer is a *psychologist-king,* a value relativist, who somehow makes a free, rational decision to devote himself to controlling individual behavior more effectively in the service of cultural survival. In Skinner's scheme there is no plan to make the controlled controllers, or to educate psychologist-kings.

Values and the Romantic Ideology

At first sight the value premises of the romantic ideology appear to be the polar opposites of Skinner's cultural transmission ideology. Opposed to social control and survival is individual freedom, freedom for the child to be himself. For example, A. S. Neill (1960) says:

How can happiness be bestowed? My own answer is: Abolish authority. Let the child be himself. Don't push him around. Don't teach him. Don't lecture him. Don't elevate him. Don't force him to do anything. (p. 297)

As we have pointed out, the romantic ideology rests on a psychology which conceives of the child as having a spontaneously growing mind. In addition, however, it rests on the ethical postulate that "the guardians of the young should merit the proud title of the defenders of the happiness and rights of children" (G. S. Hall, 1901, p. 24). The current popularity of the romantic ideology in "free school," "de-school," and "open school" movements is related to increased adult respect for the rights of children. Bereiter (1972) carries this orientation to an extreme conclusion:

Teachers are looking for a way to get out of playing God. . . . The same humanistic ethos that tells them what qualities the next generation should have also tells them that they have no right to manipulate other people or impose their goals upon them. The fact is that there are no morally safe goals for teachers any more. Only processes are safe. When it comes to goals, everything is in doubt. . . . A common expression, often thrown at me, when I have argued for what I believed children should be taught, is 'Who are we to say what this child should learn.' The basic moral problem . . . is inherent in education itself. If you are engaged in education, you are engaged in an effort to influence the course of the child's development . . . it is to determine what kinds of people they turn out to be. It is to create human beings, it is, therefore, to play God. (pp. 26-27)

This line of thought leads Bereiter to conclude:

The Godlike role of teachers in setting goals for the development of children is no longer morally tenable. A shift to informal modes of education does not remove the difficulty. This paper, then, questions the assumption that education, itself, is a good undertaking and considers the possibilities of a world in which values other than educational ones, come to the fore. (p. 25)

According to Bereiter, then, a humanistic ethical concern for the child's rights must go beyond romantic free schools, beyond de-schooling, to the abandonment of an explicit concern for education. Bereiter contrasts the modern "humanistic ethic," and its concern for the child's rights, with the earlier "liberal" concern for human rights which held education and the common school as the foundation of a free society. This earlier concern Bereiter sees expressed most cogently in Dewey's progressivism.

The historical shift in the conception of children's rights and human rights leading Bereiter to reject Dewey's position is essentially a shift from the liberal grounding of children's rights in ethical principles to the modern humanistic grounding of children's rights in the doctrine of ethical relativity.

Bereiter is led to question the moral legitimacy of education because he equates a regard for the child's liberty with a belief in ethical relativity, rather than recognizing that liberty and justice are universal ethical principles. "The teacher may try to play it safe by sticking to the middle of the road and only aiming to teach what is generally approved, but there are not enough universally endorsed values (if, indeed, there are any) to form the basis of an education" (Bereiter, 1972, p. 27). Here, he confuses an ethical position of tolerance or respect for the child's freedom with a belief in ethical relativity, not recognizing that respect for the child's liberty derives from a principle of justice rather than from a belief that all moral values are arbitrary. Respect for the child's liberty means awarding him the maximum liberty compatible with the liberty of others (and of himself when older), not refusal to deal with his values and behavior. The assumption of individual relativity of values underlying modern romantic statements of the child's liberty is also reflected in the following quote from Neill (1960):

Well, we set out to make a school in which we should allow children freedom to be themselves. In order to do this, we had to renounce all discipline, all direction, all suggestion, all moral training, all religious instruction. We have been called brave, but it did not require courage. All it required was what we had—a complete belief in the child as a good, not an evil, being. For almost forty years, this belief in the goodness of the child has never wavered; it rather has become a final faith. (p. 4)

For Neill, as for many free school advocates, value relativity does not involve what it did for Bereiter—a questioning of all conceptions of what is good in children and good for them. Neill's statement that the child is "good" is a completely non-relativist conception. It does not, however, refer to an ethical or moral principle or standard used to direct the child's education. Instead, just as in Skinner's cultural transmission ideology, the conception of the good is derived from what we have termed the psychologist's fallacy. Neill's faith in the "goodness of the child" is the belief that what children *do* want, when left to themselves, can be equated with what they *should* want from an ethical standpoint. In one way this faith is a belief that children are wired so as to act and develop compatibly with ethical norms. In another sense, however, it is an ethical postulation that decisions about what is right for children should be derived from what children do desire—that whatever children do is right.

This position begs the open question, "Why is freedom to be oneself good; by what standard is it a good thing?"

The question is raised by Dewey as follows (1938):

The objection made [to identifying the educative process with growing or developing] is that growth might take many different directions: a man, for example, who starts out on a career of burglary may grow in that direction . . . into a highly expert burglar. Hence it is argued that 'growth' is not enough; we must also specify the direction in which growth takes place, the end toward which it tends. (p. 75)

In Neill's view it is not clear whether there is a standard of development, i.e., some standard of goodness which children who grow up freely all meet, or whether children who grow up freely are good only by their own standards, even if they are thieves or villains by some other ethical standards. To the extent that there is a non-relativist criterion employed by Neill, it does not derive from, nor is it justified by, the ethical principles of philosophy. Rather, it is derived from matters of psychological fact about "mental health" and "happiness."

The merits of Summerhill are the merits of healthy free children whose lives are unspoiled by fear and hate. (Neill, 1960, p. 4)

The aim of education, in fact, the aim of life is to work joyfully and to find happiness. (Neill, 1960, p. 297).

Freedom, then, is not justified as an ethical principle but as a matter of psychological fact, leading to "mental health and happiness." These are ultimate terms, as are the terms "maximizing reinforcement" and "cultural survival" for Skinner. For other romantic educators the ultimate value terms are also psychological, e.g., "self-realization," "self-actualization," and "spontaneity." These are defined as "basic human tendencies" and are taken as good in themselves rather than being subject to the scrutiny of moral philosophy.

We have attempted to show that romantic libertarian ideologies are grounded on value-relativism and reliance on the psychologist's fallacy, just as are cultural-transmission ideologies, which see education as behavior control in the service of cultural survival. As a result of these shared premises, both romantic and cultural-transmission ideologies tend to generate a kind of elitism. In the case of Skinner, this elitism is reflected in the vision of the psychologist as a culture-designer, who "educates others" to conform to culture and maintain it but not to develop the values and knowledge which would be required for culture-designing. In the case of the romantic, the elitism is reflected in a refusal to impose intellectual and ethical values of libertarianism, equal justice, intellectual inquiry, and social reconstructionism on the child, even though these values are held to be the most important ones:

. . . Summerhill is a place in which people who have the innate ability and wish to be scholars will be scholars; while those who are only fit to sweep the streets will sweep the streets. But we have not produced a street cleaner so far. Nor do I write this snobbishly, for I would rather see a school produce a happy street cleaner than a neurotic scholar. (Neill, 1960, pp. 4-5)

In summary, in spite of their libertarian and non-indoctrinative emphases, romantic ideologies also have a tendency to be elitist or patronizing. Recalling the role of Dostoievsky's Grand Inquisitor, they see education as a process which only intends the child to be happy and adjusted rather than one which confronts the child with the ethical and intellectual problems and principles which the educator himself confronts. Skinner and Neill agree it is better for the child to be a happy pig than an unhappy Socrates. We may question, however, whether they have the right to withhold that choice.

Value Postulates of Progressivism

Progressive ideology, in turn, rests on the value postulates of ethical liberalism.[2]

---

[2] There are two main schools of ethical liberalism. The more naturalistic or utilitarian one is represented in the works of J. S. Mill, Sidgewick, Dewey, and Tufts. The other is represented

This position rejects traditional standards and value-relativism in favor of ethical universals. Further, it recognizes that value universals are ethical principles formulated and justified by the method of philosophy, not simply by the method of psychology. The ethical liberal position favors the active stimulation of the development of these principles in children. These principles are presented through a process of critical questioning which creates an awareness of the ground and limits of rational assent; they also are seen as relevant to universal trends in the child's own social and moral development. The liberal recognition of principles as *principles* clears them from confusion with psychological facts. To be concerned about children's happiness is an ethical imperative for the educator without regard to "mental health," "positive reinforcement," or other psychological terms used by educators who commit the "psychologist's fallacy." Rational ethical principles, not the values of parents or culture, are the final value-arbiters in defining educational aims. Such principles may call for consultation with parents, community, and children in formulating aims, but they do not warrant making them final judges of aims.

The liberal school recognizes that ethical principles determine the ends as well as the means of education. There is great concern not only to make schools more just, i.e., to provide equality of educational opportunity and to allow freedom of belief but also to educate so that free and just people emerge from the schools. Accordingly, liberals also conscientiously engage in moral education. It is here that the progressive and romantic diverge, in spite of a common concern for the liberty and rights of the child. For the romantic, liberty means non-interference. For the liberal, the principle of respect for liberty is itself defined as a moral aim of education. Not only are the rights of the child to be respected by the teacher, but the child's development is to be stimulated so that he may come to respect and defend his own rights and the rights of others.

Recognition of concern for liberty as a principle leads to an explicit, libertarian conception of moral education. According to Dewey and McLellan (1895),

Summing up, we may say that every teacher requires a sound knowledge of ethical and psychological principles . . . . Only psychology and ethics can take education out of the rule-of-thumb stage and elevate the school to a vital, effective institution in the *greatest of all constructions—the building of a free and powerful character.* (p. 207)

In the liberal view, educational concern for the development of a "free

---

in the works of Locke, Kant, and Rawls. A modern statement of the liberal ethical tradition in relation to education is provided by R. S. Peters (1968).

character" is rooted in the principle of liberty. For the romantic or relativist libertarian this means that "everyone has their own bag," which may or may not include liberty; and to actively stimulate the development of regard for liberty or a free character in the child is as much an imposition on the child as any other educational intervention. The progressive libertarians differ on this point. They advocate a strong rather than a weak application of liberal principles to education. Consistent application of ethical principles to education means that education *should* stimulate the development of ethical principles in students.

In regard to ethical values, the progressive ideology adds the postulates of *development* and *democracy* to the postulates of liberalism. The notion of educational democracy is one in which justice between teacher and child means joining in a community in which value decisions are made on a shared and equitable basis, rather than non-interference with the child's value-decisions. Because ethical principles function as principles, the progressive ideology is "democratic" in a sense that romantic and cultural transmission ideologies are not.

In discussing Skinner we pointed to a fundamental problem in the relation between the ideology of the relativist educator and that of the student. Traditional education did not find it a problem to reconcile the role of teacher and the role of student. Both were members of a common culture and the task of the teacher was to transmit that culture and its values to the student. In contrast, modern psychologists advocating cultural transmission ideologies do not hold this position. As social relativists they do not really believe in a common culture; instead they are in the position of transmitting values which are different both from those they believe in and those believed in by the student. At the extreme, as we mentioned earlier, Skinner proposes an ideology for ethically relative psychologist-kings or culture designers who control others. Clearly there is a contradiction between the ideology for the psychologist-king and the ideology for the child.

Romantic or radical ideologies are also unable to solve this problem. The romantic adopts what he assumes are the child's values, or takes as his value premise what is "natural" in the child rather than endorsing the culture's values. But while the adult believes in the child's freedom and creativity and wants a free, more natural society, the child neither fully comprehends nor necessarily adheres to the adult's beliefs. In addition, the romantic must strive to give the child freedom to grow even though such freedom may lead the child to become a reactionary. Like the behavior modifier, then, the romantic has an ideology, but it is different from the one which the student is supposed to develop.

The progressive is non-elitist because he attempts to get all children to develop in the direction of recognizing the principles he holds. But is this not indoctrinative? Here we need to clarify the postulates of development and democracy as they guide education.

For the progressive, the problem of offering a non-indoctrinative education which is based on ethical and epistemological principles is partially resolved by a conception that these principles represent developmentally advanced or mature stages of reasoning, judgment, and action. Because there are culturally universal stages or sequences of moral development (Kohlberg & Turiel, 1971), stimulation of the child's development to the next step in a natural direction is equivalent to a long range goal of teaching ethical principles.

Because the development of these principles is natural they are not imposed on the child—he chooses them himself. A similar developmental approach is taken toward intellectual values. Intellectual education in the progressive view is not merely a transmission of information and intellectual skills, it is the communication of patterns and methods of "scientific" reflection and inquiry. These patterns correspond to higher stages of logical reasoning, Piaget's formal operations. According to the progressive, there is an important analogy between scientific and ethical patterns of judgment or problem-solving, and there are overlapping rationales for intellectual and ethical education. In exposing the child to opportunities for reflective scientific inquiry, the teacher is guided by the principles of scientific method which the teacher himself accepts as the basis of rational reflection. Reference to such principles is non-indoctrinative if these principles are not presented as formulae to be learned ready-made or as rote patterns grounded in authority. Rather, they are part of a process of reflection by the student and teacher. A similar approach guides the process of reflection on ethical or value problems.

The problem of indoctrination is also resolved for the progressive by the concept of democracy. A concern for the child's freedom from indoctrination is part of a concern for the child's freedom to make decisions and act meaningfully. Freedom, in this context, means democracy, i.e., power and participation in a social system which recognizes basic equal rights. It is impossible for teachers not to engage in value-judgments and decisions. A concern for the liberty of the child does not create a school in which the teacher is value-neutral and any pretense of it creates "the hidden curriculum" (Kohlberg, 1969b). But it can create a school in which the teacher's value-judgments and decisions involve the students democratically.

We turn, now, to the nature and justification of these universal and intrinsically worthy aims and principles. In the next sections we attempt to indicate the way in which the concept of development, rooted in psychological study, can aid in prescribing aims of education without commission of the psychologist's fallacy. We call this the developmental-philosophic strategy for defining educational aims.

Strategies for Defining Educational Objectives and Evaluating Educational Experience

We have considered the core psychological and philosophical assumptions of the three major streams of educational ideology. Now we shall consider these assumptions as they have been used to define objectives in early education.

There appear to be three fundamental strategies for defining educational objectives, which we call "the bag of virtues" or "desirable trait" strategy, the "industrial psychology" or "prediction of success" strategy and the "developmental-philosophic" strategy. These strategies tend to be linked, respectively, with the romantic, the cultural transmission, and the progressive educational ideologies.

The romantic tends to define educational objectives in terms of a "bag of virtues"—a set of traits characterizing an ideal healthy or fully-functioning personality. Such definitions of objectives are justified by a psychiatric theory of a spontaneous, creative, or self-confident personality. This standard of value springs from the romantic form of the psychologist's fallacy. Statements of value (desirability of a character-trait) are derived from psychological propositions of fact, e.g., that a given trait is believed to represent psychological "illness" or "health."

The cultural transmission ideology defines immediate objectives in terms of standards of knowledge and behavior learned in school. It defines the long-range objective as eventual power and status in the social system (e.g., income, success). In Skinner's terms, the objective is to maximize the reinforcement each individual receives from the system, while maintaining the system. In defining objectives, this focus on prediction of later success is common to those whose interest lies in maintaining the system in its present form and those whose interest lies in equalizing opportunity for success in the system.

Within the cultural transmission school there is a second strategy for elaborating objectives which we have called the "industrial psychology" approach (Kohlberg, 1972). Psychologically, this strategy is more explicitly atheoretical than the "bag of virtues" approach; with regard to values it is more socially relativistic. Adopting the stance of the value-free consultant, it evaluates a behavior in terms of its usefulness as a means to the student's or the system's ends, and focuses on the empirical prediction of later successes. In practice, this approach has focused heavily on tests and measurements of achievement as they predict or relate to later success in the educational or social system.

The third strategy, the developmental-philosophic, is linked to the progressive ideology. The progressive believes that a liberal conception of education pursuing intrinsically worthy aims or states is the best one for everyone. Such a conception of objectives must have a psychological component. The progressive defines the psychologically valuable in developmental terms. Implied in the term "development" is the notion that a more developed psychological state is more valuable or adequate than a less developed state.

The developmental-philosophic strategy attempts to clarify, specify, and justify the concept of adequacy implicit in the concept of development. It does so through: a) elaborating a formal psychological theory of development—the cognitive-developmental theory; b) elaborating a formal ethical and epistemological theory of truth and worth linked to the psychological theory; c) relating both of these to the facts of development in a specific area; and d) describing empirical sequences of development worth cultivating.

Now we need to critically examine the three strategies. Our task is both logical and empirical. Logically, the chief question is, "Does the strategy define objectives which are intrinsically valuable or universally desirable? Can it deal with the charge that its value is relative or arbitrary?" Empirically, the major question is, "Does the strategy define objectives predicting to something of long-term value in later life?"

The Bag of Virtues Strategy

The "bag of virtues" strategy for choosing objectives is the approach which comes most naturally to educators. An example is the formulation of a Headstart list of objectives—as cited in Dr. Edith Grotberg's review (1969) offered by a panel of authorities on child development. One goal is "helping the emotional and social development of the child by encouraging self-confidence, spontaneity, curiosity and self-discipline." We may note that development is defined here in terms of trait words. From the point of view of the philosophic-developmentalist, the qualification of the term "social development" by such trait words is superfluous and misleading. The developmentalist would chart universals in preschool social development empirically and theoretically with implications for later development and would indicate the conditions which stimulate such development. Such a charting of development would make trait words like "spontaneity" and "self-confidence" unnecessary.

The justification for using trait words to qualify development as an educational end has usually been that development is too vague a term. We consider this question later. Here we need only note the arbitrariness and vagueness which underlies all efforts to use the positive connotations of ordinary trait terms of personality or character to define educational standards and values. This arbitrariness and vagueness exists in lists of mental health traits such as the Headstart list and also in lists of moral virtues composing moral character, such as the Hartshorne and May (1928-1932) objectives of "honesty, service, and self-control." Arbitrariness exists first in composing the list or "bag" of virtues itself. One member of the committee likes "self-discipline," another "spontaneity"; the committee includes both. While both words sound nice, one wonders whether cultivating "self-discipline" and cultivating "spontaneity" are consistent with one another. Second, we may note that the observable meaning of a virtue-word is relative to a conventional cultural standard which is both psychologically vague and ethically relative. The behavior that one person labels "self-discipline" another calls "lack of spontaneity." Because the observable meaning of a virtue-word is relative to a conventional cultural standard, its meaning is psychologically vague, a fact which was first demonstrated by Hartshorne and May for the virtue-word "honesty." Hartshorne and May were dismayed to discover that they could locate no such stable personality trait as honesty in school children. A child who cheated on one occasion might or might not cheat on another: cheating was for the most part situationally determined. In a factor analysis, there was no clearly identifiable factor or correlation pattern which could be called "honesty." Furthermore, "honesty" measurements did not predict to later behavior. This contradicts the commonsense notion underlying the bag of virtues approach. It turns out that dictionary terms for personality do not describe situationally general personality dispositions which are stable or predictive over development.

Related to the problem of psychological definition and measurement is the problem of the relativity of the standard of value defining "honesty" or any other virtue. Labeling a set of behaviors displayed by a child with positive or negative trait terms does not signify that they are of adaptive or ethical importance. It represents an appeal to particular community conventions, since one person's *"integrity"* is another person's *"stubbornness,"* one person's *"honesty* in expressing your true feelings" is another person's *"insensitivity* to the feelings of others."

We have criticized the "bag of virtues" approach on the grounds of *logical* questions raised by a procedure of sorting through the dictionary for trait terms with positive meaning. We need next to question two "scientific" or *psychological* assumptions, the concept of the personality trait and the concept of mental health, as they relate to the development of children. With regard to the trait assumption, longitudinal research findings lead us to question whether there are positive or adaptive childhood personality traits which are stable or predictive over time and development, even if such traits are defined by psychological rather than lexical methods. The relatively general and longitudinally stable personality traits which have been identified in earlier childhood are traits of temperament—introversion-extroversion, passivity-activity—which have been shown to be in large part hereditary temperamental traits without adaptive significance (research reviewed in Ausubel & Sullivan, 1970; Kohlberg, 1969b; Kohlberg, La Crosse & Ricks, 1971). The longitudinal research indicates that the notions of "mental health" or "mental illness" are even more questionable as concepts defining the meaning and value of personality traits. Unlike development, the term "mental health" has no clear psychological meaning when applied to children and their education. When the clinician examines a child with reference to mental health, he records the child's lags (and advances) in cognitive, social, and psychomotor development. Occasionally such lags are indicative of "illness," e.g., of an organic brain condition. But, in general, if "illness" means anything beyond retarded development it means a prognosis of continued failure to develop. Considering the child's development as an aim of education, the metaphors of health and illness add little to detailed and adequate conceptions of cognitive and social development. This also is indicated by empirical longitudinal findings (Kohlberg, LaCrosse & Ricks, 1971).

We are led to ask whether early childhood traits with apparent negative mental health implications like dependency, aggression, or anxiety, have predictive value as indicators of adult difficulties in "life adjustment" or "mental health." The answer at present is no: the mental health traits listed among the Headstart objectives, as well as those commonly included among the goals of other early education programs, have failed to show their predictive value for positive or negative adult life adjustment. Even if the behavior changes sought in such programs were achieved, the child would be no more likely than before to become a well-adjusted adult.

Secondly, from the philosophic point of view, those who espouse the mental health bag of virtues commit the psychologist's fallacy and a related fallacy, that a panel of psychiatrists or child psychiatrists such as the one defining Headstart objectives are "experts" on ethical principles or values.

In educational practice, a concern for mental health has at least meant an ethical concern for the happiness of the child; this was neglected by cultural transmission school. But ethical principles based on a concern for the child's liberty and happiness can stand on their own without a mental health bag of virtues to rationalize them.

The Industrial Psychology Rationale

Translating educational objectives into a "bag of virtues" (skills) in the intellectual domain does not run into all the difficulties which it has encountered in the social-emotional domain. This is because reasonable precision has been attained in defining and measuring intellectual skills and achievements, because there is some degree of predictability over time in these skills, and because the questions of value-relativity raised by concepts of "moral character" and "mental health" as educational objectives are not as obvious when school aims are defined in terms of intellectual skills. But concepts of intellectual skills have only appeared satisfactory because of the high empirical overlap or correlation of these skills with cognitive development (in the developmental-philosophic sense) and because of the overlap with the non-educational or "biological" constant of general intelligence. Once cognitive skills are defined and measured by educational *achievement* measures, they have little clear use in defining educational objectives.

The "achievement skills" conception is a joint product of the "bag of virtues" and "industrial psychology" approach to educational aims. We have noted that the industrial psychology approach rests on identifying and measuring relative individual success in meeting the task demands of a current job or work-position, and on identifying characteristics predicting to later success or mobility in the job-system. Its major application in education has been the development of achievement tests. While not originally developed to define operational educational goals, achievement tests have frequently been used for this purpose. The massive Coleman Report (1966) rested its entire analysis of the quality and effects of schooling on variations in achievement test scores. A number of academic early education programs, including the Bereiter and Engelmann program (1966) previously quoted, essentially define their objective as the improvement of later achievement scores.

From the ethical or philosophic point of view, the use of achievement tests to measure educational objectives rests on a compounding of one type of relativism on another. The items composing an achievement test do not derive from any epistemological principles of adequate patterns of thought and knowledge, but rather represent samples of items taught in the schools. The information taught in the schools is relative and arbitrary: Latin and Greek for one hour, computer programming for another. There is no internal logical or epistemological analysis of these items to justify their worth. Another relativistic aspect of achievement tests is "marking on the curve." This leads to what Zigler has called "defining compensatory education objectives as raising the entire country above the 50th percentile in achievement tests" (unpublished comment).

Finally, and most basically, the relativism underlying achievement tests involves predicting to success in a system without asking whether the system awards success in an ethically justifiable manner, or whether success itself is an ethically justifiable goal. The original ethical impulse in constructing the achievement test was to equalize educational opportunity by a more impartial selection system than teachers' grades, recommendations, and the quality of schools the child has previously attended. This was done with relativistic acceptance that the content and demands of the school serve as social status gating mechanisms. It is hardly surprising that the whole desire to equalize opportunity, or increase educational and occupational justice through raising educational achievement scores, has failed in every possible sense of the word "failure" (Jencks, *et al.*, 1972).

On the psychological and factual side, there have been two basic and related flaws in the assumption that achievement tests represent something of educational value. The first is the notion that correlation or prediction can be substituted for causation. The second, related notion is that success within an arbitrary system, the schools, implies success in other aspects of life. With regard to the first assumption, advocates of the industrial psychology strategy and achievement tests based on it feel that the relation between causation and prediction is unimportant. We can efficiently select those who will do well in college, become successful salesmen, or become juvenile delinquents without facing the causation issue. But if we shift from using a test or a measure of behavior as a selector to using it as the criterion for an educational objective, the problem is quite different. Unless a predictor of later achievement or adjustment is also a causal determinant of it, it cannot be used to define educational objectives.

As an example of the confusion between correlation and causation, we know that grades and achievement scores in elementary school predict to comparable scores in high school which in turn predict to comparable scores in college. The assumption is then made that the *cause* of particular achievement scores is the earlier achievement. It is assumed that a child who does not attain a second grade level of performance on reading achievement will not attain an adequate level of reading later because he is low in reading achievement at second grade.

In fact, the prediction of early to later achievement is mainly due to factors extraneous to achievement itself. Longitudinal studies show that the stability or predictive power of school achievement tests is largely due, first, to a factor of general intelligence and, second, to social class. Achievement scores correlate with I.Q. scores and both measures predict to later school achievement; early elementary achievement does not predict to later achievement any better than does I.Q. alone. In other words, bright children learn what they're taught in school faster, but learning what they're taught in school does not make them brighter nor does it necessarily mean that they will learn later material faster.

Achievement tests also fail to predict to success in later life; in fact, longitudinal studies indicate that school achievement predicts to nothing of value other than itself.

For example, in terms of future job success, high school dropouts do as well as graduates who do not attend college; high school graduates with poor achievement scores and grades do as well as those with good scores; and, college graduates with poor grades do as well as those with good grades (see Kohlberg, LaCrosse & Ricks, 1971; Jencks, *et al*, 1972).

In summary, academic achievement tests have no theoretical rationale. Their practical rationale is primarily an industrial psychology "prediction for selection." But even by industrial psychology standards the tests do not do well since they fail to predict to later life achievement.

These criticisms do not imply that schools should be unconcerned with academic learning. They do suggest: (1) a heavy element of arbitrariness in current school objectives in academic learning; (2) the inability of educational testing methods endorsed by the industrial psychology school to make these objectives less arbitrary; and (3) the invalidity of assuming that if academic achievement is good, early achievement is best. Schools should teach reading, writing, and arithmetic, but their goals and success in teaching these subjects should not be judged by skill or achievement tests.

The Developmental-Philosophic Strategy

The developmental-philosophic strategy, as opposed to the other two, can deal with the ethical question of having a standard of non-relative or universal value and with factual questions of prediction. The concept of development, as elaborated by cognitive-developmental theory, implies a standard of adequacy *internal* to, and governing, the developmental process itself. It is obvious that the notion of development must do more than merely define what comes later in time. It is not clear that what comes later must be better. As an example, if anal interests mature later in time than oral interests, this in itself is no reason for claiming that the anal interests are better than the oral interests.

Cognitive-developmental theory, however, postulates a formal internal standard of adequacy which is not merely an order of events in time. In doing so it elaborates the ordinary-language meaning of the term "development." Webster's Dictionary tells us that to develop means "to make active, to move from the original position to one providing more opportunity for effective use, to cause to grow and differentiate along lines natural of its kind; to go through a process of natural growth, differentiation, or evolution by successive changes." This suggests an internal standard of adequacy governing development; it implies that development is not just any behavior change, but a change toward greater differentiation, integration, and adaptation. Cognitive-developmental psychological theory postulates that movement through a sequential progression represents movement from a less adequate psychological state to a more adequate psychological state. The existence of this "internal standard of adequacy" is suggested by studies which show that the child prefers thinking at the next higher moral or logical stage to thinking at his own stage (or at lower stages) (Rest, 1973), and that he moves in that direction under normal conditions of stimulation.

The concept of development also implies that such an internal standard of adequacy is different than notions of adaptation based on culturally relative success or survival. As a case, we may take stages of morality. Being at the highest moral stage led Socrates and Martin Luther King to be put to death by members of their culture. Obviously, then, moral development cannot be justified as adaptive by standards of survival or of conformity to cultural standards. In terms of developmental psychological theory, however, King's morality was more adequate than the morality of most people who survive longer. Formally, King's morality was a more differentiated and integrated moral system than that of most people. It was more adequate because if all people adopted King's morality, it would resolve for everyone moral problems and conflicts unresolved by lower-stage moralities.

As the example of King suggests, the formal standard of cognitive-developmental psychological theory is not itself ultimate, but must be elaborated as a set of ethical and epistemological principles and justified by the method of philosophy and of ethics. The distinctive feature of the developmental-philosophic approach is that a philosophic conception of adequate principles is coordinated with a psychological theory of development and with the fact of development.

In contrast to "value-free" approaches, the approach suggested by Dewey and Piaget considers questions of value or adequacy at the very start. Piaget begins by establishing epistemological and logical criteria for deciding which thought structures are most adaptive and adequate for coping with complexity. Similarly, our work on ethical stages has taken a philosophic notion of adequate principles of justice (represented especially in the work of Kant and Rawls) to guide us in defining the direction of development. Epistemological and ethical principles guide psychological inquiry from the start. Thus, the strategy attempts to avoid the naturalistic fallacy of directly deriving judgments of value from judgments about the facts of development, although it assumes that the two may be systematically related. It takes as an hypothesis for empirical confirmation or refutation that development is a movement toward greater epistemological or ethical adequacy as defined by philosophic principles of adequacy.

The progressives' philosophical method differs from the approaches of philosophers of other persuasions in that the progressive or developmental method is partly empirical rather than purely analytic. It combines a prior conception of development with a prior notion of an ethical standard of adequacy; but these notions can be revised in light of the facts, including the facts of development. If the facts of development do not indicate that individuals move toward philosophically desired principles of justice, then the initial philosophic definition of the direction of development is in error, and must be revised. The analytic and normative "ought" of the developmental philosopher must take into account the facts of development, but is not simply a translation of these facts.

This method of "empirical" or "experimental" philosophy is especially central for an educational philosophy prescribing educational aims. Philosophical principles cannot be stated as ends of education until they can be stated psychologically. This means translating them into statements about a more adequate stage of development. Otherwise the rationally accepted principles of the philosopher will only be arbitrary concepts and doctrines for the child. Accordingly, to make a genuine statement of an educational end, the educational philosopher must coordinate notions of principles with understanding of the facts of development.

Development as the Aim of Education

We have attempted to clarify and justify the basic claim that developmental criteria are the best ones for defining educationally important behavior changes. We need now to clarify how the psychological study of development can concretely define educational goals. A common criticism is that the concept of development is too vague to genuinely clarify the choice of the curricular content and aims of education. A second, related criticism is that the concept of development, with its connotation of the "natural," is unsuited to determine actual educational policy.

With regard to the issue of vagueness, if the concept of development is to aid in selecting educational aims and content, this assumes that only some behavior changes out of many can be labeled developmental. We need to justify this assumption and to clarify the conditions for developmental change.

Our position has been challenged by Bereiter (1970), who claims that determining whether or not a behavior change is development is a matter of theory, not an empirical issue. For example, Piagetian research shows that fundamental arithmetical reasoning (awareness of one-to-one correspondence, of inclusion of a larger class in a sub-class, of addition and subtraction as inverse operations), usually develops naturally, without formal instruction or schooling, i.e., it constitutes development. Such reasoning can also be explicitly taught, however, following various non-developmental learning theories. Accordingly, says Bereiter, to call fundamental arithmetical reasoning developmental does not define it as a developmental educational objective distinct from non-developmental objectives like rote knowledge of the multiplication tables.

In answer, the cognitive-developmental position claims that developmental behavior change is irreversible, general over a field of responses, sequential, and hierarchical (Kohlberg, 1970). When a set of behavior changes meets all these criteria, changes are termed stages or structural reorganizations. A specific area of behavioral change like fundamental arithmetical reasoning may or may not meet these criteria. Engelmann claims to have artificially taught children the "naturally developing" operation of conservation, but Kamii (1971) found that the children so taught met Engelmann's criteria of conservation without meeting the criteria of development, e.g., the response could be later forgotten or unlearned, it was not generalized, and so forth.

When a set of responses taught artificially do not meet the criteria of natural development this is not because educational intervention is generally incompatible with developmental change. It is because the particular intervention is found to mimic development rather than to stimulate it. The issue of whether an educational change warrants the honorific label "development" is a question for empirical examination, not simply a matter of theory.

We have claimed that development can occur either naturally or as the result of a planned educational program. As was discussed earlier, development depends on experience. It is true, however, that the way in which experience stimulates development (through discrepancy and match between experienced events and information-processing structures) is not the way experience is programmed in many forms of instruction and educational intervention. It is also true that the kinds of experience leading to development must be viewed in terms of a stimulation which is general rather than highly specific in its content or meaning.

Because the experiences necessary for structural development are believed to be *universal,* it is possible for the child to develop the behavior naturally, without planned instruction. But the fact that only about half of the adult American population fully reaches Piaget's stage of formal operational reasoning and only 5% reach the highest moral stage demonstrates that natural or universal forms of development are not inevitable but depend on experience (Kuhn, Langer, Kohlberg & Haan, 1971).

If this argument is accepted, it not only answers the charge that development is a vague concept but helps answer the charge that there are kinds of development (such as growth in skill at burglary) which are not valuable.

Such questionable types of "development" do not constitute development in the sense of a universal sequence or in the sense of growth of some general aspect of personality. As stated by Dewey (1938): "That a man may grow in efficiency as a burglar . . . cannot be doubted. But from the standpoint of growth as education and education as growth the question is whether such growth promotes or retards growth in general" (p. 75).

While a coherent argument has been made for why universal developmental sequences define something of educational value, we need to consider why such sequences comprise the ultimate criteria of educational value. We also need to consider how they relate to competing educational values. How does universal structural development as an educational aim relate to ordinary definitions of information and skills central to the educational curriculum? It seems obvious that many changes or forms of learning are of value which are not universals in development. As an example, while many unschooled persons have learned to read, the capacity and motivation to read does not define a developmental universal; nonetheless, it seems to us a basic educational objective. We cannot dispose of "growth in reading" as an educational objective, as we could "growth in burglary," simply because it is not a universal in development. But we argue that the ultimate importance of learning to read can only be understood in the context of more universal forms of development. Increased capacity to read is not itself a development, although it is an attainment reflecting various aspects of development. The value or importance of reading lies in its potential contribution to further cognitive, social, and aesthetic development. As stated by Dewey (1898):

No one can estimate the benumbing and hardening effect of continued drill in reading as mere form. It should be obvious that what I have in mind is not a Philistine attack upon books and reading. The question is not how to get rid of them, but how to get their value—how to use them to their capacity as servants of the intellectual and moral life. To answer this question, we must consider what is the effect of growth in a special direction upon the attitudes and habits which alone open up avenues for development in other lines. (p. 29)

161

A developmental definition of educational objectives must not only cope with competing objectives usually defined non-developmentally, but with the fact that the universal aspects of development are multiple. Here, as in the case of evaluating non-developmental objectives, the progressive educator must consider the relation of a particular development to development in general. As an example, Kamii (1971) has defined a program of preschool intervention related to each of the chapter headings of Piaget's books: space, time, causality, number, classification, and so on. Kamii's intent in making use of all the areas of cognitive development discussed by Piaget is not to imply that each constitutes a separate, intrinsic educational objective. Rather, her interest is to make use of all aspects of the child's experience relevant to *general* Piagetian cognitive development. Such a concept of generalized cognitive-stage development is meaningful because Kohlberg and DeVries (1971) and others have shown that there is a general Piagetian cognitive-level factor distinct from psychometric general intelligence.

In contrast to the psychometric concept of intelligence, the developmental level concept of intelligence does provide a standard or a set of aims for preschool education. It does not assume a concept of fixed capacity or "intelligence quotient" constant over development. In this sense, developmental level is more like "achievement" than like "capacity," but developmental level tests differ from achievement tests in several ways. While the developmental level concept does not distinguish between achievement and capacity, it distinguishes between cognitive achievement (performance) and cognitive process (or competence). Developmental tests measure level of thought process, not the difficulty or correctness of thought product. They measure not cognitive performance but cognitive competence, the basic possession of a core concept, not the speed and agility with which the concept is expressed or used under rigid test conditions.

Psychometric and developmental level concepts of intelligence are quite different. In practice, however, the two kinds of measures are highly correlated with one another, explaining why clear theoretical and operational distinctions between the two concepts of intelligence have not been made until recently. Factor-analytic findings now can provide an empirical basis for this distinction (Kohlberg & DeVries, 1971). While psychometric measures of general intelligence and of "primary mental abilities" at mental age six correlate with Piagetian measures of cognitive level, there is also a common factor to all developmental level tests. This factor is independent of general intelligence or of any special psychometric ability. In other words, it is possible to distinguish between psychometric capacity and developmental level concepts or measures of intelligence. Given the empirical distinction, cognitive stage measures provide a rational standard for educational intervention where psychometric intelligence tests do not. This is true for the following reasons:

1. The core structure defined by stage tests is in theory and experiment more amenable to educational intervention—Piagetian theory is a theory of stage movement occurring through *experience* of structural disequilibrium.

2. Piagetian performance predicts later development independent of a fixed biological rate or capacity factor, as demonstrated by evidence for longitudinal stability or prediction independent of I.Q. Because Piaget items define invariant sequences, development to one stage facilitates development to the next.

3. Piagetian test content has cognitive value in its own right. If a child is able to think causally instead of magically about phenomena, for instance, his ability has a cognitive value apart from arbitrary cultural demands—it is not a mere indicator of brightness, like knowing the word "envelope" or "amanuensis." This is reflected in the fact that Piaget test scores are qualitative; they are not arbitrary points on a curve. The capacity to engage in concrete logical reasoning is a definite attainment, being at mental age six is not. We can ask that all children reason in terms of logical operations; we cannot ask that all children have high I.Q.'s.

4. This cognitive value is culturally universal, the sequence of development occurs in every culture and subculture.

The existence of a general level factor in cognitive development allows us to put particular universal sequences of cognitive development into perspective as educational aims. The worth of a development in any particular cognitive sequence is determined by its contribution to the whole of cognitive development.

We must now consider the relation of developmental aims of education to the notion of developmental acceleration as an educational objective. We indicated that a concept of stages as "natural" does not mean that they are inevitable; many individuals fail to attain the higher stages of logical and moral reasoning. Accordingly, the aim of the developmental educator is not the acceleration of development but the eventual adult attainment of the highest stage. In this sense, the developmentalist is not interested in *stage-acceleration*, but in avoiding *stage-retardation*. Moral development research reviewed elsewhere suggests that there is what approaches an optimal period for movement from one stage to the next (Kohlberg & Turiel, 1973). When a child has just attained a given stage, he is unlikely to respond to stimulation toward movement to the next stage. In addition, after a long period of use of a given stage of thought, a child tends to "stabilize" at that stage and develops screening mechanisms for contradictory stimulation. Accordingly, it has been found that both very young and very old children at a given stage (compared to the age-norm for that stage) are less responsive or less able to assimilate stimulation at the next higher stage than children at the age-norm for that stage. The notion of an "open period" is not age-specific, it is individual. A child late in reaching Stage 2 may be "open" to Stage 3 at an age beyond that of another child who reached Stage 2 earlier. Nevertheless, gross age-periods may be defined which are "open periods" for movement from one stage to the next. Avoidance of retardation as an educational aim means presenting stimulation in these periods where the possibility for development is still open.

We need to consider a related distinction between *acceleration* and *decalage* as an aim of education. Piaget distinguishes between the appearance of a stage and its "horizontal *decalage*," its spread or generalization across the range of basic physical and social actions, concepts, and objects to which the stage potentially applies. As a simple example, concrete logic or conservation is first noted in the concept of mass and only later in weight and volume. Accordingly, acceleration of the stage of concrete operations is one educational enterprise and the encouragement of *decalage* of concrete reasoning to a new concept or phenomenon is another. It is the latter which is most relevant to education. Education is concerned not so much with age of onset of a child's capacity for concrete logical thought, but with the possession of a logical mind—the degree to which he has organized his experience or his world in a logical fashion.

It is likely that the occurrence of such horizontal *decalage,* rather than age of first appearance of concrete operations, predicts to later formal operational thought. Formal reasoning develops because concrete reasoning represents a poor, though partially successful, strategy for solving many problems. The child who has never explored the limits of concrete logical reasoning and lives in a world determined by arbitrary unexplained events and forces, will see the limits of the partial solutions of concrete logic as set by intangible forces, rather than looking for a more adequate logic to deal with unexplained problems.

We have so far discussed development only as general cognitive development. According to cognitive-developmental theory there is always a cognitive component to development, even in social, moral, and aesthetic areas. Development, however, is broader than cognitive-logical development. One central area is moral development, as defined by invariant stages of moral reasoning (Kohlberg & Turiel, 1971, 1973). On the one hand, these stages have a cognitive component; attainment of a given Piaget cognitive stage is a necessary, though not sufficient, condition for the parallel moral stage. On the other hand, moral reasoning stages relate to action, principled moral reasoning has been found to be a precondition for principled moral action (Kohlberg and Turiel, 1973). For reasons elaborated throughout this paper, the stimulation of moral development through the stages represents a rational and ethical focus of education related to, but broadening, an educational focus upon cognitive development as such (Kohlberg & Turiel, 1971). Programs effective in stimulating moral development have been successfully demonstrated (Blatt & Kohlberg, 1973).

While developmental moral education widens the focus of cognitive-developmental education beyond the purely cognitive, there is a still broader unity, called ego-development, of which both cognitive and moral development are part (Loevinger, Wessler & Redmore, 1970). Particularly in the earlier childhood years, it is difficult to distinguish moral development from ego-development. Cognitive development, in the Piagetian sense, is also related to ego development, since both concern the child's core beliefs about the physical and social world. Much recent research demonstrates that the development of the ego, as attitudes and beliefs about the self, involves step-by-step parallel development of attitudes and beliefs about the physical and social world. Further, it indicates definite stages of ego-development, defined by Loevinger *et al.* (1970), van den Daele (1970) and others, which imply step-by-step parallels to Piaget's cognitive stages, although they include more social emotional content. In general, attainment of a Piagetian cognitive stage is a necessary but not sufficient condition for attainment of the parallel ego stage. All children at a given ego stage must have attained the parallel cognitive stage, but not all children at a cognitive stage will have organized their self-concept and social experience at the corresponding ego stage. Thus, a general concept of ego-development as a universal sequential phenomenon is becoming an empirically meaningful guide to defining broad educational objectives. Furthermore, experimental educational programs to stimulate ego-development have been piloted with some definite success at both the preschool and the high school levels (van den Daele, 1970; Sprinthall & Mosher, 1970).

Thus, education for general cognitive development, and perhaps even education for moral development, must be judged by its contribution to a more general concept of ego-development. In saying this, we must remember that "ego-development" is the psychologist's term for a sequence which also must have a philosophic rationale. One pole of ego-development is self-awareness; the parallel pole is awareness of the world. Increasing awareness is not only "cognitive," it is moral, aesthetic, and metaphysical; it is the awareness of new meanings in life.

Finally, we need to note that in the realm of ego-development, a focus upon "horizontal *decalage*" rather than acceleration is especially salient. The distinction reflects in a more precise and viable fashion the concern of maturational or romantic stage-theorists for an educational focus upon "healthy" passage through stages, rather than their acceleration. In maturational theories of personality stages, age leads to a new stage regardless of experience and re-organizations at previous stages. As a result, education and experience become valuable not for movement to a new stage, but for healthy or *successful integration* of the concerns of a stage. Onset of the next stage occurs regardless of experience; it is only healthy integration of the stages which is contingent on experience and which should be the focus for education. Without accepting this contention, cognitive-developmental theory would agree that premature development to a higher ego stage without a corresponding *decalage* throughout the child's world and life presents problems. In psychoanalytic maturational terms, the dangers of uneven or premature ego development are expressed as defects in ego-strength with consequent vulnerability to regression. In cognitive-developmental terms, inadequate "horizontal *decalage*" represents a somewhat similar phenomenon. While the relation of "ego-strength" to logical and moral *decalage* is not well understood, there are many reasons to believe they are related. A child who continues to think in magical or egocentric terms in some areas of cognition and morality is likely to be vulnerable to something like "regression" under stress later in life.

In conclusion, if a broad concept of development, conceived in stage-sequential terms, is still vague as a definer of educational ends, it is not due to the inherent narrowness or vagueness of the concept. Rather, it is due to the fact that researchers have only recently begun the kind of longitudinal and educational research needed to make the concept precise and useable. When Dewey advocated education as development at the turn of the century, most American educational psychologists turned instead to industrial psychology or to the mental health bag of virtues. If the results of the cognitive-developmental research of the last decades are still limited, they indicate real promise for finally translating Dewey's vision into a precise reality.

Summary and Conclusions

The present paper essentially recapitulates the progressive position first formulated by John Dewey. This position has been clarified psychologically by the work of Piaget and his followers; its philosophic premises have been advanced by the work of modern analytic philosophers like Hare, Rawls, and Peters. The progressive view of education makes the following claims:

1. That the aims of education may be identified with development, both intellectual and moral.

2. That education so conceived supplies the conditions for passing through an order of connected stages.

3. That such a developmental definition of educational aims and processes requires both the method of philosophy or ethics and the method of psychology or science. The justification of education as development requires a philosophic statement explaining why a higher stage is a better or a more adequate stage. In addition, before one can define a set of educational goals based on a philosophical statement of ethical, scientific, or logical principles one must be able to translate it into a statement about psychological stages of development.

4. This, in turn, implies that the understanding of logical and ethical principles is a central aim of education. This understanding is the philosophic counterpart of the psychological statement that the aim of education is the development of the individual through cognitive and moral stages. It is characteristic of higher cognitive and moral stages that the child himself constructs logical and ethical principles; these, in turn, are elaborated by science and philosophy.

5. A notion of education as attainment of higher stages of development, involving an understanding of principles, was central to "aristocratic" Platonic doctrines of liberal education. This conception is also central to Dewey's notion of a democratic education. The democratic educational end for all humans must be "the development of a free and powerful character." Nothing less than democratic education will prepare free people for factual

and moral choices which they will inevitably confront in society. The democratic educator must be guided by a set of psychological and ethical principles which he openly presents to his students, inviting criticism as well as understanding. The alternative is the "educator-king," such as the behavior-modifier with an ideology of controlling behavior, or the teacher-psychiatrist with an ideology of "improving" students' mental health. Neither exposes his ideology to the students, allowing them to evaluate its merit for themselves.

6. A notion of education for development and education for principles is liberal, democratic, and non-indoctrinative. It relies on open methods of stimulation through a sequence of stages, in a direction of movement which is universal for all children. In this sense, it is natural.

The progressive position appears idealistic rather than pragmatic, industrial-vocational, or adjustment-orientated, as is often charged by critics of progressivism who view it as ignoring "excellence." But Dewey's idealism is supported by Piagetian psychological findings which indicate that all children, not only well-born college students, are "philosophers" intent on organizing their lives into universal patterns of meaning. It is supported by findings that most students seem to move forward in developmentally oriented educational programs. Furthermore, the idealism of the developmental position is compatible with the notion that the child is involved in a process of both academic and vocational education. Dewey denied that educational experience stimulating intellectual and moral development could be equated with academic schooling. He claimed that practical or vocational education as well as academic education could contribute to cognitive and moral development; it should be for all children, not only for the poor or the "slow." Our educational system currently faces a choice between two forms of injustice, the first an imposition of an arbitrary academic education on all, the second a division into a superior academic track and an inferior vocational track. The developmental conception remains the only rationale for solving these injustices, and for providing the basis for a truly democratic educational process.

References

Ausubel, D., & Sullivan, E. *Theory and problems of child development.* New York: Grune and Stratton, 1970.

Bereiter, C. Educational implications of Kohlberg's cognitive-developmental view. *Interchange,* 1 (2, 1970), 25-32.

Bereiter, C. Moral alternatives to education. *Interchange,* 3 (1, 1972), 25-41.

Bereiter, C. *Must we educate?* Engelwood Cliffs, N. J.: Prentice-Hall, in press.

Bereiter, C., & Engelmann, S. *Teaching disadvantaged children in the preschool.* Engelwood Cliffs, N. J.: Prentice-Hall, 1966.

Berkowitz, L. *Development of motives and values in a child.* New York: Basic Books, 1964.

Bettelheim, B. On moral education. In T. Sizer (Ed.), *Moral education.* Cambridge, Mass.: Harvard University Press, 1970.

Blatt, M., & Kohlberg, L. Effects of classroom discussion upon children's level of moral judgment. In Kohlberg & Turiel (Eds.), *Recent research in moral development.* New York: Holt, Rinehart and Winston, 1973.

Brandt, R. B. *Ethical theory.* Engelwood Cliffs, N.J.: Prentice-Hall, 1956.

Coleman, J. S. *et al. Equality of educational opportunity.* Washington, D.C.: U. S. Dept. of Health, Education and Welfare, Office of Education, 1966.

Dewey, J. The primary-education fetish. *The Forum.* Washington, D. C.: U. S. Government Printing Office, May, 1898.

Dewey, J. *Experience and education.* New York: Collier, 1963 (originally written in 1938).

Dewey, J. & McLellan, J. The psychology of number. In R. Archambault (Ed.), *John Dewey on education: Selected writings.* New York: Random House, 1964.

Freud, A. The ego and the mechanisms of defense. London: Hogarth Press, 1937.

Grotberg, E. *Review of research, 1965 to 1969.* Office of Economic Opportunity Pamphlet 6108-13. Washington, D.C.: Research and Evaluation Office, Project Head Start, Office of Economic Opportunity, 1969.

Group for the Advancement of Psychiatry. *Psychopathological disorders in childhood: Theoretical considerations and a proposed classification.* Formulated by the Committee on Child Psychiatry, GAP Report, 62 (6, 1966), 173-343.

Hall, G. S. The ideal school based on child study. *The Forum,* 32, 1901.

Hartshorne, H., & May, M. A. *Studies in the nature of character.* Vol. 1. Studies in deceit. Vol. 2. Studies in service and self-control. Vol. 3. Studies in organization of character. New York: Macmillan, 1928-1930.

Jencks, C., *et al. Inequality: A reassessment of the effect of family and schooling in America.* New York: Basic Books, 1972.

Kamii, C. Evaluating pupil learning in preschool education: Socio-emotional, perceptual-motor, and cognitive objectives. In B. S. Bloom, J. T. Hastings, & G. Madaus (Eds.), *Formative and summative evaluation of student learning.* New York: McGraw-Hill, 1971.

Kohlberg, L. Early education: A cognitive-developmental view. *Child Development,* 39 (December, 1968), 1013-1062.

Kohlberg, L. The moral atmosphere of the school. Paper delivered at Association for Supervision and Curriculum Development Conference on the "Unstudied Curriculum." Washington, D.C., January 9, 1969a (printed in A.A.S.C. Yearbook, 1970).

Kohlberg, L. Stage and sequence: The cognitive-developmental approach to socialization. In D. Goslin (Ed.), *Handbook of socialization theory and research.* New York: Rand McNally, 1969b.

Kohlberg, L. Reply to Bereiter's statement on Kohlberg's cognitive-developmental view. *Interchange,* 1 (2, 1970), 40-48.

Kohlberg, L. From is to ought: How to commit the naturalistic fallacy and get away with it in the study of moral development. In T. Mischel (Ed.), *Cognitive development and epistemology.* New York: Academic Press, 1971.

Kohlberg, L. The contribution of developmental psychology to education: Examples from moral education. Forthcoming in *The Educational Psychologist.*

Kohlberg, L., LaCrosse, R., & Ricks, D. The predictability of adult mental health from childhood behavior. In B. Wolman (Ed.), *Handbook of child psychopathology.* New York: McGraw-Hill, 1971.

Kohlberg, L. & DeVries, R. Relations between Piaget and psychometric assessments of intelligence. In C. Lavatelli (Ed.), *The natural curriculum.* E.R.I.C., 1971. Urbana, Ill.: Revised version to be published as a chapter in L. Kohlberg & R. Mayer, *Early education, a cognitive-developmental view.* Chicago: Dryden Press, in press.

Kohlberg, L., & Turiel, E. Moral development and moral education. In G. Lesser (Ed.), *Psychology and educational practice.* Chicago: Scott Foresman, 1971.

Kohlberg, L., & Turiel, E. (Eds.). *Recent research in moral development.* New York: Holt, Rinehart and Winston, 1973.

Kuhn, D., Langer, J., Kohlberg, L., & Haan, N. The development of formal operations in logical and moral judgment. Unpublished mimeo monograph, Columbia University, 1971.

Langer, J. *Theories of development.* New York: Holt, Rinehart and Winston, 1969.

Loevinger, J., Wessler, R., & Redmore, C. *Measuring ego development.* San Francisco: Jossey-Bass, 1970.

Mead, G. H. *Movements of thought in the nineteenth century.* Chicago: University of Chicago Press, 1936.

Neill, A. S. *Summerhill.* New York: Hart, 1960.

Peters, R. S. *Ethics and education.* Chicago: Scott Foresman, 1968.

Piaget, J. The general problem of the psychobiological development of the child. In J. M. Tanner & B. Inhelder (Eds.), *Discussion on child development.* Vol. 4. New York: International Universities Press, 1960.

Rawls, J. *A theory of justice.* Cambridge, Mass.: Harvard University Press, 1971.

Rest, J. Comprehension preference and spontaneous usage in moral judgment. In L. Kohlberg & E. Turiel (Eds.), *Recent research in moral development.* New York: Holt, Rinehart and Winston, 1973.

Skinner, B. F. *Beyond freedom and dignity.* New York: Alfred A. Knopf, 1971.

Sprinthall, N. A., & Mosher, R. L. Psychological education in secondary schools: A program to promote individual and human development. *American Psychologist,* 25 (October, 1970), 911-924.

Turiel, E. Developmental processes in the child's moral thinking. In P. Mussen, J. Langer, & M. Covington (Eds.), *New Directions in developmental psychology.* New York: Holt, Rinehart and Winston, 1969.

van den Daele, L. Preschool intervention with social learning. *Journal of Negro Education,* 39 (Fall, 1970), 296-304.

Hierarchical Theories
of Development
in Education and Psychology

D. C. PHILLIPS
Stanford University

MAVIS E. KELLY
Monash University

The authors examine the much-touted hierarchical theories of development and argue that their underlying assumptions have not been adequately examined. One special concern is the claim that the order of stages of development must be invariant; another is the problem of clarifying the contribution that earlier stages make to succeeding stages. Reviewing the works of Piaget and Inhelder, Kohlberg, Jensen, Erikson, and Gagné, the authors maintain that it is unclear whether their theories are empirically or conceptually grounded. Because of such obscurities, they argue, a good many of the assumptions currently accepted in developmental psychology are dubious.

Although he is not noted for his contribution to psychology, Chairman Mao Tse-tung has written a passage that is of some relevance to the field:

> Lacking an analytical approach, many of our comrades do not want to go deeply into complex matters, to analyze and study them over and over again.... From now on we should remedy this state of affairs.[1]

[1] Mao Tse-tung, *Quotations from Chairman Mao Tse-tung* (Peking: Foreign Languages Press, 1966), p. 215.

Harvard Educational Review   Vol. 45   No. 3   August 1975, 351–375.

171

A good illustration—but one the Chairman probably did not have in mind—is the readiness with which psychologists and educational researchers have accepted theories of development embodying hierarchies.

Erik Erikson has formulated a hierarchy of stages in the development of the mature human personality. Havighurst has his sequence of developmental tasks and Gesell his photographs of typical children of different ages. Piaget, Inhelder and Kohlberg have devised many variations on the theme of an invariant sequence of stages in the development of logical operations in the individual. Jensen is interested in a hierarchical model of intellectual abilities, and Gagné has formulated a theory of learning hierarchies. These psychologists have all been influential, but it is time, heeding the Chairman, to pause and examine some of the fundamental assumptions underlying hierarchical theories in developmental psychology and education.

While these theories are similar in certain respects, one dimension along which they vary is in their analysis of the relationship between levels or stages. Some postulate temporal sequences without specifying any particular relation between levels. Other hierarchies are based on substitution or replacement of one stage by another. There are theories which assume that higher levels incorporate the lower levels. Still others attempt to provide a causal explanation of higher levels in terms of lower levels. And of course, there are various combinations of these theories. All such theories fall within the scope of the present discussion, provided that they embody the assumption that their classificatory scheme also reflects a developmental sequence. Clearly, however, a hierarchical theory need not be developmental.

Hierarchical theories may be potentially useful in understanding human development. At the present time, however, the scientific status of such theories is obscure. In the flurry of experimental research on child development, it is not always clear what type of evidence would count as confirmation or refutation of such a theory, or indeed whether empirical research is relevant at all. These and related issues have not been totally ignored in the literature, but discussion has been hampered by the failure to draw some important distinctions and to make explicit certain underlying assumptions.

Ontogenetic and Phylogenetic Hierarchies

There has been a tendency in the study of child development to assume that ontogenetic hierarchies (which pertain to individual development) must parallel phylogenetic ones (which pertain to the pattern of evolution of the species). This confusion has a venerable history dating back at least to the Romantic period, and there are a number of striking instances of its continued presence. In one of the world's most widely read books, Dr. Benjamin Spock describes the growth of the human infant in these terms:

> Each child as he develops is retracing the whole history of mankind, physically and spiritually, step by step. A baby starts off in the womb as a single tiny cell, just the way the first living thing appeared in the ocean. Weeks later, as he lies in the amniotic fluid in the womb, he has gills like a fish. Toward the end of his first year of life, when he learns to clamber to his feet, he's celebrating that period millions of years ago when man's ancestors got up off all fours. . . .[2]

In other words, during both its embryological and later development the individual child retraces the evolutionary history of the race. As Ernst Haeckel elegantly put it in his famous law, "ontogeny recapitulates phylogeny."[3]

Dr. Spock is by no means alone in espousing this doctrine; Arthur Jensen[4] and Jean Piaget explicitly adhere to a form of recapitulationism in their theories of development. However, Piaget offers some supporting arguments and introduces some modifications. Embryological development does not merely recapitulate phylogenesis, he states, for sometimes embryological events may themselves help to shape the path of further evolution. In a similar spirit he argues that characteristics displayed by the child may provide clues about adults from earlier historical periods or from contemporary primitive societies.[5] As he puts it in *Genetic Epistemology:*

> The fundamental hypothesis of genetic epistemology is that there is a parallelism between the progress made in the logical and rational organization of knowledge and the corresponding formative logical processes . . . . Of course the most fruitful, most obvious field of study would be reconstituting human history—the history of human thinking in prehistoric man. . . . Since this field of biogenesis is not available to us, we shall do as biologists do and turn to ontogenesis.[6]

In this respect Piaget is comparable to G. Stanley Hall, the pioneering figure in the history of the American child-study movement, who in 1909 wrote that "from

[2] Benjamin Spock, *Baby and Child Care* (New York: Pocket Books, 1963), p. 229.

[3] This law is discussed in J. F. Cleverley and D. C. Phillips, *From Locke to Spock* (Carlton South: Melbourne University Press, 1976), ch. 4, and also in Robert E. Grinder, *A History of Genetic Psychology* (New York: Wiley, 1967).

[4] Arthur R. Jensen, "Hierarchical Theories of Mental Ability," in *On Intelligence,* ed. W. Bryan Dockrell (London: Methuen, 1969), p. 143.

[5] Jean Piaget, *Biology and Knowledge* (Chicago: University of Chicago Press, 1971), p. 83.

[6] Jean Piaget, *Genetic Epistemology* (New York: Columbia University Press, 1970), p. 13.

one point of view, infancy, childhood and youth are three bunches of keys to un-lock the past history of the race."[7]

Hall and Piaget may be correct in assuming a relationship between the stages of ontogenesis and those of phylogenesis, but on the other hand there is no *a priori* reason to make this supposition. The processes of development of the in-dividual child and of evolutionary development of the human species are quite distinguishable. Thus, the notion of recapitulation which links the two is an em-pirical hypothesis, and it must be supported in some way by evidence. There are grounds, however, for believing that it lacks this backing. For one, the serious weaknesses of this notion were largely established over sixty years ago by E. L. Thorndike.[8] In William Kessen's words:

> Nothing much is left of this radical notion now.... The late nineteenth-century notion of parallels between animal and man remains in the academic literature only as a half joking reference.... [9]

However, Piaget, for one, is not joking. The recapitulation hypothesis has in-fluenced both his methodology and his approach to theory construction. For in-stance, the fact that Piaget regards the growth of logic in the child as paralleling the evolution of human intelligence is one of several reasons for his apparent lack of concern for the normal complexities of experimental research. Since the development of logic in all individuals is assumed to follow the pattern of the evolution of knowledge, then any child can be used to provide the data for his theory. Piaget's basic assumptions make it unnecessary for him to seek a larger data base.

Hierarchical Classification and Developmental Hierarchies

Paralleling the tendency to confuse or conflate ontogenetic and phylogenetic hierarchies is the tendency to posit a straightforward sequence—such as simple to complex—in which individual growth or development or learning takes place. It has been comforting to find this simple logic apparently widely reflected in other parts of nature. Such examples as "The Great Chain of Being," and later in evolu-tionary theory, conjectures about the development of human societies, and the

---

[7] Granville Stanley Hall, "Evolution and Psychology," in *Health, Growth and Heredity: G. Stanley Hall on Natural Education,* eds. Charles E. Strickland and Charles Burgess (New York: Teachers College Press, 1965), p. 47.

[8] Edward L. Thorndike, "Objections to the Theory of Recapitulation," rpt. in Robert E. Grinder, *A History of Genetic Psychology* (New York: Wiley, 1967).

[9] William Kessen, *The Child* (New York: Wiley, 1965), p. 116.

development pattern of the various intellectual disciplines, all attest to the appeal of straightforward sequences.

The central issues emerge with great clarity in the case of the eighteenth-century French naturalist Lamarck, who argued that reason supported the classification of animals that he had devised:

> If indeed it is true that all living bodies are productions of nature, we are driven to the belief that she can only have produced them one after another and not all in a moment. Now, if she shaped them one after another, there are grounds for thinking that she began exclusively with the simplest, and only produced at the very end the most complex organisations both of the animal and vegetable kingdoms.[10]

With some modernization of the language, this passage could well have come from a twentieth-century psychological treatise.

Lamarck's hierarchical classification of animals, ranging from the simplest to the most complex, embodied a second major assumption. He believed that a classificatory scheme should reflect the order in which the entities under consideration came into being. However, this is not mandatory. It is possible to classify or organize entities into a hierarchy that is based on some characteristic other than their order of creation—some structural or behavioral feature, for example. The fact is that if by some criterion of simplicity A is simpler than B and B is simpler than C, it is not necessarily the case that these three have been produced in the order A-B-C. It is quite feasible that they have been produced in some other order, say C-B-A. This possibility is illustrated by the case of the tapeworm which, according to modern evolutionary theory, is one of several relatively simple degenerate parasites that have evolved from structurally more complex precursors. Thus, if it is found that three entities were produced in the order X-Y-Z, it does not follow that X is simpler than Y or Z. Yet, the danger exists that the order of production will *become* the criterion of simplicity, making the whole analysis self-supportingly circular.

One area of psychology which provides a clear illustration of these points is the study of the structure of human intellectual abilities. Not all theories in this area are developmental or even hierarchical. For instance, Guilford distinguishes a number of independent abilities and places them in a classificatory matrix which does not refer to their order of development in either the individual or the spe-

---

[10] Jean-Baptiste de Lamarck, *Zoological Philosophy*, trans. Hugh Elliot (1809; rpt. New York: Hafner, 1963), p. 129.

cies.[11] Burt[12] and Vernon[13] have produced models which order human abilities in hierarchies going from specific to general, but which in essence are not developmental. Partly inspired by this work, Arthur Jensen[14] has produced a theory of intellectual abilities which involves a hierarchical classification of abilities from simple to complex, but he adds an explanation of the development of intelligence in terms of increasing complexity in intellectual processing.

A hierarchical classification of mental abilities from simple to complex may well be convenient and parsimonious, but Jensen extends his analysis to cover phylogenetic and ontogenetic hierarchies and produces a theory of development of Level I (simple or associative) and Level II (complex or conceptual) abilities. At the phylogenetic level Jensen envisages a hierarchy of abilities which is "best characterised in terms of increasing complexity of adaptive capabilities and increasing breadth of transfer of learning as we move from 'lower' to 'higher' organisms."[15] Furthermore, his analysis of child development, quite apart from encompassing the dubious recapitulation hypothesis, is made in terms of a hierarchical progression with "certain capabilities regularly preceding others in their order of appearance."[16] It is not surprising to find that he places simple associative abilities at the beginning of the developmental sequence and intelligence or abstract and conceptual abilities at the end.

Unlike Lamarck, but like other prominent students of individual differences, Jensen employs factor analysis rather than simple "reason" to develop his hierarchical classificatory scheme. The description of abilities which results from the use of factor analysis is determined by the method of analysis as well as by the tests and the subjects used. The theoretical interests of the investigator also play a role in shaping an interpretation of the material. Jensen overlooks difficulties here, and he does not seriously consider the possibility that other hierarchies (such as the hierarchy of generality proposed by Burt and Vernon, or a hierarchy of increasing economy in information processing, or increasing memory capacity) might adequately explain his data. And yet he does, in one place, admit that no one classification is "compelled by nature."[17] Considering the difficulties in attributing differences in performance between young and older children primarily

11 Joy P. Guilford, "Three Faces of Intellect," *American Psychologist*, 14 (1959), pp. 469–79.
12 Cyril Burt, *The Factors of the Mind* (London: University of London Press, 1940).
13 Phillip Vernon, *The Structure of Human Abilities* (New York: Wiley, 1950).
14 Jensen, p. 143.
15 Jensen, p. 140.
16 Jensen, p. 143.
17 Jensen, p. 130.

to differences in their ability to handle complex materials, Jensen's conclusion that a hierarchy of increasing intellectual complexity is involved in this development is hasty. There is a danger, as pointed out earlier, that the order of appearance of abilities in development will become the criterion of complexity.

Invariance Within Hierarchies

Those who construct developmental hierarchies are fond of maintaining that the order of appearance of the stages is invariant. At present there are no serious opposing theories which specify a number of developmental stages which the growing child can pass through in any order.

It is, of course, the term "invariant" that is troublesome. In one usage this has the force of an empirical concept; that is, none of the subjects considered in investigations of these theories have been found to depart significantly from whichever hierarchical pattern is under examination. An alternative usage implies that the regularity is somewhat more watertight; it is in some sense *necessary* that the stages occur in a particular order.

It is not always clear in which of these senses the term "invariant" is being used. Consider as an example Erik Erikson's schema covering the development of a "lasting ego-identity." The child is depicted as passing through eight stages, each of which normally adds a new quality (or set of qualities) to the ego through the child's "decisive encounters" with the people and the things constituting his or her environment.[18] As the growing child progresses up the hierarchy gaining new qualities, each of the ones previously gained continues to develop further. Erikson writes:

> What we must try to chart, then, is the approximate sequence of stages when according to clinical and common knowledge the nervous excitability as well as the coordination of the "erogeneous" organs and the selective reactivity of significant people in the environment are apt to produce decisive encounters.[19]

How are these stages to be discovered? Evidently by means of an eclectic set of techniques, although there can be little doubt that the main point of departure for Erikson's work was Freud's theory of sexuality, which depicted the individual as developing through the oral, anal and genital stages.[20] In neither theory do the earlier stages appear to be necessary precursors of the later ones: the oral is not

18 Erik Erikson, *Childhood and Society* (Harmondsworth: Penguin Books, 1970), ch. 7.
19 Erikson, pp. 61, 66.
20 Erikson's debt to Sigmund and Anna Freud is discussed in *Dialogue with Erik Erikson*, ed. Richard I. Evans (New York: Dutton, 1969).

part of the *meaning* of the anal or genital. It is not a conceptual confusion to speculate that the anal stage could come before the oral.

So if there are several possible paths by which a complex system can arrive at a given final state such as lasting ego-identity (systems theorists encapsulate this possibility in their principle of equifinality), then the fact that only one of these paths is used—if it is a fact—is interesting and calls for explanation. Simply to claim that this particular developmental path is necessary in some sense does not constitute an explanation. However, if a theory is forthcoming to account for development along a sole path, then *in this context* one stage along the path may be said to be necessary for the appearance of a later stage. But the theory must be genuinely explanatory; it cannot merely describe in new terms how development occurs along a particular path. The psychoanalytic theories that Erikson and Freud adduce to explain the pattern of development face serious difficulties here.

The theory of genetic programming has been put forward as another candidate. Certainly Gesell and, in a modified form, Jensen, assume a degree of genetic determination which could account for the necessary order of development. On the other hand, there are many theorists who place emphasis upon the environmental determinants of behavior or who hold an interactionist position, but who just as readily claim that there is an invariant order of stages. Robert Gagné and the Piagetians fall into this group.

Some psychologists have gathered experimental evidence in support of a necessary, invariant pattern of development without realizing that the higher-order capabilities of their hierarchies, or the tasks used to test them, have been defined in such a way as to incorporate lower-level tasks. Flavell and Wohlwill give one of the few discussions of this problem in the literature:

> The existence of these relations poses something of a conundrum for the developmental psychologist, however. We are accustomed to thinking of ourselves as students of nature, not of logic, and we seek to discover, rather than reason out, the developmental connections between acquisitions. If somebody predicts that a pair of acquisitions A and B emerge in a fixed and invariant order for all children, our immediate inclination is to want to test the prediction empirically. In the case of acquisitions linked by Implicative Mediation, however, it is hard to see any justification for any kind of empirical test.[21]

This issue of the mistaken empirical investigation of implicative or definitional or

[21] John H. Flavell and Joachim F. Wohlwill, "Formal and Functional Aspects of Cognitive Development," in *Studies in Cognitive Development*, eds. David Elkind and John H. Flavell (New York: Oxford University Press, 1969), p. 86.

conceptual linkages warrants further discussion. After all, the mistake is serious and is on a par with doing a survey to determine how many bachelors in San Francisco are unmarried—it can be known beforehand with certainty that all of them are in this condition.

Subject-Matter Hierarchies

As children grow, they may appear to move through an invariant sequence of stages marked by their ability to perform different tasks and master progressively more abstract subject matter. It is true that inferences about capabilities can be drawn only on the basis of performance of some specified tasks. But it is possible that, where individual growth is correlated with mastery of hierarchically-ordered subject material such as basic and higher mathematics, the stages of development of the child will be assumed to be identical with some such ordering of this material. But this assumption is fallacious; the ordering of subject matter provides very dubious evidence about the order of child development, particularly when the higher-order tasks within the subject field are constructed in such a way as to assume the presence of lower-level tasks. These points can be illustrated with reference to the work of Robert Gagné.

Gagné theorizes within the bounds of the behaviorist assumption that development is the sum total of learned experiences. The growth of the central nervous system is acknowledged, but is not explicitly included in the explanation of development. From this position Gagné moves to a hierarchical theory of development based on an analysis of subject matter. With reference to his eightfold classification of learning types, Gagné writes:

> Each of the eight varieties of learning conditions, whether it occurs more or less accidentally or is deliberately employed in formal instruction, establishes a different kind of capability in the learner. . . . But in all cases, the capability itself embodies an identifiable intellectual skill. . . . People do not learn in a general sense, but always in the sense of a change in behavior that can be described in terms of an observable type of human performance.[22]

Gagné has approached the problem of human learning and its contribution to development from the point of view of determining the prerequisites for specific learning tasks. Thus, item A might be a prerequisite for learning item B so that B can only be mastered after A; but then B itself may be a prerequisite for C, and C

---

22 Robert M. Gagné, *The Conditions of Learning,* 2nd ed. (London: Holt, Rinehart and Winston, 1973), p. 237.

for D, and so on in a hierarchical fashion. Gagné introduces his theory of pre-requisites for learning in the following way:

> From where does the student begin, and where is he going? What are the specific prerequisites for learning, and what will he be able to learn next? ... What is meant by "prerequisite" is not that fourth-grade social studies must precede fifth-grade social studies. Rather, the meaning is that learning to pronounce foreign words must precede learning to use them in sentences; or that learning to count numerically must precede learning to add numbers.[23]

The central issue is how such prerequisites of learning are to be identified: does some theory exist which can provide criteria for locating prerequisites? A cursory examination of Gagné's work might suggest that this is the case, for at times he writes as if the whole matter of hierarchies can be fruitfully treated in terms of transfer of learning:

> A learning hierarchy, then, identifies a set of intellectual skills that are ordered in a manner indicating substantial amounts of positive transfer from those skills of lower position to connected ones of higher position.[24]

Now, whether or not transfer of learning occurs in a given context is, as Gagné has said, a psychological question.[25] Thus, it is a problem which can be finally settled only by experimental evidence. Gagné has expended much effort making this point, often citing his own research as well as that of others.[26] In general, his experimental designs appear at first sight to parallel some that are used by biologists to study the stages of development of an embryo: a crucial set of cells is destroyed or manipulated in some way, and the effects of this change on subsequent development are observed. Gagné thus examines students who have mastered a higher-order task in a subject in order to ascertain if they have also mastered the necessary lower-order precursors. He also studies those students who have not mastered the lower-level tasks to see if they can successfully handle the higher-level one.

Unfortunately, there is a serious flaw in all this work, as becomes apparent when Gagné's ideas are considered in the context of a mathematical example:

> Determining the prerequisites for any given rule may be accomplished by asking the question, What would the student have to know how to do in order to be

23 Gagné, p. 26.
24 Gagné, p. 239.
25 Gagné, p. 203.
26 Gagné, pp. 206–07.

instructed in this rule? For example, if he is to learn rule IIc, "Identify and draw the intersection of lines or parts of lines taken two at a time, as more than one point," he must know the rules that govern the construction of lines (IVa) and intersections of sets of points (IVb) and also the rules pertaining to various parts of lines, including the line segment (IIIa), the ray (IIIb), and the half-line (IIIc). The reason is that the higher-order rule *incorporates* these other rules as a part of it. . . . [27]

The point is that experimentation is redundant here, for Gagné is focusing not on a psychological or contingent matter but on a conceptual (or, in a loose sense, a logical) one. And redundant is probably not the correct term either, for it is not simply that it is *unnecessary* to experiment. Experimentation is totally irrelevant; *whatever* results the experimentation turns up, it remains necessarily true that in order to be able to identify the intersection of two lines *as* an intersection of lines, one must first know what intersections and lines are.

To put the point another way, consider a skill X which is defined as "the ability to carry out operation A followed by operation B on material M." Experimentation is not the procedure to be followed here to determine whether or not it is the case that all individuals who can perform X can also perform A followed by B. The procedure to be followed is one akin to philosophical analysis, for it follows from the *meaning* of X that it involves the ability to perform A followed by B. Gagné comes close to appreciating this when he writes that "the rule or problem-solving task to be learned was analyzed into simpler capabilities that needed to be learned as prerequisites,"[28] but a page later he confuses the issue by stating that each "subordinate capability has been identified as such because it is known (or initially, hypothesized) to contribute positive transfer to the learning of the superordinate capability . . . ."[29]

This discussion helps to clarify other issues that can be found in the literature inspired by Gagné's work. In the first place, Gagné himself is pleased that he found strong evidence for the existence of certain hierarchies, as for instance, in the learning of mathematics.[30] It should now be apparent that he was bound to discover this for he was dealing with a conceptual truth. But of course Gagné does not realize this, and he sometimes makes the serious error of talking as if there was

[27] Gagné, p. 207.
[28] Gagné, pp. 237–38.
[29] Gagné, p. 239.
[30] Gagné, pp. 206–07.

only a *trend* for mastery of a higher element in the hierarchy to be related to mastery of lower elements.[31]

Another issue concerns the content of subject matter hierarchies. Gagné distinguishes between intellectual skills such as the ability to perform specific mathematical operations and the ability to recall facts; he is convinced of the validity of learning hierarchies for the former but expresses doubts about the latter.[32] There can be little question that Gagné is correct to have reservations here, and again his correctness can be appreciated without recourse to experimental evidence of the kind that Kolb and White have obtained.[33] Facts such as "the Battle of Hastings occurred in 1066" and "William the Conqueror defeated Harold in the Battle of Hastings" are not conceptually related in the way that the learning of skill X was related to the learning of skills A and B. It is simply not part of the *meaning* of "the Battle of Hastings" that it was fought in 1066 or that during it Harold was defeated by William the Conqueror—these are *facts* about the battle. At the present time there seems no good reason to believe that the learning of one fact (such as a statement embodying some facts concerning the year 1066) depends upon the mastery of some prior fact.

The final issue to be raised in connection with Gagné concerns the correct labeling of his theory. He regards this theory as falling within the province of psychology and his expositions of it are to be found in the journals of that discipline. However, the existence of Gagné's hierarchies of skills is not a psychological issue. They are not to be discovered by experiment but by an analysis of material within such subject-areas as mathematics and physics. The pursuer of Gagnéan hierarchies needs the skills and knowledge of a physicist or mathematician rather than those of a psychologist.

Conceptual Hierarchies

Unlike Gagné, Jensen does not assume that the abilities he describes in his hierarchical account of development are the result of specific learning. Rather, he sees Level I and Level II abilities as being genetically and independently determined. Neither does Jensen construct a hierarchy of tasks in the manner of Gagné. Nevertheless, his analysis of the hierarchical relationship between Level I and Level II abilities is flawed by similar conceptual confusions. He describes the abilities as follows:

[31] This is discussed in Richard White, "A Limit to the Application of Learning Hierarchies," *Australian Journal of Education*, 17 (June 1973), pp. 153–55.

[32] White, pp. 153–55.

[33] White, pp. 153–55.

If Level I phenotypes are defined by scores on digit span and laboratory measures of rote learning, and Level II is defined by scores on standard intelligence tests, particularly those with the highest g loading such as the Progressive Matrices, and by laboratory tasks involving conceptual learning and abstract problem solving, there is ample evidence that these two classes of tasks, Level I and Level II, are factorially distinct.[34]

This analysis is sound enough, but Jensen makes an assumption which confuses the issue and contradicts the claim that the abilities are independent. He assumes that the relation between the levels is such that Level I abilities are necessary, but not sufficient, for the attainment of Level II:

It also seems to make sense psychologically to suppose that basic learning and short term memory processes are involved in performance on a complex Level II task, such as the Progressive Matrices, although the complex inductive reasoning strategies called for by the matrices would not be called for in success in Level I tests such as digit span and serial rote learning.[35]

If Jensen is correct here, and a cursory analysis of his other Level I–Level II tasks such as forward and backward digit span seems to support his argument, then what is involved are not two separate types of ability, Level I (e.g. ability A) and Level II (e.g. ability C). Rather, the situation is that there is Level I (ability A) and Level II (abilities A + B = ability C). This being the case, it would not be at all surprising to find that subjects who do well on tests at Level II (A + B) also do well on tests at Level I (A), although the reverse need not be true: Level I is necessary for Level II but not vice-versa.

Piaget, Inhelder, and Kohlberg also maintain that development occurs in an invariant sequence of stages such that the lower levels are necessary for the occurrence of higher levels in the hierarchy. Piaget attempts to provide an account of the hierarchical development of logical structures from an interactionist position. He writes:

To characterize the stages of cognitive development we therefore need to integrate two necessary conditions without introducing any contradictions. These conditions for stages are (a) that they must be defined to guarantee a constant order of succession, and (b) that the definition allow for progressive construction without entailing total preformation.[36]

[34] Jensen, p. 166.
[35] Jensen, p. 159.
[36] Jean Piaget, "Piaget's Theory," in *Manual of Child Psychology*, ed. Paul H. Mussen, 3rd ed. (New York: Wiley, 1970), vol. 1, p. 710.

The claim that the stages "must be defined to guarantee a constant order of succession" is disturbing, for it implies that a guarantee of invariant order is written into the theory. Alternative orders are thus ruled out on an *a priori* basis. Other statements by Piaget on this question are ambiguous; it is not clear to what extent invariance is empirically or conceptually grounded:

> If we restrict ourselves to major structures, it is strikingly obvious that cognitive stages have a sequential property, that is, they appear in a fixed order of succession because each one of them is necessary for the formulation of the following one.[37]

This issue needs to be pursued in order to ascertain whether, in common with Gagné and Jensen, Piaget has proposed an implicative relationship between the levels of his developmental hierarchy.

One of the key properties of the Piagetian concept of hierarchy is the dialectic of progressive differentiation and integration which operates both between and within stages:

> overall structures are integrative and non-interchangeable. Each results from the preceding one, integrating it as a subordinate structure, and prepares for the subsequent one, into which it is sooner or later itself integrated.[38]

The processes of restructuring and coordination which characterize integration have been most fully described by Piaget in terms of the coordinations which occur at the sensorimotor stage. Looking and listening are coordinated into "things heard," which is in turn a subordinate level in various means-end relationships, and so on.

It is of course an essential property that coordination cannot occur between subordinate levels until they are present in the child's repertoire of responses. If, in determining the prerequisites for a particular coordination, the levels are defined in a way that implies the presence of the subordinates, then it is a logical rather than an empirical matter that C follows the emergence of A and B. There may, however, be scope for research to ascertain whether A precedes B or B precedes A, or if they occur simultaneously.

In addition, Piaget's account of development marks out four broad stages (the sensorimotor, preoperational, concrete operational, and formal operational stages) such that integration results in a significant shift in the child's logic when transition from one stage to the next occurs. This shift is sometimes so dramatic that,

37 Piaget, "Piaget's Theory," p. 711.
38 Jean Piaget and Barbel Inhelder, *The Psychology of the Child,* trans. Helen Weaver (New York: Basic Books, 1973), p. 153.

for example, the change from preoperational to concrete operational thought results in qualitatively different processes of reasoning. Indeed, writers such as Flavell and Wohlwill have been inclined to characterize this dramatic shift as a substitution hierarchy in which concrete operations supersede preoperational thought.[39]

Piaget maintains that the order of development through the four stages is invariant:

> A stage system of this kind . . . makes up a sequential process: it is not possible to arrive at "concrete" operations without undergoing some sensorimotor preparation (which explains why, for example, blind people, having badly coordinated action schema, may be retarded). It is also impossible to progress to propositional operations without support from previous concrete operations, etc.[40]

There seems to be no escape from the conclusion that Piaget's "invariance" is a mixture of the necessary and the empirical. While his famous empirical case studies have failed to produce examples of children whose behavior deviates from the hierarchical sequence, it is apparent that he is claiming much more than this: it is *impossible* to operate at one level without having been through the preceding levels.

As an illustration of the ambiguous mixture of the necessary and the empirical that has been built into Piaget's theory, consider the case of transitive inference. If A is greater than B (in some respect such as weight), and B is greater than C, then A is greater than C. If a child could not solve a problem using this mode of inference in a concrete case, then Piaget would likely predict that he or she would be unable to solve a variety of problems using this mode, let alone be able to solve abstract transitive problems. On the one hand, it is possible for this prediction to be made on *a priori* grounds, for it could then become part of what is *meant* by using a mode of reasoning in abstract cases that simple, concrete cases must have been mastered first. It will be recalled that Jensen's Level II abilities (such as A + B) were a similar case, for they included Level I abilities (such as A) as a necessary, but not sufficient, condition. On the other hand, it is possible to interpret abstractness and concreteness in such a way that one must not necessarily occur before the other—the possibility can be left open that a mode of reasoning in abstract cases could be mastered before concrete instances were met. (After all, blind people can learn to master color concepts—"red and yellow give orange,"

[39] Flavell and Wohlwill, p. 85.
[40] Piaget, *Biology and Knowledge*, p. 18.

"red is a warm color," and so on—without having met concrete instances of these concepts.)

Yet another possibility is that one stage must occur before another, not because it has been defined in this way, but because Piaget's general theory provides an overarching framework from which a certain order of stages can be shown to follow. While it could be argued that Piaget's self-regulation model aspires to take on this overarching role, in its present state of development it does not provide a satisfactory explanation of invariant order. It is difficult to imagine how it could be shown that assimilation, accommodation, and equilibration do not affect development, since their presence is inferred from the very behaviors they purport to explain. Furthermore, it is not sufficient to claim as Piaget does that "such equilibration processes, such self-regulations . . . yield necessities . . . . "[41] As Jerome Bruner has written:

> It is not the rather easy conception of equilibrium-dis-equilibrium that has contributed to our understanding of growth. . . . What is overwhelmingly important is the utility and power of his descriptive work. But in no sense does this formal description constitute an explanation or a psychological description of the processes of growth.[42]

Lawrence Kohlberg, following Piaget, believes that cognitive stages are real entities, not descriptive fictions, and that their order is invariant. In his paper "Cognitive Stages and Preschool Education," he attempts to support his belief with evidence drawn from his research on dreams. Kohlberg informs his readers that there is a hierarchy of six stages in the development of the concept of a dream. First, children come to realize that the objects in the dream are not physically present; then they recognize that dream objects are invisible to others; third, they recognize that the dream comes from inside themselves; then they see that it also goes on inside them; fifth, they realize that dream objects are thoughts; and finally they realize that dreams are self-created by their own thoughts and are not imposed from without.[43]

The empirical evidence to which Kohlberg appeals in order to show that the order is invariant falls far short of establishing his conclusion. Ninety children were questioned about their dreams, with the dual aims of establishing where they were located within the six-stage hierarchy and whether or not they had

41 Jean Piaget, *Structuralism* (London: Routledge and Kegan Paul, 1971), p. 90.
42 Jerome S. Bruner, *Toward a Theory of Instruction* (New York: Norton, 1968), p. 7.
43 Lawrence Kohlberg, "Cognitive Stages and Preschool Education," *Human Development*, 9 (1966), p. 7.

passed through all the stages prior to their present one. Kohlberg reproduces a few protocols to illustrate the technique, among them an interview with four-and-a-half-year-old Stevie:

> (Where does the dream come from? Where are dreams made, where do they come from?)
>
> "I don't know."
>
> (Do they come from within you or from outside of you?)
> "From inside your eyeball."
>
> (Who makes the dreams come forth? Is it you or somebody else?)
> "Your sister."
>
> (While you are dreaming, where is your dream, where does it go or what place is it in?)
>
> "It's in your eyeball. Then it comes out."[44]

From this interview, Kohlberg concludes that Stevie is past stage 3 (dreams have an internal origin) but has not reached stage 6 (dreams are not self-caused). The reader starts to wonder about the interviews Kohlberg has not reprinted, especially since he reports that "only" in eighteen of the ninety cases do children appear to have been at a higher stage of the hierarchy without having yet attained one of the lower stages. Although these eighteen cases are 20 percent of his sample, Kohlberg asserts that his evidence establishes that the order of attaining the concept of a dream is invariant! It is of course possible to argue that the measurement was faulty and that if it were improved invariance would be established. However, the other alternative—that the situation is one of variance rather than invariance—is an equally viable explanation.[45]

The other interesting thing about this "dream hierarchy" is its complete lack of surprise: it is precisely what one would expect. When it is realized that the objects you have been dreaming about are not present in the room, then you might think they are like television pictures—immaterial but visible to others. But if they were not seen, then they must have been both immaterial and internal. And so the logic unfolds; the stages reflect the common-sense order in which one would form, test, and refute the possible hypotheses, moving steadily toward the conception

---

44 Kohlberg, "Cognitive Stages," p. 8.
45 A discussion of the issues involved in assessing invariance of stages is given by William Kurtines and Esther G. Greif, "The Development of Moral Thought and Evaluation of Kohlberg's Approach," *Psychological Bulletin*, 81, No. 8 (1974), pp. 433–70.

of dreams held by adults within one's culture. This is simply following what Sir Karl Popper called the method of conjectures and refutations.[46] Why then does Kohlberg refuse to say this? Why does he maintain that the order is invariant, which implies that it *could not* be different? As he writes:

> The concept of stage implies an invariance of sequence in development, a regularity of stepwise progression regardless of cultural teaching or circumstance. Cultural teaching and experience can speed up or slow down development but it cannot change its order or sequence.[47]

Hierarchies and Experience

As children move through the hierarchy of developmental stages, their stock of experience is continually increasing. There is a possibility, then, that their development can be explained along the lines pioneered by the philosopher John Locke in the closing years of the seventeenth century.

In *An Essay Concerning Human Understanding,* Locke pictured the newborn child as a blank tablet totally devoid of ideas. Only experience could be the source of simple ideas, he argued, and all complex ideas were compounded from these simple elements. Locke's work suggested that if a child were studied over a period of time, the development of all of that child's ideas could be traced from their origins in sensory experience. Indeed, this is what Dietrich Tiedemann attempted to do in his historic study of 1787.[48] Locke's essay also raised the possibility that the pattern of individual development will vary across the population, as individuals are likely to have different trains of experience and different innate abilities to bring to bear upon their simple ideas. This possibility was developed along socially egalitarian lines by Locke's intellectual descendants, including Condillac and Helvetius in pre-revolutionary France.[49] They believed that if the key factor in human development was experience, then men could be re-educated so that inequalities arising from disparate early experiences would be eliminated —man would be perfectible through education.[50]

This general view, which relates development to a continuing stream of experience, is one which has both strong supporters and opponents in the modern

[46] Karl Popper, *Conjectures and Refutations,* 2nd ed. (London: Routledge and Kegan Paul, 1965).

[47] Kohlberg, "Cognitive States," p. 6.

[48] Suzanne Langer and Carl Murchison, "Tiedemann's Observations on the Development of the Mental Faculties of Children," *Pedagogical Seminary and Journal of Genetic Psychology,* 34, No. 2 (June 1927), pp. 205–30.

[49] Cleverley and Phillips, ch. 2.

[50] John Passmore, *The Perfectibility of Man* (London: Duckworth, 1970), especially chs. 8–9.

world. On the one hand, the behaviorist school stresses the role of the environment. Founding father John B. Watson even went so far as to claim:

> The behaviorists believe that there is nothing from within to develop. If you start with a healthy body, the right number of fingers and toes, eyes, and the few elementary movements that are present at birth, you do not need anything else in the way of raw material to make a man, be that man a genius, a cultured gentleman, a rowdy, or a thug.[51]

In *Science and Human Behavior*, B. F. Skinner argues that "operant conditioning shapes behavior as a sculptor shapes a lump of clay."[52]

Jerome Bruner is nearer the middle ground. He recognizes that development is not an unbroken incremental process but takes place in a step-like series of stages. Influences from outside the developing child are so crucial that unless a theory of development is linked to both a theory of knowledge and of instruction, it is bound to be trivial.[53]

On the other hand there is Piaget, who has commented that the "excellent psychologist, J. Bruner, has gone so far as to state that you can teach anything to any child at any age if only you set about it in the right way."[54] Piaget rejects this, his first reason being that as development takes place in several major steps, there are certain things that are beyond the grasp of a child until the earliest of these steps have been surmounted. However, he also holds that experience—the influence of the outside environment—"does not explain everything." Piaget argues that:

> Some of the concepts which appear at the beginning of the stage of concrete operations are such that I cannot see how they could be drawn from experience.[55]

The example he gives concerns the concept of substance. Consider a child who has rolled a ball of plasticene into a sausage shape and who is asked if it now has the same amount of material, the same weight, and the same volume as before. Piaget found that at about the age of eight the child will answer that there is the same amount of plasticene. Some time later the child realizes that weight is conserved; and at still a later age, that volume is conserved. Here then is a paradox:

---

[51] John B. Watson, *Psychological Care of Infant and Child* (London: Allen and Unwin, 1928), pp. 25–26.
[52] B. F. Skinner, *Science and Behavior* (New York: Free Press, 1965), p. 91.
[53] Bruner, p. 21. See also pages 7 and 27.
[54] Piaget, *Biology and Knowledge*, p. 20.
[55] Jean Piaget, "Development and Learning," in *Readings in Child Behavior and Development*, eds. Celia S. Lavatelli and Faith Stendler, 3rd ed. (New York: Harcourt, Brace Jovanovich, 1972), p. 40.

the child is first able to conserve substance, but as yet has no conception of constancy of weight or volume—both of which are prerequisites for any empirical derivation of constancy of the former.

> So I would ask you where the idea of the conservation of substance can come from. What is a constant and invariant substance when it doesn't yet have a constant weight or a constant volume? ... No experiment, no experience, can show the child that there is the same amount of substance. ... He knows that something is conserved but he doesn't know what. It is not yet the weight, it is not yet the volume; it is simply a logical form—a logical necessity.[56]

It is a pity that the whole argument is built upon the flimsy basis of several eight-year-old plasticene modelers remarking that "there is the same amount of plasticene," for it is evident that the children conserved plasticene, not substance. Piaget, with adult insight, realizes that plasticene is a substance and if substance is conserved during changes of shape, then both weight and volume will be conserved. But perhaps the children believed the same amount of plasticene was present because they knew that none had either been removed or added.[57] Certainly the shape of the plasticene had been changed; yet to a child who does not define substance in the manner of a scientifically knowledgeable adult, it may not be significant that some other features may also have changed. In more sophisticated terms, it is possible that weight or volume are functions of shape or length. After all, it must be remembered that it was with hypotheses of this sort that the great early scientist Archimedes was concerned. It might be the case that it is only when children have their attention drawn to this set of problems that they start to notice things which are relevant to the growth of their knowledge. Again, in Sir Karl Popper's terms, they start to make conjectures and then refute them by observations and simple experiments[58]—which of course are partly a function of experience. An older child, with more experience, has had an opportunity to refute more false hypotheses and advance nearer to the truth than has a younger child.

This discussion is not aimed at proving that Piaget is wrong, but it is intended to show that rival explanations of the phenomena are possible. Neither of the arguments offered by Piaget is sufficient to establish that development, even though it may occur in a hierarchy of discrete stages, cannot be explained solely in terms of the ever-increasing stock of experience of the growing child.

[56] Piaget, "Development and Learning," p. 40.

[57] John Wilson refers to Piaget's example of conservation when discussing the distinction between conceptual and empirical truths, *Philosophy and Educational Research* (Buckinghamshire: National Foundation for Educational Research in England and Wales, 1972), pp. 15–16.

[58] Popper, *Conjectures and Refutations.*

Lawrence Kohlberg, writing from what purports to be a Piagetian perspective, has carried the discussion further. He reports on several experiments aimed at establishing whether specific training is effective in teaching children conservation concepts, and whether intelligent children can conserve such properties as weight earlier than others:

> Our interpretation is not that Piaget's stages represent age-fixed maturational unfoldings independent of psychometric ability but that cognitive-structural development depends upon massive general experience, a requirement which the "innately" bright child cannot short circuit.[59]

This conclusion is not quite as exciting as it first seems, for Kohlberg admits that specific instances of conservation can be taught; but by conservation he means something much more general:

> This constitutes the root meaning of the notion of cognitive structure. If the child has developed a concept of conservation, we expect that he will not lose it even in the face of contrary stimulation or social pressure. We also expect that he will invoke or apply the concept under conditions appropriate to the meaning of the concept rather than in terms of situational and sensory parameters extraneous to its meaning.[60]

If knowledge of conservation in this wide sense is not innate, then it certainly would be acquired only after a massive amount of experience or a great deal of teaching. Kohlberg is thus right almost by definition. On the other hand, he is surely wrong to expect an unshakeable faith in such things as conservation; empirical notions must always be subject to change in the light of fresh experience, and the community of practitioners of science have considerable influence over the conceptual apparatus of particular individuals, as Thomas Kuhn and others have shown.[61]

However, for Kohlberg as well as for Piaget, "massive general experience" is not enough to explain the hierarchical pattern of human development. Kohlberg argues that if the child passes through several significantly different intellectual stages, then his development cannot result directly from adult teaching, for other-

[59] Lawrence Kohlberg, "Early Education: A Cognitive Developmental View," in *Readings in Child Behavior and Development*, eds. Celia S. Lavatelli and Faith Stendler, 3rd ed. (New York: Harcourt, Brace Jovanovich, 1972), p. 508. Similar points are made in Lawrence Kohlberg and Rochelle Mayer, "Development as the Aim of Education," *Harvard Educational Review*, 42 (1972), especially pp. 455–59.

[60] Kohlberg, "Early Education," p. 509.

[61] Thomas S. Kuhn, *Structure of Scientific Revolutions* (Chicago: University of Chicago Press, 1963).

wise he should mirror adult thought patterns from the beginning. Moreover, if the "quantity" of experience was the only significant difference between the child and the adult, then it would be expected that the child's intellectual structure would be similar to that of the adult and differ from it only in its incompleteness. However, as the child's intellectual structure does seem to be qualitatively different from that of the adult, and as this structure apparently is the same for all children, then

> . . . it is extremely difficult to view the child's mental structure as a direct learning of the external structure. Furthermore, if the adult's mental structure depends upon sequential transformations of the child's mental structure, it, too, cannot directly reflect the current structure of the outer cultural or physical world.[62]

This is a good line of argument, but it does not quite succeed. Again, this is not necessarily to say that the conclusions are wrong, but the grounds Kohlberg offers are not conclusive. For the first part of his argument to be persuasive, it has to be established that in their teaching, adults—and parents in particular—actually concentrate on structure, basic logical patterns, and the rules governing formation and use of concepts. Unless they do, it would be no surprise that children do not immediately acquire this structure, and it cannot be concluded that it is impossible for them to acquire it if it were to be taught to them. Common experience would appear to refute Kohlberg here. Adults normally teach such things as "this is plasticene" and "this is a glass of water," but they do not usually teach abstract concepts such as substance, mass, and volume (including its conservation through changes of shape, as measured by the method of displacement). They may point out to their youngsters that plasticene can be changed from a ball shape into a sausage or that water can be poured from a vessel of one shape into another, but they rarely add to the lesson that the law of conservation of matter holds—for the very good reason that a three- or four-year-old will not be particularly interested in this. And of course the child would first need to be taught what the concepts of law, matter, and conservation entail.

The remainder of Kohlberg's argument fares even worse. He is not correct in assuming that qualitatively different stages of development cannot be accounted for solely in terms of the child having had less experience than the adult. The nineteenth-century associationists, for example, compared the accumulation of sensory experience (or rather, the ideas arising from this experience) with the combining of atoms into molecules having new, qualitatively different or emergent

---

[62] Kohlberg, "Early Education," p. 506.

properties, as for example, the combination of hydrogen and oxygen to form water.[63] This "mental chemistry," as it became known, was therefore able to account for the sudden appearance of complex conceptions which were qualitatively different from their precursors. This theory certainly has its problems, but they are not dealt with by the assertion that there is an invariant hierarchy of stages of development. Finally, Kohlberg's ultimate conclusion, that if the thought patterns of adults are arrived at through a sequence of stages then these patterns cannot be regarded as matching reality in some way, seems entirely spurious. The question of the origin of man's ideas (which includes the question of the pattern of their development) is one thing, and the question of the validity of these ideas is quite another.

If Kohlberg, together with Piaget, rejects experience as the sole force shaping individual development, what is substituted in its place? In a word: interaction. The growing child, with his developing neural machinery, is interacting with his environment and is thus undergoing experience. But the physical and social entities within the environment have a structure themselves which may exert a crucial influence, and the concepts necessary for adequate dealings with these entities may be complex and may only be formed after some logically necessary simpler concepts have been formed. Furthermore, children's intellectual structures may only develop if they notice some discrepancy between their current concepts and the experiences they are undergoing. Therefore, developmental theorists who hold an interactionist conception must indulge in three types of analysis: they must perform a structural analysis of the items constituting the environment, they must perform a logical analysis of concepts, and they must analyze the degree of discrepancy between the "child's action system or expectancies and the experienced event."[64] Perhaps it is no accident, then, that Piaget uses the techniques of modern logic and is also a structuralist in the contemporary holistic sense of this term. Yet it is interesting to note the conclusion of Kohlberg's discussion: "While these three modes of analysis are foreign to the habits of associationistic learning theorists, they are not totally incompatible in principle with them."[65]

Summary and Conclusion

Hierarchical theories of development will not be particularly useful frameworks

---

[63] Excerpts from the relevant associationists are reprinted in Jean J. Mandler and George Mandler, eds., *Thinking: From Association to Gestalt* (New York: Wiley, 1964).

[64] Kohlberg, "Early Education," pp. 506–07.

[65] Kohlberg, "Early Education," p. 507.

for research if the relationship between the levels is an implicative one, that is, if by definition the higher levels presuppose the existence of the lower ones. Related to this is the question of whether or not the order of appearance of the stages is invariant, for this, too, can be effectively closed to research.

In these respects, the major developmental theories discussed in this paper appear to be less than satisfactory. Failure to remove implicative relationships renders experimental work unnecessary; it is bound to confirm the theory for there is no possibility of falsification. As the writings of Karl Popper have indicated, it is a serious mistake to regard the apparent certainty of a theory as a sign of scientific strength.

Both variance and invariance in the order of appearance of behaviors are interesting phenomena worthy of investigation and both warrant genuine scientific explanation. In this context, to hold that the order is not only invariant but that it is also necessary is puzzling: a hierarchical theory is not a better theory simply because it asserts that the order of appearance of the stages is a necessary rather than an empirical matter. Such an assertion will most likely be made in the context of some overarching theory of the determinants of behavior.

Theorists arguing from the genetic, environmentalist, and interactionist positions have similar views on invariance, which is surprising in view of the different roles they assign to experience in affecting the course of development. Experience can be extremely variable from one person to another, though there may well be some cultural uniformities in the rate of presentation and overall patterning of a child's experience. To hold that the stages of development must occur in a fixed order, it must also be held that a child could not be affected by a different pattern of experience. In that case, some reasons would need to be forthcoming to account for this rigidity on the part of the child. Piagetian structuralism is by far the most elaborate attempt to maintain both an interactionist position and a necessary hierarchy of stages. Without postulating genetic predetermination, however, it falls short of resolving all the problems.

It may well be unfair to claim that developmental theories are part folklore and part science, but it is not unfair to point out that a good many of the assumptions that have crept into modern developmental psychology are dubious. William Kessen has perhaps made the best diagnosis of the ills that beset the field, and it is interesting to note that he comes close to agreeing with Mao:

> The defining problem of cognitive development is to comprehend how an organism of a particular kind, in encounters with phenomena defined in a particular way, constructs the world. For a task of this range, it is not possible to duck the

specification of philosophical—particularly epistemological—underpinnings for a psychological theory. The danger that our conclusions about the development of human knowledge may derive in large measure from the preconceptions of the nature of man and the nature of reality that we stuffed—or worse, let slip—into our initial construction of the psychological task (a danger that I believe to be clear and present in all current attempts to understand cognitive development) requires that we take a long uncomfortable look at our governing presuppositions.[66]

---

[66] William Kessen, "Questions for a Theory of Cognitive Development," in *Concept of Development: Monographs of the Society for Research in Child Development*, ed. Harold W. Stevenson, 31, No. 5 (1966), p. 61.

Education for Cognitive Development

ROBERT SELMAN
Harvard University

In this review of Thinking Goes to School, *Robert Selman critiques the attempt by Furth and Wachs to develop a program of elementary education based on Piaget's theory of cognitive development. To set the Furth and Wachs effort in context, Selman first considers the educational implications that can be derived from Piagetian theory and then considers the degree of congruency between the Furth and Wachs program and the theory. Selman also describes a primary school curriculum that he and his colleagues developed from their work on the development of children's social reasoning.*

THINKING GOES TO SCHOOL: PIAGET'S THEORY IN PRACTICE
by Hans Furth and Harry Wachs.
New York: Oxford University Press, 1974. 296 pp. $8.95.

Although it is commonly recognized that children see the world differently than adults, it is less obvious that children are not simply ignorant or unaware of certain facts about the world, but that they have their own original theories and interpretations of the social and physical events in their lives. Children structure their experience; each general restructuring or reorganization of experience can be conceptualized as a stage of cognitive development.

About fifteen years ago the impact of these ideas, which were made more precise by the Swiss psychologist and philosopher Jean Piaget, penetrated the circles of psychology in this country. Structural-developmental psychology has since become a highly respected, although controversial, approach to the scientific study of cognition and knowledge. The basic principle of this theory is that it is useful to think of the child's reasoning process as developing through an ordered, knowable, universal sequence of stages.

The flurry of intellectual excitement and discovery which marks the emergence of a new approach has by and large subsided. However, in the realm of social and educational implications, structural-developmental theory still generates controversy. With regard to social development, whether the Piagetian approach is applicable to the whole child, not just to his cognitive behavior, is hotly debated. In education, debate focuses on whether the very nature of Piagetian-type stages makes them impervious to outside influence or stimulation, and hence to educational intervention. These two closely related issues are the subject of concern for many American psychologists, particularly for

Harvard Educational Review Vol. 45 No. 1 February 1975, 127–134.

those concerned with the practical or educational application of the theory, and the implications of Piagetian theory for social development and educational practice. In this review, I will deal with these issues in two ways: first, by considering the attempt of Hans Furth and Harry Wachs to develop a program of social and cognitive elementary education based on Piaget's developmental principles; second, by briefly describing our own approach to these issues as a partial alternative to their approach.

Furth and Wachs's book, *Thinking Goes to School: Piaget's Theory in Practice,* is one of a deluge of attempts to apply Piagetian theory to education.[1] Cognitive-developmental approaches to science education, preschool education and moral education are now joined by Furth and Wachs's popular attempt to encompass all aspects of the elementary years of schooling. Up to now the impetus for educational application of developmental psychology has come not from educators but from psychologists themselves, most of whom have done basic research within the developmental framework. For example, Lawrence Kohlberg views the Piagetian approach as a restatement of Dewey's progressive education but with a firmer grounding in empirical method. Kohlberg argues that the Piaget-Dewey philosophy is the axis around which American education should rotate.[2]

To the extent that psychologists have shown their ability to interpret Piaget accurately, this is a potentially valuable trend. The danger lies in the potential naiveté of the developmental psychologist turned educator when it comes to implementation.

Two basic questions need to be asked of each new wave in developmental educa-

tion. First, how adequately is Piaget's developmental descriptive theory reinterpreted as an educational theory applicable to planned intervention? Second, how carefully thought out and how useful to teaching is the educational program which purports to use a Piagetian approach? These concerns guide this critique of the Furth and Wachs book.

In order to examine the first question, let us introduce some of the distinctive characteristics of Piaget's theory. Piaget has posited the following characteristics for stage-development theory:

1. The existence of *stages* implies distinct or qualitative differences in children's modes of thinking or of solving the same problem.

2. These different modes of thought form a *universal and invariant sequence,* order, or succession in individual development. While cultural factors may speed up, slow down, or stop development, they do not change its sequence.

3. Each of these different and sequential modes of thought forms a *structural whole.* A given stage-response on a task does not just represent a specific response determined by knowledge and familiarity with that task or tasks similar to it; rather it represents an underlying thought-organization.

4. Cognitive stages are *hierarchical integrations.* Stages form an order of increasingly differentiated and integrated structures to fulfill a common function.

These characteristics clearly have import for the application of Piaget's developmental theory to the field of education. For example, if Piagetian stages form an invariant sequence, we know that a child whose reasoning is generally concrete operational across a wide range of problems may be ready to move to formal operations. If our educational aim is to further the child's cognitive ability in the logical domain, our job is to develop activities with which the child can interact so that he may construct for himself the more adequate formal mode of reasoning. Simi-

---

[1] See, for example, Milton Schwebel and Jane Raph, *Piaget in the Classroom* (New York: Basic Books, 1973).
[2] Lawrence Kohlberg, "Development as the Aim of Education," *Harvard Educational Review,* 42 (November 1972), pp. 449-496.

larly, the assumption of structural whole-ness is important to the significance of Piaget's theory for education. If a child responds to one particular problem with formally operational thought, that in and of itself is of limited significance. But if the child's formally operational response to a specific problem generally indicates the child's thought organization (as the assumption of structural wholeness im-plies), this is far more significant. In other words, the assumption of structural wholeness implies that a Piagetian mea-sure of logical reasoning has great predic-tive power from the problem at hand to other problems in the logical reasoning realm.

Some observers have been skeptical of the possibilities of reinterpreting Piage-tian developmental theory in terms of educational practice. For example, given that Piagetian stages represent a universal and invariant sequence in the develop-ment of cognition, some critics ask why something which will develop anyway should be taught. In fact, they ask whether one can teach or accelerate the emergence of developmental concepts or abilities at all.[3] Furth and Wachs respond by noting that it is necessary to examine the role of variability in this theory. (Universality of sequence does not imply that advance-ment through stages is predetermined. Experience plays a critical part in concep-tual stage development. One way to clarify the role of experience within a theory of universal stage development is to recog-nize that certain forms of experience are universal across cultures; for example, the experience of a dropped ball falling or of people having social relations. Yet al-though these forms of experience are cul-turally universal, individuals do not ex-

perience them in a predetermined man-ner. The provision of certain facilitating experiences can help children progress through a developmental sequence. The number and kind of experiences have an important effect on the rate and extent of development. Research, including Furth's previous study of deaf and blind chil-dren,[4] supports the hypothesis of univer-sality of logical thought sequence, while also sustaining the hypothesis of variabil-ity in rate of stage development. Finally, within each individual there is variation in level of reasoning depending on the con-cept or domain reasoned about. These as-pects of structural developmental theory bear directly on education, indicating the potential of intervention using a Piagetian framework. Furth and Wachs argue co-gently for the applicability of the theory.

Perhaps the most compelling implica-tion of Piaget's theory for education is that it supports an argument that some stages of thinking are more adequate than others, both philosophically and psychologically, and seeks to trace the development of these stages. But not all knowledge is sub-sumed under stage analysis. Furth and Wachs make a distinction between "Piage-tian development" as representative of ac-tive thought or of reasoning process and "learning" as representative of basic fact or skill acquisition. They then introduce the concepts of high- versus low-level reasoning, relative to the child's own stage of development, to stress that activities need to stimulate thinking at a high-level. The teacher's task is to present activities with which each child can naturally in-teract and which can stimulate the child to move to the next level.

Furth and Wachs also outline the educa-tional implications of Piaget's concept of décalage which refers to an individual's operating at different cognitive stages at different times or in different realms.

---

[3] Siegfried Engelmann, "Does the Piagetian Approach Imply Instruction?" in *CTB/McGraw-Hill Conference on Ordinal Scales of Cog-nitive Development, Monterey, Calif. and Carmel, Calif. 1969, Measurement and Piaget,* ed. Donald Ross Green, Marguerite P. Ford, and George P. Flamer (New York: McGraw Hill, 1971), pp. 118-127.

[4] Hans G. Furth and James Youniss, "Think-ing in Deaf Adolescents: Language and Formal Operations," *Journal of Communication Disorders,* 2 (1969), pp. 195-202.

This concept is often employed in a defensive manner by some followers of Piaget to explain away differences in the way an individual reasons across various Piagetian tasks. In light of the assumed structural wholeness of stages, some might expect more homogeneity in level of reasoning. But the principle of structural wholeness does not demand absolute homogeneity within the child. The claim of structured wholeness refers to a common structure that can be used to analyze the child's reasoning across a range of categories of experience. It does not mean that a given child functions at a given stage across all experiences. Structured wholeness refers to the nature of reasoning in general, not to the state of a given child. While we would not expect the child's thinking to vary widely across stages on different tasks, it is natural to expect reasoning to vary across adjacent stages on tasks of greater or lesser difficulty.

Given this interpretation of structural wholeness and décalage, Furth and Wachs begin with the common-sense observation that the child does not think at a uniform level, either across all tasks or on the same type of task at different times. Reasoning is an interaction between the level of the thinker and the level of difficulty of that thought about. The implication is that the activity should have flexibility over time and across a range of levels. Thinking games or activities should not have right and wrong solutions—they should have more or less adequate solutions. From these theoretical principles, Furth and Wachs generate the following educational guidelines:

1. an emphasis on thinking as development, not as learned facts;
2. a need for specific and structured activities, each of which has flexibility for manipulation at a number of levels of interaction;
3. the stimulation of reason, through challenge, to the higher levels of reasoning;
4. a child-task orientation rather than child-teacher orientation;
5. peer-group interaction, particularly in social areas, as stimulation for intellectual conflict and therefore for growth.

These guidelines are described in the first five chapters of *Thinking Goes to School*. Most of the remaining nine chapters of the book are an elaboration of how guidelines can be implemented; they contain specific examples of activities designed to stimulate thinking across sensori-motor, logical and social domains. The authors express a fear that teachers may follow these examples in a cookbook fashion, without perceiving developmental potential in other activities. My fear is that neither the authors nor the tasks on the whole accurately communicate to the uninitiated reader the nature of true developmental activities or curriculum. Developmental activities are not as easy to devise as the authors imply, and seldom do Furth and Wachs clearly describe a method for doing so.

Many of the thinking activities prescribed in *Thinking Goes to School* will be recognized by learning disability teachers as part of their established techniques—reading readiness, movement and kinesthetic coordination, visual-, auditory- and haptic-motor training—but these are not necessarily developmental in the Piagetian sense. In a true Piagetian stage-development sequence, subsequent stages are dependent on previous ones; all children go through the stages in the same order and without skipping stages; and each stage represents a qualitative advance over the previous one. Although Furth and Wachs describe each of their suggested tasks with variations that make them seem logically harder or easier, seldom do the authors specify how a child's interactions with a task represent a specific level of thinking. Nor do they specify how a progression in a certain activity necessitates a higher level of reasoning, beyond the fact that the more difficult activity described is self-evidently more complex. For example, the authors describe three "stages" in a balance-board activity, part of movement and kinesthetic coordination (pp. 101-106). The child develops "side balance" by standing on one side of a balance board while the teacher exerts pressure on the other side. Then the child develops "front-back balance" by standing in front and compensating for pressure applied to the back. Finally, the child straddles the board and balances it by himself to gain bilateral balance. Although it may be evident that each so-called stage consists of a more difficult activity, it is hard to see what is uniquely Piagetian about this development. How does the subsequent stage derive from the prior one? Do all children learn side balance before front-back balance? Is front-back balance necessary to bilateral balance? Does anyone ever learn bilateral balance first? These questions are unasked and unanswered. Furthermore, this is not really a task with which children can independently interact at their own level and strive to the next, but a series of tasks of greater difficulty set up and varied by the teacher. The concept of stage is attached to the balance-board task, whereas it should be seen as the interaction between the child and the task.

What is developmental about the activities? Although Furth and Wachs adequately translate Piaget's theory into educational philosophy and the activities described have a certain educational face validity, the problem is that the program described does not really clarify the application of theory to classroom activities. It fails to spell out how the tasks represent Piagetian stages and how changes represent Piagetian development. Therefore the educator is left with only a cookbook; from what is described, one cannot connect the child's advances on tasks to development within the child. How does going from front-back balance to bilateral balance indicate anything more than practice, greater skill acquisition, or physical maturity?

This critique can be clarified by reference to our attempt to develop a Piagetian model for social thinking procedures with elementary school children. This effort is based upon current research which suggests that stage progression in social reasoning occurs through mechanisms similar to those proposed by Piaget in logical-mathematical thought.[5] The development of social reasoning involves experiences of conflict in the child's attempt to apply his current level of thought to social problems, and exposure to moderately higher levels of thought. The aim of our research, following Piaget's framework, is descriptive—to describe a sequence of levels of social thought from the egocentric to the sociocentric. The educational application in the domain of social development is based upon evidence of a natural progression of social thought from an initial level at which the child confuses the perspectives of self and other (level 0), to subsequent levels of development at which he realizes that other's subjective thoughts and feelings are distinct from self's (level 1); that other can consider the self's subjective attitudes and feelings (level 2); that self and other can view self's and other's point of view mutually and simultaneously (level 3); and that there is a general social viewpoint that transcends individual perspectives (level 4).

For the last three years we have been developing a curriculum model for primary-school children based on this research. The assumption of this curriculum is that children's functioning in areas such as social problem-solving, interpersonal awareness, communication and persuasion skills, and moral thought and behavior can be improved by helping children apply their level of social reasoning

[5] Robert Selman, "The Development of Socio-Cognitive Understanding: A Guide to Educational and Clinical Practice," in *Morality: Theory, Research and Social Issues*, ed. Thomas Lickona (New York: Holt, Rinehart and Winston, 1976.

to these areas and by helping to stimulate movement through the levels.

With these considerations in mind we constructed a set of dilemmas designed to stimulate the child's ability to perceive and understand perspectives other than his own. The dilemmas are presented to children through filmstrips and recordings. Although filmstrips differ in specific content, the form of each is similar. Each presents a dramatic story involving children of primary school age in conflict over two or more ideas. Each story emphasizes taking another person's perspective as part of the resolution of the dilemma. Rather than presenting a resolution to the dilemma, each story provides arguments both for and against the suggested resolutions to the dilemma. Both pro and con reasons are presented at a range of levels of social development so that the dilemma will stimulate children to advance into more complex stages of social reasoning regardless of their initial stage. For example, one dilemma focusing on interpersonal awareness depicts two boys who are trying to figure out what to get a friend for his birthday:

Greg has already bought some checkers for Mike, but Tom can't decide whether to get Mike a football or a little toy truck. The boys see Mike across the street and decide to hint around to see what he'd like for his birthday.

Greg and Tom ask Mike about trucks and football, but nothing seems to interest him. He's very sad because his dog, Pepper, has been lost for two weeks. When Greg suggests that Mike could get a new dog, Mike says he doesn't even like to look at other dogs because they make him miss Pepper so much. He runs off home, nearly crying.

Greg and Tom are left with the dilemma of what to get Mike. On their way to the toy store, they pass a store with a sign in the toy store, they pass a store with a sign in the window—"Puppies for Sale." There are only two dogs left. Tom has to make up his mind whether to get Mike a puppy before the last two are sold.

The presentation of the particular filmstrip is only a small part of the total instruction. The teacher then asks the children to discuss in small groups what should be done to resolve the dilemma, to give reasons for each choice and to debate about whether some reasons are more adequate than others. Role-playing and class debates are also used. Teachers are encouraged to use these discussions as models for dealing with real-life dilemmas that arise in class. They are helped by a teacher-training film which discusses how different reasoning reflects different stages.

Although the classroom techniques we advocate do not differ greatly from those advocated by Furth and Wachs, and we, like them, advocate these dilemmas only as paradigms of an educational process, there is one important difference between the two programs. In contrast to the Furth and Wachs approach, the filmstrip series not only presents tasks that are clearly developmental in nature, but also describes what is developmental about the children's responses.

Here, for example, is a conversation which followed the previously described filmstrip dilemma:

Alex—age 10
I think it's important because like um, if you buy something ah, something for the other person, that he doesn't like, he might get mad at you or something and not be your friend or something and then you'd just be down one friend and. . . So if I did that I'd be in trouble.

Jane—age 10
Yeh, but that not gonna make them not friends. His friend will understand. Besides, I think that um, he should buy the puppy because in a month or two he's going to be wanting one. He just said that because he lost his dog and he's sad. I think he should buy it and he'll start to like the dog and after a few days he'll

stop thinking about Pepper once he gets another thing he loves a lot.

In this example, Alex has a very concrete and moment-to-moment conception of friendship. Jane rejects Alex's level of reasoning because of her awareness that friendship is based on the expectations of each person towards the other, not on a specific act such as exchanging gifts. Her reasoning represents one stage above Alex's and provides stimulation for him, as well as for herself. This discussion also exemplifies an important aspect of Piagetian stages of reasoning: children at higher levels usually reject lower-level reasoning as immature or inadequate. Points such as these are presented to teachers in the training filmstrip.

Pilot testing of our social dilemmas indicates that children often disagree how the conflicts should be resolved and have difficulty making up their minds on the best resolution. It is precisely this kind of conflict which should help children develop into advanced forms of social reasoning. However, in describing our own work, I am not advocating that education aim simply at the acceleration of children through Piagetian stages on Piagetian-type tasks. That would be a limited educational perspective. However, since Piaget's conception of development is difficult to communicate, a writer labeling activities as Piagetian should make clear to the reader exactly what is developmental about them. This requires explanation of activities in terms which clearly indicate how a child's interaction with an activity reflects a given level of development and how a given level of development is more or less adequate than another. This is missing in Furth and Wachs's book.

Nevertheless there are valuable insights in *Thinking Goes to School*. Furth and Wachs challenge the reader to sharpen his conception of "thinking": first by emphasizing that thinking involves action as well as reflection; second by specifying that thought is involved in sensorimotor activities; third by showing that the physical

activities need not be thought of as mere gymnastics drill; and fourth by showing that thought is more than verbalization. Furth and Wachs use Piagetian theory to lend validity to activities other than reading and math in the elementary grades. The collaboration of developmental psychologist and clinician leads to some good results. There is nothing wrong with vintage wine in a new bottle; that is, worthwhile sensorimotor exercises cast loosely within a Piagetian framework.

But the authors face a dilemma. On the one hand, they do not want a "teacher proof" cookbook; on the other, they want to be concrete, to get away from the standard, "Here are some general ideas for you teachers, go out and transform your school. . . ." Both extremes are offensive to them and to the Piagetian conception of development, which involves active construction on the part of the teacher as well as the child. But the middle ground the authors seek is elusive—they might have had better success if they could have shown how to link qualitative or Piagetian levels of reasoning to levels of performance in each of the games or activities they present.

My critique of *Thinking Goes to School* may read harshly, but it is the harshness of someone who generally agrees with Furth and Wachs that Piagetian theory has great educational potential. Yet I do not agree that presenting a host of tasks with only general ties to Piagetian theory is the most effective way to realize this potential. Developmental psychologists cannot afford to dip their toe into education only to withdraw it proclaiming themselves educators. If we psychologists are going to see ourselves as educators, we must do more than consult for school systems or develop curriculum. We must recognize the same constraints and responsibilities for the education of children as those to whom we direct our advice. Only then might we become aware of the difficulties in translating a developmental theory into an educational reality.

Notes on Contributors

PATRICIA TEAGUE ASHTON is Assistant Professor of Foundations of Education at the University of Florida, Gainsville. Her current research interest is the development of social responsibility in children.

ELEANOR DUCKWORTH, who frequently serves as English translator of Jean Piaget's lectures, is the founding Director of the Lighthouse Learning Program of the Atlantic Institute of Education in Halifax, Nova Scotia. She has recently completed a doctoral thesis entitled *The African Primary Science Program: An Evaluation* at the University of Geneva where she is also Chargee D'Enseignement.

DAVID ELKIND is Professor of Psychology, Psychiatry and Education, and Director of the Mt. Hope School at the University of Rochester. He is the author of numerous articles and books, including *Children and Adolescents* and *Child Development and Education: A Piagetian Perspective*.

JOHN C. GIBBS is a Research Associate at the Center for Moral Education, Harvard University. A former instructor in psychology at McMaster University, Hamilton, Ontario, he is currently interested in the analysis of conflictual discussions in moral judgment development.

CAROL GILLIGAN, an Assistant Professor of Education at Harvard University, has written extensively on adolescent development in collaboration with Lawrence Kohlberg. Professor Gilligan is currently engaged in research on moral development in women and the developmental transition from adolescence to adulthood.

MAVIS E. KELLY is a graduate research student in the Faculty of Education of Monash University, Australia. Her research interests are in the measurement of cognitive development and the educational implications of Piagetian theory.

LAWRENCE KOHLBERG is Professor of Education and Social Psychology, Harvard University. Professor Kohlberg is well known for applying a cognitive-developmental approach to moral education. He has written numerous articles on moral development and moral education.

DEANNA KUHN is Associate Professor in the Laboratory of Human Development at Harvard University. She is author of numerous articles and *Development: Becoming Who We Are*. Her current research interests include experimental studies of the development of advanced logical reasoning.

ROGER LANDRUM is with The Potomac Institute in Washington, D.C. as study director for a committee examining federal youth policy, youth unemployment, and national service opportunities. He has taught at the University of Nigeria, Yale, and Harvard and is interested in educational research and developmental theory.

ROCHELLE MAYER is currently Program Associate in the Follow Through Division of the Bank Street College of Education. She is interested in developing alternatives to standardized achievement tests for assessing children's competencies and has recently co-authored *BRACE: An Instrument for Systematic Observation of Verbal Communication and Behavior in Educational Settings.*

D. C. PHILLIPS is Associate Professor of Education and Philosophy at Stanford University. He is author of numerous articles on philosophy of education and social science and several books, the most recent of which is *Holistic Thought in Social Science.*

ROBERT L. SELMAN is Lecturer in Education at Harvard University and is also affiliated with the Judge Baker Child Guidance Center. A recipient of a National Institute of Mental Health Career Scientist Award, he is presently concerned with children's development of interpersonal reasoning and maturity.